VIEWS TO
DINE BY

FODOR'S TRAVEL GUIDES

are compiled, researched, and edited by an international team of travel writers, field correspondents, and editors. The series, which now almost covers the globe, was founded by Eugene Fodor in 1936.

OFFICES
New York & London

Fodor's Views to Dine By:

Editor: Gail Chasan

FODOR'S

VIEWS TO DINE BY

AROUND THE WORLD

Jerome E. Klein

FODOR'S TRAVEL GUIDES
New York & London

The following Fodor's Guides are current; most are also available in a British
edition published by Hodder & Stoughton.

Country and Area Guides

Australia, New Zealand
  & the South Pacific
Austria
Bahamas
Belgium & Luxembourg
Bermuda
Brazil
Canada
Canada's Maritime
  Provinces
Caribbean
Central America
Eastern Europe
Egypt
Europe
France
Germany
Great Britain
Greece
Holland
India, Nepal &
  Sri Lanka
Ireland
Israel
Italy
Japan
Jordan & the Holy Land
Kenya
Korea
Mexico
New Zealand
North Africa
People's Republic
  of China
Portugal
Province of Quebec
Scandinavia
Scotland
South America
South Pacific
Southeast Asia
Soviet Union
Spain
Sweden
Switzerland
Turkey
Yugoslavia

City Guides

Amsterdam
Beijing, Guangzhou,
  Shanghai
Boston
Chicago
Dallas & Fort Worth
Greater Miami & the
  Gold Coast
Hong Kong
Houston & Galveston
Lisbon
London
Los Angeles
Madrid
Mexico City &
  Acapulco
Munich
New Orleans
New York City
Paris
Philadelphia
Rome
San Diego
San Francisco
Singapore
Stockholm, Copenhagen,
  Oslo, Helsinki &
  Reykjavik
Sydney
Tokyo
Toronto
Vienna
Washington, D.C.

U.S.A. Guides

Alaska
Arizona
California
Cape Cod
Chesapeake
Colorado
Far West
Florida
Hawaii
I–95: Maine to Miami
New England

New Mexico
New York State
Pacific North Coast
South
Texas
U.S.A.
Virginia

Budget Travel

American Cities (30)
Britain
Canada
Caribbean
Europe
France
Germany
Hawaii
Italy
Japan
London
Mexico
Spain

Fun Guides

Acapulco
Bahamas
Las Vegas
London
Maui
Montreal
New Orleans
New York City
The Orlando Area
Paris
Puerto Rico
Rio
St. Martin/Sint Maarten
San Francisco
Waikiki

Special-Interest Guides

Selected Hotels of Europe
Ski Resorts of North
  America
Views to Dine by around
  the World

I've never enjoyed a view alone; therefore, it is fitting for me to dedicate this book to the one who has shared these views with me—my wife, Jean.

Acknowledgments

I wish to express my appreciation first to the more than 3,000 readers who have written through the years giving me suggestions and complaints about what I left out, pushing me to do yet another edition of this book. Next, I would like to thank the owners of the fine restaurants we visited for helping to create this edition. These are wonderful people who work hard at the art of pleasing patrons every day. They have to be very special to do that, and in this book are many who have done it well for nearly half a century.

The names that follow are of people who went out of their way to be of help. I've tried to include everyone who deserves mention; to those I've inadvertently left out, I apologize with the hope that the finished product is something of an appeasement. I'm especially grateful to Linda C. Gwinn, Leading Hotels of the World; Mimi Baer, Hilton International Hotels; Kim Derderian, Market Share; Claude Terrail, La Tour d'Argent; Becky Farmerie, Robinson, Yesawich, & Pepperdine; Mabel M. Ting, Hong Kong Tourist Association; Joyce Fredo, Venice Simplon-Orient-Express; Michele Paget, Greater Victoria Visitors and Convention Bureau; Michele Holter, Westin Hotels; Priscilla Hoye, Marriott Marquis, New York; Mary Kay Warner, Burson-Marsteller; Jessica Miller, Hilton International; Elvira Quarin, Greater Vancouver Convention & Visitors Bureau; Ann Neville, Belgian National Tourist Association; Marge Brooker, San Francisco Convention and Visitors Bureau; Francoise Garnier, Bristol, Paris; Susan Bruno, The Colonial Williamsburg Foundation; Joyce Johnson and Mark Shea, Cole & Weber; Bob Wheatley and Jim McFarland, Cole & Weber; Patti Cook, Communications-Pacific; Beverly Gianna, New Orleans Convention and Visitors Bureau; Melina Hung, Hong Kong Tourist Association; Donna Simmons, Hyatt International Corporation; Beth Preddy and Susanna Miller, Karen Escalera Associates; Leesa Lovelace, Mandarin International Hotels Limited; Pornsri Luphaiboon, Oriental Bangkok; Mark Allem, Pier 39; Carmen Roy, Ritz Madrid; Catherine Bouvet, Plaza Athenée; Sallu Moncrieff, Shangri-La Hotel, Hong Kong; Erika Faisst, Swiss National Tourist Office; Thomas G. Murphy, Washington D.C. Convention & Visitors Bureau; Mrs. Louella Barrett, London Hilton on Park Lane.

Discover the Europe only the natives know.

Avis features GM cars. Opel Corsa

Get a free "Personally Yours" itinerary when you rent from Avis.

Highlights of Germany. Undiscovered Spain. Irish castles and palaces. And much more.

Personally Yours[SM] is a customized itinerary, tailored to your own special interests, featuring detailed driving instructions, hotel and restaurant suggestions...plus out-of-the-way places only the natives know about. Be sure to ask for *Personally Yours* when you reserve in advance.

Avis tries harder to make you feel right at home in Europe. Starting with low SuperValue Rates on a wide variety of cars. And your very own personalized itinerary. No wonder we're Europe's largest car rental company. Call your travel consultant, or Avis at **1-800-331-2112.**

Avis. So easy.[SM]

Table of Contents

Introduction

When Lot fled Sodom and Gomorrah, his wife stopped to admire the view. And when Hannibal crossed the Alps, he and his men encamped on a high level so they might enjoy the view as they ate.

Travelers from time immemorial have paused in their journeys to dine at spots enabling them to take in grand views. Such respites offered them an opportunity to reflect upon the land left behind, and, just as important, to contemplate the challenge of unknown vistas still to come.

Our search for views to dine by started when we first began traveling to new parts of our country and world. After arriving, we always tried to have our first dinner at a fine restaurant with an all-inclusive view. My wife, Jean, and I would look at the city or village, or the river or lake, and plan our activities for the next few days. Not surprisingly, our superior vantage points gave us a better grasp of the situation and a more comfortable and exciting start in our enjoyment of a new place.

Much has happened since the book with this title first appeared in 1961. So much so, in fact, that more than three-quarters of the views appearing in this year's edition were not in that earlier book. We do repeat such grand classic views as that of Notre Dame from the Tour d'Argent in Paris and of the city of Paris from the Jules Verne in the Eiffel Tower. To these we add an entirely new crop of exciting views to dine by—for example, Hong Kong from the Plume restaurant of the Regent, or New York City from Windows on the World, 107 floors above street level—and many others that simply did not exist in the 1960s.

Keep in mind as well that so many more restaurants have come into being which serve grand views along with their cuisine that this book contains only a small portion of the great views to dine by around the world.

More than three thousand readers were kind enough to send us some 6,000 suggestions of views to dine by which were not mentioned in the four editions of this title published from 1961 through 1964. We have tried to visit those we found interesting during the past quarter century. These and others we found on our own have contributed to the making of this book.

The interest in dining with a view has grown, we'd like to think, partially because of our book and also because people have become more aware of its joys. In fact, some restaurateurs mentioned in previous editions told us that they had received so many requests for "view tables" from our readers that they tore down some walls so more could be offered. Perhaps most flattering of all, a number of hotel, restaurant, and airport designers asked for my suggestions during the design stage of many new projects.

Most of the views to dine by selected for this book have been enjoyed by my wife and myself. Some we have heard about so often from so many readers and friends that we have long-standing plans to visit them as soon as we can; the information we obtained on these establishments, in advance of a visit, is shared with you in this book.

Now, with the publication of such an extensive compendium of views to dine by, we can answer the question we most often try to avoid: which is our favorite? This book is filled with them. The most exciting view is of Hong Kong, New York, Vancouver, Paris, London, Portofino, Amsterdam, Copenhagen, Vienna, Brussels, Venice, New Orleans, Florence, Rome, Tokyo, San Francisco, Marbella, Lisbon, Bangkok, Madrid, and—do you get the idea? The list is endless. This is a beautiful world, full of wonderful views to dine by, and, to us, the greatest hobby of all is to experience as many of them as possible.

If you like to travel but hate to walk a lot (like us!), this is the hobby for you. We are relaxed but ardent and unashamed tourists. After more than twenty-five years of traveling and writing about it, our preferred style of sightseeing is to see the world from our lunch, dinner, breakfast, or tea table. At any repast, you'll find carefully selected spots from which you can see the best parts of a city, village, harbor, seacoast, or mountain. You can see royalty enjoying a stroll in their backyard while you leisurely dine in a restaurant far above them, or wild animals at their favorite watering hole while you watch from a lovely dining room built on stilts above.

In reviewing our earlier edition of *Views to Dine By,* one critic got carried away and enthusiastically proclaimed that "this book proves the theory that wherever you find a truly great view—anywhere in the world almost—you will find, a short distance away, a truly great restaurant sharing it." We wish this were true. Not every great view is complemented by the cuisine it deserves. Many restaurants, particularly highly commercial ones or those overlooking popular tourist attractions, do not always have good food or service. Yet there are times when even mediocre or meager food is a small price to pay for the pleasure of relaxing at a table to enjoy an exceptional vista. Be assured, however, that many of the world's truly great restaurants are in this book, and if their food was great when we tried it, we don't hesitate to say so. And where the view is truly exceptional although the food may not be, we've tried to point that out, too.

At the beginning of every article discussing a restaurant and its view, we've given the names of the chef and the maitre d'. We find this to be very helpful. When you make your reservation, do ask for the maitre d' by name, and tell him that you read about him in our book and that you'd appreciate a table with a view. Most will try to accommodate you. We've also indicated where reservations are necessary, and have included telephone numbers. Most hotel and city restaurants require jackets or jackets and ties, particularly at dinner time. At resorts, and in some more relaxed areas in some cities, attractive casual dress is welcome.

Prices given, generally for a three-course meal without wine or liquor, were accurate at press time and are subject to change, usually upwards. Please be aware that in many parts of the world a gratuity or service charge will automatically be added to your bill; you might want to check the policy at individual locations. If you want to save some money and still enjoy a good view and a good meal, note particularly the places offering lunch or Sunday brunch. The cost at most dining rooms for one of these meals is sometimes half the price of a comparable dinner, and you usually get the same meal (albeit with slightly smaller portions).

Credit card information is also provided at the beginning of each listing. We considered Visa, MasterCard, American Express, Diner's Club, and Carte Blanche to be major credit cards; the notation "all major credit cards" is used when at least three of these five are accepted. In addition, other credit cards particular to the region in which a restaurant is located may be accepted as well. Of course, restaurants reserve the right to change their credit card policies at any given time.

Where we have enjoyed the food, we try to tell what we or friends—or even dining neighbors—have enjoyed. That doesn't mean you shouldn't try anything else. You'll find that the maitre d' is glad to work honestly for his tip and will give you an honest answer as to which of the restaurant's specialties are particularly good on that day.

In some instances, an important part of the grand view to dine by might be the decor of the restaurant—several of the world's most beautiful dining rooms are in this book—or the beautiful and artistic way the food is prepared, arranged on your plate, and served. In this book we tell of some of the world's truly greatest gastronomical artists.

So enjoy the feast for the taste buds and for the eyes that this book offers. And please tell us what you find in your travels so we and other readers may enjoy more great views to dine by around the world.

PALM BEACH

The Mill Restaurant

L.G. Smith Boulevard 330
Palm Beach
P.O. Box 162
Oranjestad
Aruba, N.A.
Telephone: 2–6300

All major credit cards
Dinner
Reservations recommended
Jacket preferred
Liquor served
Dinner: $18 to $28
*   full 3 courses, without wine*
Chef: Rudolph Ratzenboch
Maitre d': Christian Mongellez

This restaurant, built in the Netherlands in 1804, was dismantled and shipped to Aruba in 1959 and reconstructed in 1960. It has been run by William W. Waldron since 1974.

Located just a few hundred yards from some of the major hotels, along the main highway, the Mill Restaurant is quite a contrast to those modern structures and is one of Aruba's most frequently photographed tourist sites.

The restaurant's interior contains original oil paintings of mill scenes, authentic Delft plates, antique Dutch wall tile paintings, and exceptional decorative artifacts, including water pumps and copper kettles.

The food, prepared by Austrian-born Master Chef Ratzenboch, is quite an attraction. The restaurant has won an award from the American Culinary Association in an international competition held by the ACA and the World Congress. Among the favorites are Shrimp Scampi, Red Snapper Creole, Lobster Bisque, and Roast Duck. Most of the guests are from Europe, Latin America, and the United States. Maitre d' Mongellez's extensive knowledge of wines can be most helpful when trying to decide on the right one to complement your meal.

MELBOURNE

Le Restaurant
The Regent of Melbourne
25 Collins Street
Melbourne
Australia
Telephone: 63 0321

All major credit cards
Lunch and dinner
Reservations recommended
Jacket required
Liquor served
Dinner: $35 to $50
*   full 3 courses, without win*
Lunch: $22 to $35
Chef: Klaus Lemm
Maitre d': Peter Olschyna

Le Restaurant is located in the Regent of Melbourne, a magnificent luxury hotel which begins on the 35th floor of one of the spectacular twin towers comprising the Collins Place Complex. This complex, the largest single construction project ever undertaken in Australia, was designed by I.M. Pei and Partners, New York architects, with Robert Lym, their interior designer in charge, and was finished in 1981. So American know-how had much to do with this dramatic structure of which Le Restaurant is a part.

One of the hotel's two main restaurants, Le Restaurant has a commanding view over most of Melbourne and the distant Dangenong Mountain Ranges. The restaurant's pale colors and low-key atmosphere were established so as not to compete with the magnificent view. Next to Le Restaurant is Le Cafe, offering guests an informal all-day dining service. It, too, has a spectacular panorama of the city skyline.

Le Restaurant is open for dinner, Monday through Saturday, from 7 P.M. until midnight, and for a *table d'hôte* luncheon Monday through Friday. It has earned two hats for the past three years from Australia's *A.G.E. Good Food Guide* for its fine cuisine.

SYDNEY

Kable's at the Regent of Sydney

199 George Street
P.O. Box N185
The Rocks, Level II
Sydney 2000
Australia
Telephone: 238–0000

All major credit cards
Lunch and dinner
Reservations suggested
Jacket required
Liquor served
Chef: Serge Dansereau
Maitre d': Willy Hashka

Situated on the second level of the 620-room Regent of Sydney is one of the city's most popular restaurants, offering a selection of views of beautiful Sydney Harbor, over the balcony into the atrium-style lobby of the hotel, and through the Circular Quay, the city's bustling ferry and transport terminal.

Chef Dansereau takes pride in his cuisine, bringing to the tables the highest quality of local fruit, vegetables, fish, and meat each day. He prides himself on the fact that the only freezers in his kitchens are for ice cream and some pastry products (which are made on the premises). The menu always features two hot entrées, one of which is always seafood, a vegetable and meat entrée, three cold entrées, and Iranian caviar. The main course selection includes lobster, or, when it is not available, a shellfish such as scampi or Balmain Bugs.

The dessert tables are laden with an assortment of French pastries, tortes, and other specialties including fresh seasonal fruits (mangoes, raspberries, strawberries, and kiwis).

Guests seem to enjoy the fresh fruit sorbets and ice creams, which are also made everyday in Kable's kitchen.

CARINTHIA

Castle Hochosterwitz

A 9314 Hochosterwitz
Carinthia
Austria
Telephones: 04213–2010 or 2020

No credit cards
Lunch
Reservations not accepted
Jacket not required
Liquor served
Lunch: $5 to $15
without wine

Castle Hochosterwitz, located in one of the most beautiful valleys of Austria's Carinthian province, is wrapped around a steep limestone rock which overlooks the neighboring mountains, hills, and verdant countryside. Guests and hosts will point to and name the mountains for you—the Saualpe, the Friesacher, and the Gurktaler, the Ulrichsberg, the Magdalensberg, the Görlitzen, and the Villack alps, as well as the picturesque Duchy town of the province of St. Veit. The region also features other castles and ruins, such as Mansberg, Taggenbrunn, and Kraiger castles, all combining to form a unique panorama.

Castle Hochosterwitz is one of the most impressive castles in Austria. There are 14 gates leading gradually up the mountain, bridging deep gorges, cleverly leaning on the carved rock wall and opening at various points at squares where weapons were kept, until the main castle is reached at the mountain's top. The structure is a remarkable example of medieval fortress construction, meaning that it was built during the 14th and 15th centuries. The museum is fascinating, and, in the courtyard, the guards and servants are garbed in traditional armor and medieval costumes.

The food is satisfactory, but that's not what we come here for. The castle itself and the view are what matter. So have a glass of wine and enjoy!

KITZBÜHEL

Hotel Tennerhof

Griesenauweg 26
A-6370 Kitzbühel, Tirol
Austria
Telephone: 05356–3181

All major credit cards
Breakfast, lunch, and dinner
Reservations recommended
Jacket required
Liquor served
Dinner: $17 to $20
full 3 courses, without wine
Lunch: $13 to $16
Chef: Mr. Oberhammer
Maitre d': Mr. André

Tennerhof is a centuries-old Tyrolean farmhouse, located on the sunny side of the village of Kitzbühel. It was gradually turned into the extremely comfortable hotel it is today. The house is furnished with classic Tyrolean care and taste and offers good living and complete relaxation in a beautiful garden setting. It is carefully maintained by its proud owners, Mr. and Mrs. L.V. Pasquali.

The view from the dining room windows is of the mountains, the countryside, the village, and the pool. The restaurant is excellent, featuring fresh vegetables and spices from the Tennerhof garden. Among the popular main dishes are Home Marinated Salmon and

Saddle of Lamb. For dessert, try the Soufflée au Citron, which has been awarded five stars in the *Gault* guide, which listed the Hotel Tennerhof as having one of the thirty best kitchens in Austria.

Easy to reach, this restaurant is a 15 minute walk from the town center and is above the Horn cable car station.

ST. WOLFGANG

Romantikrestaurant Und Hotel
Im Weissen Rössl Am Wolfgangsee
(Romantic Restaurant and
White Horse Inn on the Wolfgang Lake)

A-5360 St. Wolfgang
Salzkammergut
Austria
Telephone: 06138–2306–61

All major credit cards
Breakfast, lunch, and dinner
Reservations if possible
Jacket preferred; dress: leisurely
but correct
Liquor served
Dinner: $10 to $18
full 3 courses, without wine
Lunch: $8 to $15
Chef: Günther Urbanek
Maitre d': Michel Emaulaz

This lovely romantic spot served as inspiration for the 1898 comedy entitled *At the White Horse Inn.* The play was a farce about the headwaiter of an inn who was madly in love with the sprightly landlady. It was written so that the theater in all its parts appeared to be a beautiful Tyrolean landscape, which is, indeed, the view to dine by here.

The village of St. Wolfgang, where this restaurant is located, has an ancient history. It was named for the Bishop of Regensburg, who was appointed to that post by the German Emperor in 972. In 982, the Bishop came to this spot and remained until 987; during his years in St. Wolfgang he built a small chapel in a cave where he meditated and worshiped. Indeed, as you dine on the terrace of the White Horse Inn, it is not difficult to imagine the inspiration the Bishop must have felt. Of course, there was no village and no inn then—only the placid lake and the mountains.

The earliest record of the White Horse Inn dates back to 1440, when the first of five houses gradually joined together was used as an inn. By 1878 the place looked much as it does today. In 1912 it became the property of the Peter family, which has been in the brewery and inn business in St. Wolfgang for almost three centuries.

The restaurant from which we enjoy the view is built out over the lake on stilts. It is a major attraction for celebrities, movie stars, heads of state and other politicians and leaders from around the world, and, particularly during the day, hordes of tourists. Helmut Peter asked us to say that during the daytime, when there are many sightseers, you should ask to sit on the Emperor Terrace. During the day, park your car on the opposite side of the lake and take Ferry Boat V-XI. In the evening, use the parking lot at the entrance to the village of St. Wolfgang. From there it is just three minutes via a pedestrian walk to the restaurant.

Remember, this is a busy and very popular place; luckily, the view makes braving the crowds worthwhile. The food is typically Austrian, including fish from the lake, venison, and of course, Austrian sweets. The delightful specialties of the house which we recommend include Abersee Fish Soup, Smoked Char Mousse, Lamb's Lettuce with Fillet of Chamois, Fillet of Pork with Spinach in a Caul, Chanterelles and Homemade Whole Wheat Noodles, and finally, Wild Strawberry Charlotte. About five percent of the guests are local people, ten percent are Americans, and the rest are an international mix.

SALZBURG

Festungs Restaurant

Hohensalzburg
Mönchsberg 34
Salzburg
Austria
Telephone: 06 62–41 7 80

American Express
Lunch and dinner
Reservations recommended
Jacket not required at lunch
Liquor served
Dinner: $12 to $20
 full 3 courses, without wine
Lunch: $9 to $14
Chef: Albert Brugger
Maitre d': Gerald Feichtinger

No matter where you are in Salzburg you have a great view. But you can see it all from the Festungs Restaurant atop the Hohensalzburg. The Hohensalzburg dominates Salzburg in much the same manner as the fortress dominates another musical city, Edinburgh: the structures can be seen from almost anywhere in town.

The Schraffl family runs the restaurant with pride. Few restaurants have a more international representation of guests, and none have more music lovers. During the summer, this being Salzburg, there are concerts every evening featuring the works of Mozart. Three times a week there are Austrian folklore evenings featuring famous Salzburg performers. The restaurant is open from 10 A.M. until midnight, from April through October. Among the dining favorites are *Festungsplatte* (Mixed Grill), *Salzburger Bauernschuaus/Pfifferlingen* (yellow mushrooms), veal, pork, and the famous *Salzburger Nockerl*. These are but a few of the items offered on a large and varied menu.

Restaurant of the Hotel Kobenzl

Gaisberg 11
5020 Salzburg
Austria
Telephone: 0662–21776 or 20275

American Express, Visa
Breakfast, lunch, and dinner
Reservations requested
Jacket requested
Liquor served
Dinner: $15 to $25
    full 3 courses, without wine
Lunch: $15 to $25
Chef: Franz Eder
Maitre d's: Peter and Gunter

About 2,500 feet above the festival city of Salzburg, sitting on Mount Gaisberg, is the lovely Hotel Kobenzl, comfortably run by the Herzog family.

On clear, sunny days the terraces are filled with guests; many of them are famous. In the summer of 1984, Prime Minister Margaret Thatcher of England joined several members of the Austrian government for lunch—to talk, to dine, to relax and enjoy the view. When Thatcher noticed conductor James Levine sitting nearby, she wanted to approach him and thank him for a beautiful *Magic Flute* performance which he had conducted and she had enjoyed. However, the security people did not want her to leave her table, so the Herzogs were asked to tell Levine what was happening. He, of course, went straight to her table. Other famous patrons have included Brooke Shields, former president Richard Nixon, and Henry Kissinger.

Such affairs of state and culture should not, however, obscure the main reason for coming to these comfortable surroundings: the view itself. In addition to the greenery

surrounding the hotel, one can see all of Salzburg and its surrounding mountains, rocks, and forests. The view extends all the way from the mountain chains in the south to the lakes in the north. Cattle grazing below complete the countryside portrait.

Mr. and Mrs. R. and M. Herzog, their youngest son, Peter, and their daughter, Matianne, the baroness of Buseck, do their best to create a home-like atmosphere for their mostly-German guests (many Americans dine here as well). Their establishment is actually a farmhouse dating from the 17th century. Until 1925 it was also an inn where people from Salzburg came for a snack and a drink; a few guest rooms were available as well. Through the years it was enlarged, and in 1959 the Herzog family took over, eventually tripling its size, enhancing its cuisine, and doing as little as possible to disturb the visual splendor for which it has become known.

VIENNA

Cafe-Restaurant Landtmann

Dr. Karl-Luegerring 4
1010 Vienna
Austria
Telephone: 63 91 28 or 63 06 21

All major credit cards
Breakfast, lunch, and dinner
Reservations recommended
Jacket required in the dining room
Liquor served
Dinner: $12 to $28
  full 3 courses, without wine
Lunch: $12 to $28
Chef/Owner: Herbert Querfeld

Part of the view to dine by in this popular coffeehouse is the mixture of guests who dine here. Among the regulars are the actors of the nearby Burgtheater, the senators, congressmen, and other politicians of Austria (since the restaurant is near the House of Parliament and the Chancellery), artists, and students. There is also the usual assortment of tourists from around the world. This typical Viennese melange makes the Landtmann all the more fascinating. The visual panorama is of the famous and fashionable Ringstrasse of Vienna on which the café is located. [In the spring through the fall, the outside terrace offers that view.] The diner can enjoy a splendid view of the Burgtheater, the Town Hall, and the University, and despite being situated in the middle of a big city, can breathe the fresh air from the Volksgarten and the park surrounding the Town Hall.

The 110-year old Landtmann Cafe has been managed by the Querfeld family since 1976, and portions of it have undergone substantial renovation. Both the famous Viennese Coffeehouse with its Biedermeier Room, which is the favorite spot for talking business, and the terrace, where coffee and cakes are enjoyed in great quantities over idle chatter, have been restored to their original cozy and distinctive atmosphere.

The Landtmann can seat 282 guests, plus another 200 on the terrace. The terrace offers the most informal atmosphere and the best views, which can be enjoyed for the price of a cup of coffee—if you wish, *mit schlag* (with whipped cream on top!)—and a piece of luscious pastry. The interior dining rooms, the elegant Biedermeier Room, and the Green Drawing Room offer a great variety of Viennese specialties, including *Erdäpfel-Suppe* (Potato Soup), *Fiaker-Gulasch* (Coachman's Goulash), *Salonbeuschel* (cooked heart, lungs, liver, and sweetbread of a calf, finely sliced and heated in a savory sauce), and *Zwiebel-Rostbraten* (Sirloin Steak with Onions). Keep in mind, however, that in Vienna the great event is to select from the *Mehlspeisen* (Desserts).

As you sip your coffee, consider for a moment that at one time, perhaps, the chair in which you are seated may have been occupied by the duke of Windsor, Queen Juliana of the Netherlands, Pandit Nehru, Sir Laurence Olivier, August Piccard, Robert Stolz, Axel Munthe, or any of the other famous personages who have signed the Golden Book of the Cafe Landtmann.

Cafe-Restaurant Landtmann is open from 8 A.M. until midnight, seven days a week, for breakfast, lunch, afternoon coffee, dinner, and after-theater supper.

Bahamas

ELEUTHERA

Cotton Bay Club Dining Room

Cotton Bay Beach & Golf Club
Rock Sound
Eleuthera
Bahamas
Telephone: 809–334–2101/2156

All major credit cards
Breakfast, lunch, and dinner
Reservations necessary
Jacket and tie required after six P.M.,
    December 15 to April 15
Liquor served
Dinner: $30
    full 3 courses, without wine
Lunch: $4.50 to $7.50
Chef: Gerhard Kampichler
Maitre d': Sammy Culmer

    This restaurant offers the sea, the sky, and serenity. The Cotton Bay Beach & Golf Club is a private, self-contained resort nestled away on Eleuthera, one of the most beautiful of the Family Islands of the Bahamas.

    Eleuthera, derived from the Greek word for freedom, is blessed with natural beauty that has been relatively untouched since the island was settled in 1647. From the white sand beaches to the myriad shades of blue and green of the clear ocean water to the majestic white-roofed homes dotting the hills, you are surrounded by a plenitude of views to dine and recline by.

    The cuisine is a delightful mix of Continental, American, and Bahamian, prepared by a skilled Austrian chef. Favorites on the menu include lobster and a variety of fish and seafood dishes, all very fresh.

NASSAU

Baccarat's Restaurant

The Royal Bahamian
Cable Beach
Nassau
Bahamas
Telephone: 809–327–6400

All major credit cards
Dinner
Reservations required
Jacket preferred
Liquor served
Dinner: $35 to $60
    full 3 courses, without wine
General Manager: Philip Wood

The Balmoral Beach Club, the grand old colonial resort which served heads of state, tycoons, and the rich and famous, has been renamed the Royal Bahamian after $9 million of restoration work done by the Dallas-based Wyndham Corporation. Owned by the Bahamian government and managed by Wyndham, it now has 170 luxurious guest rooms in an establishment that offers the best of Bahama past and present.

There are two adjoining restaurants. The Baccarat serves haute cuisine in an elegant atmosphere with full European-style service. It features a French menu, with seafood and veal specialties; the house favorite is *Carre d'Agneau Villette*—rack of lamb dusted with exotic herbs, then roasted and broiled. The Cafe Royal seats 136 and is set outside amid sweeping palm trees and offers a view overlooking the swimming pool (as does the Baccarat) from the tables along its fully opened side wall.

Buena Vista Restaurant

Delancy Street
P.O. Box N 564
Nassau
Bahamas
Telephone: 809–322–2811

All major credit cards
Dinner
Reservations recommended
Jacket suggested
Dinner: $28 to $35
full 3 courses, without wine
Chef/Co-Owner: Jimmy Perez
Manager/Co-Owner: Stan Bocus
Maitre d': Charles Rolls

Dining in the Buena Vista Restaurant, on three levels of outdoor dining terraces, surrounded by native flowers and palms, is delightful. This restaurant occupies a 200-year-old colonial mansion on five acres of lush tropical land and is one of the finest and oldest restaurants in Nassau.

The dining room is reminiscent of an era of casual elegance, such as the one during which the mansion was built. Dining at the Buena Vista is an unhurried experience, featuring plentiful native foods and elegant service. The candlelight reflects off the polished wood floors of the dining room, and the tables are set with fine crystal and china.

Among the favorite main dishes are Bahamian Lobster Buena Vista, *Tournedos aux Chanterelles, Filet Mignon aux Deux Poivres, Cailles Desosses "Rossini," Aupreme de Poulet,* and *Mignonnettes de Veau.*

A favorite dessert is Mrs. Hsuck's Orange Pancakes. Other desserts include chocolate mousse, or, for two, Baked Alaska, *Soufflé Grand Marnier,* or *Cerises Jubilé* (dark sweet cherries flamed in liqueurs, served with vanilla ice cream and whipped cream).

Belgium

BRUGES

Duc de Bourgogne

Huidenvettersplein 12
8000 Bruges
Belgium
Telephone: 050–33–20–38/39

All major credit cards
Lunch and dinner; breakfast for hotel guests only
Reservations requested
Jacket requested but not required
Liquor served
Dinner: $40 to $50
 full 3 courses, without wine
Lunch: $40 to $50
Chef: Jules Pieters
Maitre d': Angelo Ribas

Certainly the best way to see Bruges is on foot. Everything in this small, picturesque town is within walking distance, and the city, with its narrow, winding back streets, is inviting for explorers. This is one of Europe's loveliest cities, really an open-air museum of medieval churches, elegant houses, cobbled streets, the *Grote Markt,* and, most of all, the picturesque canals. Boat trips lasting half an hour can be taken in the summer months.

Another way to enjoy the canals is to have lunch or dinner at the Duc de Bourgogne restaurant, located at a scenic bend on a narrow canal. Even more important, this is *the* restaurant in Bruges offering *haute cuisine* in a romantic setting. It is richly furnished, with magnificent tapestries and candlelit tables. Most tables do not, however, have a view of the canal, so ask, when you make your reservation, for a window table.

About half the guests are Americans, about forty percent are from Belgium, and the remaining ten percent come from all over Europe, according to Willy van de Vijver, the proprietor. Favorite entrées include all kinds of fresh seafood and local baby vegetables. The favorite dessert is probably the *Peche Pompadour.*

Because of the narrow, one-way streets, it is not easy to reach the restaurant by car. Parking is also difficult. The best thing to do is to park your car in an underground parking space at the nearby fish market and take the two-minute walk to the restaurant. Anyone in the fish market will point you in the right direction.

BRUSSELS

Chalet Robinson

Sentier de l'Embarcadére
en l'ile du Bois de la Cambre
1050 Brussels
Belgium
Telephone: 02–374–30–13

All major credit cards
Lunch and dinner
Reservations not necessary
Jacket not required
Liquor served
Dinner: $12 to $25
    full 3 courses, without wine
Lunch: $8 to $20
Chef: J.J. Huart
Maitre d': Deligne Julien

A delightful spot within Brussels, this restaurant is situated on a man-made island built about a century ago in the middle of the lake. It was built for King Leopold II of Belgium and has been, since then, a favorite meeting and relaxation spot for politicians. As proprietor Daniel Van der Poorten says, "It is also a favorite of lovers, tourists, and businessmen." Movie and musical celebrities have dined here as well.

Chalet Robinson's setting, the island in the middle of a lake in the middle of the *Bois de Cambre,* can be compared to Central Park in New York, Hyde Park in London, and the Bois de Boulogne in Paris. The park is situated at the edge of *La Foret de Soigne,* a large forest on the outskirts of Brussels. It is located just between Franklin Roosevelt Avenue, well known for its embassies and perhaps the most beautiful avenue in Brussels, and Waterloo Road, named for the battle that Napoléon Bonaparte lost when fighting the British. Many Americans live in the area because they find it quiet, attractive, and not too far from the heart of Brussels, where many of them work.

Like so much of the food in Brussels, Chalet Robinson's is excellent. Among the favorites are *Scampi a la Facon du Chef* and *Supreme de Turbotin au Citron et Coboulette.* The favorites among the desserts are the freshly made sorbets.

En Plein Ciel

Hilton International Brussels
38, Boulevard de Waterloo
1000 Brussels
Belgium
02–513–88–77

All major credit cards
Lunch and dinner
Reservations required
Jacket and tie required
Liquor served
Dinner: $35 to $50
*   full 3 courses, without wine*
Lunch: $20 to $25
Chef: Michel Theurel
Maitre d': Jacques Vingerhoets

The name of this restaurant describes the feeling you inevitably get when you look out of its broad windows at most of the fascinating ancient/modern city of Brussels. Translated from the French, En Plein Ciel means "in the middle of the sky," and, at 27 floors above one of the busiest and most fashionable streets of the city, it is the highest dining room in Brussels. On a clear day you can see much of the city and some of the surrounding areas.

It is hard to pull oneself away from the view, but once you catch sight of the elaborate luncheon buffet served each day, with its beautiful salads, fish, and cold meats (artistically arranged by the crew of Chef Theurel), you'll find this view entirely appetizing as well. The *Gault Millau* guide gave the cuisine a rating of two red hats.

In the evening, *En Plein Ciel* becomes an elegant dining room, with its guests dressed appropriately. Unlike most hotel dining rooms, this is also a favorite of local people, who like to dine here on their own but who particularly enjoy bringing visitors so they can give them both a bird's eye view of Brussels and a sampling of fine Belgian cuisine.

Among the favorites on the dinner menu are *Petite Salad Coquille St. Jacques, Fantaisie de bar aux Huitres,* and the most expensive entrée, *Fantaisie de Langoustines aux*

Morilles a la Creme. It is not easy to select dessert from so many appealing choices; some people simply point at the trolley and find themselves delighted with whatever they receive. One suggested favorite is *Chibouze aux Prunes,* served as you've never tasted them before!

There is music for dancing or listening pleasure. Many people come after an evening at a concert or the theater and dance until En Plein Ciel closes at one in the morning. Then, too, the view of the twinkling lights of the ancient city of Brussels is a pleasant prelude to sleep.

DAMME

De Drie Zilveren Kannen
Markt 9
8340 Damme
Belgium
Telephones: 050–35–56–77 or 50–06–63

All major credit cards
Lunch and dinner
Reservations necessary
Jacket not required
Liquor served
Dinner: $20 to $35
    full 3 courses, without wine
Lunch: the same
Chef: Willaert Rudy
Maitre d's: Deslypebe and Delbeke

Damme, near the grand canal town of Bruges, is one of those quaint and delightful little Belgian villages you should see if you are in the area. Founded sometime in the middle of the 12th century, when it became the outer harbor for what had become the world market city of Bruges, Damme got its name from being situated at the end of the Zwin, a large estuary into the North Sea, on a dike *(dam).* As Damme became a flourishing seaport, sailors, merchants, brokers, bankers, and artisans settled there. By the 13th century it had market rights for wine and herring, and in the Middle Ages it was the most important wine market in Northern Europe.

The town likes food and drink and has everything from intimate little bistros to top-class restaurants. Die Drie Zilveren Kannen, which means "the Three Silver Jugs," is one of the latter. With only six tables, it is a small but excellent dining spot that has been in operation for thirty-five years. It was one of the first restaurants in Damme, founded by the grandmother of the present proprietors when she was sixty years old; she began with a modest menu of bread, ham, and cheese. Then she added eel, and at last it became a restaurant of "a certain class." It is situated at the market place and its very old interior is filled with lovely antiques.

The restaurant's name derives from Belgium's early days, when the poor drank their wine from jugs made of stone while the rich, seated on the other side of the tavern, drank theirs from silver jugs. Such overt class differences are a thing of the past, but the implied spirit of refined ways lives on.

The view inside is delightful, and from a few good vantage points you can see outside to the ancient market place of Damme and its 15th century gothic-style Town Hall.

Among the favorites on the menu of De Drie Zilveren Kannen are *Gratin de Saumon a la Ciboulet, Gratin de Huitres ou Champagne,* and *Turbot Blanc de la Loin aux Pommes.*

DURBUY

Le Sanglier des Ardennes

Rue Comte Theodule d'Ursel gg
5480 Durbuy
Belgium
Telephone: 086–21–10–88

All major credit cards
Breakfast, lunch, and dinner
Reservations necessary
Jacket not required
Liquor served
Dinner: $17 to $41
*   full 3 courses, without wine*
Lunch: the same
Chef: Maurice Caerdinael
Maitre d': Paul Alexandre

One of the best of the many delightful inns and restaurants in Durbuy, a medieval hamlet tucked into the steep crevices cut by the River Ourthe in the Ardennes Forest of eastern Belgium, is Sanglier des Ardennes and its annex, Le Vieux-Durbuy.

The solid old stone inn imparts a 17th century ambience, with its low beamed ceilings and deeply set windows, heavy oak doors matching the beams, its use of charming printed fabrics, and the ceramic candelabra.

Like so much of Belgian cuisine, the food here has earned recognition with the

Premier Prix Culinair de Belgigue. Among the delectable choices from the menu are the local grilled fish, the Haunch of Boar, Young Rabbit with Carrots, White Fowl Steamed with Leeks, and Sanglier ham in oak leaves. One guest said we should "order anything that comes with *beurre au cresson,* a rich emerald-colored velvety sauce whose delicate flavor perfectly accompanies any kind of white fish." No wonder *Michelin* has given Sanglier des Ardennes three stars.

Nearby at Trois Ponts, at the confluence of three rivers (including the Ourthe), is the high point in the middle of the country where fir and pine forests appear to be thick dark rugs over the saddles of the hills. The lush, sloping meadows are dotted with orchards and herds of grazing pedigree cattle—wherever you look you'll think a painting has come to life.

HERBEUMONT

Hostellerie du Prieure de Conques
Route de Florenville, 176
B-6803 Herbeumont sur Semois
Belgium
Telephone: 061–41–14–17

All major credit cards
Breakfast, lunch, and dinner
Reservations necessary
Jacket required
Liquor served
Dinner: $25 to $50
    full 3 courses, without wine
Lunch: $20 to $40
Chef: Etienne van Boxel
Proprietors: Mr. & Mrs. De Naeyer

On the banks of the Semois River, in the heart of the vast forest of the Ardennes, on the fringe of La Gaume, exists an 18th century priory with magnificent furnishings, excellent food, and delightful views of its surroundings, including its informal gardens.

Your hosts are proud of the quietness of the place, of the old-time courtesy, and, most certainly, of its excellent French gastronomy. Among the favorites from a generous menu are such items as *Flan de Truite au Coulis de Homard, Aiquillette de Caneton au Vinaiore de Framboise,* and *Bavarois aux Poires.*

Less than ten percent of the guests here are Americans, and about a third are local people. The rest are Dutch, French, and German.

LIEGE

Au Vieux Liege
Quai de la Goffe, 41
4000 Liege
Belgium
Telephone: 041–23–77–48

All major credit cards
Lunch and dinner
Reservations suggested
Jacket not required
Liquor served
Dinner: $20 to $30
    full 3 courses, without wine
Lunch: the same
Chef: Cornet
Maitre d': Herbertz

This restaurant is situated along the Meuse, a short distance downstream from the *Pont des Arches,* in an ancient building that is an architectural treasure. Built in 1594, the building is called the *Maison Havart* and is considered one of the most striking examples of the civil architecture of Liege. We found it charming, especially as we realized that this attractive old brick building has been standing for about four centuries.

The restaurant, located inside, features high ceilings covered with thick ancient beams and delightful, blue-tiled fireplaces. Gobert, an eminent Liege historian, is correct in saying that the present owners of *Au Vieux Liege* have good taste and high artistic values of the past, and that the restaurant, "in spite of its utilitarian side has become not only a museum, but a living museum where the Wallon language has a friendly sound between these venerable walls, where local dishes and fine wines bring to a zenith the tasteful character of the charming hospitality one finds here."

Au Vieux Liege has a typically fine Belgian menu, where everything is very fresh and the vegetables are young, tender, and sweet. A typical menu might start with a *Creme de Legumes* or a *Bisque de Tourteaux,* followed by *Escalope de Saumon au Concasse de Tomates* or a *Brioche de Poisson Farcie.* As a main course, the choices include *Viande Rouge Flambeé aux Baies et Poivres Varies, Canard Sauvage aux Cerises,* and *Agneau au Jus de Truffles.* Then, for dessert, opt for *Granité au Chocolat* or *Coupe de Sabayon Glacé,* or choose from an *assortiment de sorbets.* This is only a small portion of the items available from a rich and varied menu.

MARTUE

Hostellerie du Vieux Moulin

6821 Martue
(Florenville sur Semois)
Belgium
Telephone: 061–31–10–76

All major credit cards
Lunch and dinner
Reservations recommended
Jacket requested
Liquor served
Meals: $30
    full 3 courses, without wine
Chef: Idem
Maitre d': Raymond Vandenberg

The Hostellerie du Vieux Moulin is a completely refurbished old mill which dates back to the 18th century. It is delightfully situated in the beautiful valley of the river Semois, at Martue, an ancient hamlet of the Gaume region, a short distance from the tourist center at Florenville. The main attraction in this area is the magnificent and vast forest of the Ardennes.

The dining room prides itself on providing typically Belgian gastronomic delights; the weekends featuring game and venison in season are a special pleasure.

RIO DE JANEIRO

Petronius Restaurant

Caesar Park Hotel Ipanema
Ipanema Beach
Avenida Vieira Souto 460
22420 Rio de Janeiro
Brazil
Telephone: 021–287–3122

All major credit cards
Dinner
Reservations required
Jacket not required
Liquor served
Dinner: $20 to $35
full 3 courses, without wine
Chef: Bertrand Bovier
Maitre d': Mauricio de Carvalho

Although the views of the Atlantic Ocean, the beautiful Ipanema Beach next to the famous Copacabana Beach, and the low mountains jutting into the ocean are better from the Toberius, the rooftop coffee shop of the Caesar Park Hotel, we suggest you dine at the brand new Petronius restaurant, which has the same magnificent Rio de Janeiro view from the second floor.

In July 1985, the new Petronius restaurant was opened after it was redesigned by Sig Bergamin, who opted for an art nouveau decor, with light shades predominant. The concept behind it is the informal but elegant style of the *cariocas* (people who are born in Rio). The decor includes large tropical flower arrangements, china, linen, and vases adorning each table, and aquariums with colorful fish. The large panoramic windows bringing in the beautiful beach of Ipanema top off the design with a resounding "wow!"

Bertrand Bovier, the restaurant's Swiss chef, has a menu offering a variety of fish and crustaceans, featuring live lobsters taken from tanks right to the stove for grilling. Starters include soufflés and soups. Main dishes include grilled lobsters and shrimps and a bountiful seafood Imperial Tray. Bowls of mixed fresh green salad are served as well. Suggested desserts include *Rhum-Topf* and a tantalizing assortment of pastry. Small cups made of chocolate containing chantilly cream and chartreuse or cognac are served along with espresso at the end of the meal.

British Virgin Islands

PETER ISLAND

The Beach Bar

Peter Island
British Virgin Islands
Telephone: 809–494–2561

All major credit cards
Lunch and dinner
Reservations not necessary
Dress: informal
Liquor served
Dinner: $34.50 à la carte
Lunch: $12 à la carte
Chef: Wilfred Stout

Peter Island Resort is a 52-room complex occupying two-thirds of Peter Island, one of the larger of the fifty-some islands that comprise the British Virgin Islands. The resort is a 1,050-acre estate offering 104 guests Robinson Crusoe-style seclusion on a palm-fringed beach along Deadman Bay, where Blackbeard, the pirate, left fifteen men and a bottle of rum.

The Beach Bar is a restaurant with a view overlooking Deadman Bay (considered one of the Caribbean's most beautiful beaches), the small islands dotting the Caribbean waters, and the colorful yachts and sailboats. Diners have the option of sitting under cover or outside on the terrace, just a few steps from the water. This resort was recently modernized and improved, with the Beach Bar opening in 1984.

Not a gourmet dining room but offering good food in an informal tropical setting, the Beach Bar features a wide selection of salads and pastas, along with barbecued burgers, chicken, spareribs, and other popular repasts. Sundown cocktails and casual dinners are the preferred choices here.

BRITISH COLUMBIA

NORTH VANCOUVER

Ship of the Seven Seas

Anchored at the foot of Lonsdale Avenue
North Vancouver
British Columbia
Canada
Telephones: 604–987–3344/5/6

All major credit cards
Lunch and dinner
Reservations necessary
Jacket optional
Liquor served
Dinner: $12 to $26
  full 3 courses, without wine
Lunch: $5 to $9
Chefs: Maria Cusano
  Rena Arcuri
Maitre d': Barbara Turnbull

Ferries make fine restaurants. Here in North Vancouver is the Ship of the Seven Seas, formerly North Vancouver Ferry Number 5, one of Canada's most unusual restaurants. It is luxurious and colorful and one of the area's most interesting eating spots. It has a splendid view of the city, the harbor, the neighboring drydock and tugboats, and the famous Sea Bus right next door.

The Seven Seas Buffet is the main attraction. It, too, is a view to dine by. You can fill your plate from a choice of sixty different dishes, including such delights as domestic salmon, crab, shrimp, scallops, prawns, oysters, other Pacific Ocean fish as well as such exotic sea items as octopus, smoked eel, and conch from the Gulf of Mexico. The buffet also offers a complete selection of salads, trimmings, and chicken, as well as a spread of desserts, including fresh fruit, light cakes, puddings, fruit jello, and fruit salad.

The fee for the buffet allows the guest to visit the buffet tables (one cold, one hot) as many times as desired. Or guests may sample the delectable menu of individually prepared seafood or meat dishes from a complete dinner menu.

To get to this restaurant, the conventional way is to drive over the Lions Gate Bridge from downtown Vancouver. But boarding the Sea Bus at the foot of Granville Street in Vancouver is more fun. You have a delightful but fast tour of the harbor, and when you dock in North Vancouver, the Ship of the Seven Seas is only a few steps away.

SOOKE

The Sooke Harbour House

1528 Whiffen Spit Road
R. R. #4
Sooke
British Columbia V0S 1N0
Canada
Telephone: 604–642–3421

All major credit cards
Breakfast, dinner, and Sunday lunch
Reservations advised
Jacket recommended
Liquor served
Dinner: $20 to $45
  full 3 courses, without wine
Lunch: $5 to $20
Chef: Pia Carroll
Maitre d': Sinclair Philip

Set on a bluff above the surf of southern Vancouver Island, the Sooke Harbour House looks out on the small harbor of Sooke, nearly landlocked by the sandy, mile-long Whiffen Spit on one side and by *Juan de Fuca* Strait and the Olympic Mountains on the other.

Sooke Harbour House

It is a dynamic, always-changing view. Harbor seals sun themselves on floating logs, otters frolic, cormorants dry their wings on abandoned pilings, wild Trumpeter swans float by, and bald eagles glide overhead. And because Sooke is also a fishing port, colorful commercial fishing vessels either lay their crab traps in the bay or make their way around red and green government markers to the end of the Whiffen Spit before heading west out to sea.

The Spit is covered with wild flowers, golden hues of Scots broom, wild chives, wild roses, and wind swept pines. The snow-capped Olympic Mountains in the distance range in altitude from 5,000 to 8,000 feet.

The Sooke Harbour House, erected in 1928, features wonderfully fresh food, with 80 percent of the vegetables grown in the gardens on the premises. Fishermen in nearby waters call the restaurant by radio when something unusual is caught and rush the catch right from the boats to the kitchen to be prepared for immediate serving. The menu—which changes constantly—includes endless varieties of fresh fish, plus vegetables, fruits, and herbs. A big round table offers a predinner buffet of unusual seafood appetizers, ranging from Smoked Lingcod and Fresh and Salted Salmon Eggs to Red Rock Crab and Marinated Octopus. The local Northwest Pacific cuisine features, of course, salmon, sturgeon, abalone, sea urchin, shrimp, and local game, plus vegetables and wild mushrooms. Pretty as a picture are the edible flower salads. This dining room has won the *Chaine des Rotisseurs* medallion, the Sea Urchin Award for contributions to Northwestern Cuisine, the 1982 International Culinary Arts Competition, and others.

The desserts here feature some of the fruit grown in the garden. One favorite is the Blueberry Mousse.

VANCOUVER

Il Giardino di Umberto

1382 Hornby Street
Vancouver
British Columbia
Canada
Telephone: 604–669–2422

All major credit cards
Lunch and dinner
Reservations recommended
Dress: casual
Liquor served
Dinner: $25 to $40
*   full 3 courses, without wine*
Lunch: $15 to $20
Chef: Olivier Arm
Maitre d': Chico Tjehdor

Umberto Menghi opened his first restaurant in Vancouver in 1973. *Il Giardino* is his third, opened in 1976.

It is particularly pleasant in summer, when nearly all the guests dine in the Mediterranean Garden. There's a family atmosphere here: everyone seems to know everyone else, and soon, even though we were strangers, we were able to meet and talk with many fellow patrons. This restaurant is regarded by many as Umberto's finest achievement. A local columnist unhesitantly calls it the best restaurant in the country. Even in winter it is a delight, for with the decor, Umberto brings the garden inside.

The cuisine concentrates on game, such as duck, partridge, pheasant, rabbit, and quail. One unique dish is the cannelloni stuffed with ground reindeer meat that is flown in from Inuvik. Other specialties include *Filetto di Capriolo Pepato* (fillet of reindeer in pepper and brandy sauce) and egg fettuccine tossed with one teaspoon of orange juice, reduced with white wine, tossed with julienne of green beans, tomato concasse, and parmesan cheese.

The Pelican Bay Restaurant

The Granville Island Hotel
1253 Johnston Street
Granville Island
Vancouver
British Columbia V6H 3R9
Canada
Telephone: 604–683–7373

All major credit cards
Lunch, dinner, and Saturday
*   and Sunday brunch*
Reservations advised
Dress: casual, no jeans
Liquor served
Dinner: $30 to $40
*   full 3 courses, without wine*
Lunch: $10 to $15
Chef: John Cochran
Food and Beverage Manager:
*   George Walker*

The Pelican Bay Restaurant offers one of the more interesting views in a city full of views. From May 2 through October 13 of 1986, the most exciting view from this restaurant is of Expo 86, the World Exposition in Vancouver. Expo 86 celebrates Vancouver's centennial, and it is situated about 300 yards across the water from the Granville Island

Hotel. Even without the exposition, diners enjoy looking at the water, leisure boats, and the city skyline, against the backdrop of snow-capped mountains.

Granville Island, a delightful part of Vancouver, has theater as well as boating as a major attraction. The Granville Island Hotel is the only hotel on this island, and it is a marina as well with moorage facilities for up to 50 yachts throughout the year. It is the second "boatel" in Vancouver; the first is the Westin Bayshore Inn.

The Granville Island Hotel is small and one of the Canadian West Coast's most unusual. It has a sweeping reception area with lofty ceilings and tiered stories overlooking the central Pelican Bay restaurant and lounge area. The front of the building points upward and, when approached from the water, looks like the prow of a boat. It is beautifully modern, with plenty of glass and light and a profusion of plants.

This hotel is at the heart of all the Granville Island attractions—the Arts Club Theatre, the Public Market, the gallery shops, and other bohemian attractions. It is near the new British Columbia Place development (with a 60,000-seat stadium) and is adjacent to the Amphitheatre park, a center of the island's entertainment events during the summer months.

In 1985, the Pelican Bay menu won first prize in a British Columbia Hotel Association competition. Among the favorite main dishes are Chicken Dijonaise and a *Hôte* Seafood Salad. For dessert, Rhubarb Mousse is the featured item.

Salmon House on the Hill

2229 Folkstone Way
West Vancouver
British Columbia V7S 2Y6
Canada
Telephone: 604–926–3212

All major credit cards
Lunch, dinner, and Sunday brunch
Reservations suggested
Jacket preferred
Liquor served
Dinner: $12 to $20
  full 3 courses, without wine
Lunch: $6 to $12
Manager: Pierre Barbey

There are many views to dine by in Vancouver, but most of them look westward. One of the best views, looking southeast to Vancouver itself and much more, can be seen from a delightful restaurant atop a hill in West Vancouver.

The Salmon House on the Hill is just off the Upper Levels Highway in West Vancouver. It commands a stunning view of Howe Sound, English Bay, and a bit of the Burrard Inlet, and on a clear day you can see beyond to Mount Baker, Mount Rainier, and more of the snow-capped mountains. Day or night, the view is breathtaking.

The building which houses the restaurant is built of natural British Columbia cedar, and the decor features attractive West Indian artifacts. It has picture windows and seats 160 guests on two levels, with a small adjoining lounge. All spots offer view opportunities.

Opened in 1976, the Salmon House on the Hill was originally a convenient eating establishment for residents of the condominiums and apartments of a development aptly called Panorama Village. But its reputation as a fine restaurant spread rapidly and now it is considered one of the top restaurants in Greater Vancouver.

Our favorites are the house salmon specialties. We recommend the Smoked Salmon as an appetizer. As a main course, we suggest Barbecued Salmon, a succulent fillet done over sweet smoke of alderwood (as is common in this area) served with cheddar cheese and a side of potatoes with the restaurant's own blend of natural brown rice and herbs. Swiss-born manager Pierre Barbey says that he also gets lots of calls for the restaurant's shrimp salad and the vegetarian plate. Other interesting items include an oyster omelet called Hangtown Fry. For those who prefer meat there are daily specials such as Beef Stroganoff, Cornish Hen, Roast Rib Eye of Beef, and others. If you want a little of everything, try the Salmon House Platter, which includes salmon, beef, and Cornish game hen.

Served with all dinners are Bannock Bread (an Indian bread of the area), fresh country butter, Wild Blueberry Ice Cream, or Cranberry Sherbet. Other great desserts served include the Salmon House's "World-Renowned Apple Cobbler," Cheesecake with Raspberry Sauce, and Bavarian Chocolate Cream with Tia Maria.

The Teahouse Restaurant
at Ferguson Point

Stanley Park
Vancouver
British Columbia
Canada
Telephone: 604–669–3281

All major credit cards
Lunch, dinner, and
*   Saturday and Sunday brunch*
Reservations required
Jacket not required
Liquor served
Dinner: $15 to $20
*   full 3 courses, without wine*
Lunch: $10 to $15
Chef: Lucien Couet
Maitre d's: David Richard and
*   Felix Zurbuchen*

This restaurant, once a simple teahouse, is now one of Vancouver's most popular dining spots. Undoubtedly, the view overlooking English Bay and the Straits of Georgia has much to do with this. As you look north you see the Northshore Mountains, including peaks called the "lions" which are snowcapped almost year-round. These slope west toward Howe Sound and Bowden Island. Looking southwest, you see the University District. On clear days you can see the distant mountains of Vancouver Island and part of the Gulf Islands more than thirty miles away.

Among the starters on the menu are Stuffed Mushrooms and *Pâté de Volaille*. Main dishes include Barbecued Prawns and Rack of Lamb as well as the regular Teahouse menu of seafood and French country specialties.

Stanley Park, where this restaurant is situated, occupies over 1,000 acres in the heart of the city. It has an unspoiled wilderness, a fine aquarium, and a Shakespearean Garden which features every flower the great Bard mentioned in his works. There's a beautiful rose garden as well.

VICTORIA

The Captain's Palace

309 Belleville Street
Victoria
British Columbia V8V 1X2
Canada
Telephone: 604–388–9191

All major credit cards
Breakfast, lunch, and dinner
Reservations suggested
Jacket requested
Liquor served
Dinner: $20
*   full 3 courses, without wine*
Lunch: $9
Chef: Patrick Savory
Maitre d': John Yong

What a setting for a delightful view of old Victoria! Victoria is a wonderfully English city with a colorful past. The Captain's Palace is the perfect place to experience that treasured legacy.

This magnificent Victorian mansion, with its quaint pepper-shaker tower and surrounding open veranda, was originally built in 1897 for W.J. Pendray, a prominent person in the history and development of this beautiful city. Every detail of the home, from the hand-painted frescoes by Mueller and Sterne to the elaborate stained-glass windows and doors, is an echo of the opulence of the late 1890s and has been faithfully restored and preserved by the host of the Captain's Palace, Florence, and her late husband, Bill Prior.

The foyer door leads you into a wood-panelled receiving room where you'll most likely see a glowing fire in the picturesque hand-painted ceramic-tiled fireplace. Guests may have cocktails or after-dinner liqueurs in this cozy area.

Each room of The Captain's Palace has its own character. The library has a unique hidden panel door. The original family dining room and music room feature frescoed ceilings and walls, a fireplace with an oak mantel, and a built-in buffet that displays the

Priors' antique collection. The glassed-in porch overlooks the rose garden and is a favorite for breakfast. Members of the serving staff add to the overall flavor of the place by wearing costumes of the Victorian era.

The Captain's Palace offers a view of the bustling Inner Harbour of Victoria and of the ships which connect Vancouver Island to the United States, the British Columbian mainland, and the city of Vancouver. These ships dock almost at the restaurant's doorstep. From here you look directly across the harbor to the "Old Town"; there is also a fine view of the majestic Empress Hotel, built in the same era as the Captain's Palace by the Canadian Pacific Railroad.

Many famous people have dined here, and the guest book includes the signatures of Burt Lancaster, Margaret O'Brien, Darren McGavin, Andy Devine, Cheryl Ladd, and many others.

You can get a gift at dinner, too. The "house drink" is served in a ceramic replica of the Captain's Palace which you may take home as a souvenir.

A favorite on the very good menu is Pacific Stew, a collection of seafood delectables in a blanket of tarragon and cognac cream. For dessert, consider puff pastry filled with Chantilly liqueur, floating on a pond of chocolate sauce. The cuisine generally features fresh seafood as well as sizzling steaks, tempting chicken, and crisp salads. The dessert table presents you with some tough choices!

The Captain's Table is easy to find; it is located on the left side of the harbor as you look from the Empress Hotel, just opposite the berth of the ship, the *Princess Marguerite*.

Parrot House Restaurant

Chateau Victoria
740 Burdett Avenue
Victoria
British Columbia V8W 1B2
Canada
Telephone: 604-382-9258

All major credit cards
Breakfast and dinner
Reservations necessary
Jacket not required
Liquor served
Dinner: $20 to $35
 full 3 courses, without wine
Chef: Gilbert Noussitou
Maitre d': Joseph Roese

The Parrott House Restaurant is Victoria's only rooftop restaurant, situated atop the Chateau Victoria—a modern and modest skyscraper hotel.

The restaurant provides a full-circle panorama of the city, the Juan de Fuca Strait, and the majestic Olympic Mountains. The view of the harbor is delightful because it is always so busy and colorful. At night, the lights of the harbor and on the Parliament building provide a lovely show.

The cuisine is very good. Among the more popular main dishes which use locally available products are Roast Duckling in Orange Cointreau Sauce, Roasted Rack of Lamb with Dijon mustard and Fresh Herbs, Shrimp- and Crab-Filled Rainbow Trout, and Poached Salmon in Cream and Sorrel. For meat lovers there's Chateaubriand, a succulent cut of prime beef tenderloin broiled to taste and served with garden fresh vegetables and

Parrot House

Bernaise sauce. Favorite desserts include the dark mousse, made with fine Belgian chocolate flavored with Cointreau, or Crepes Lady Janes (for two), made from ice cream and fresh fruits and flambéed at your table.

The Parrot House Restaurant is so called for the legendary parrot named Louis who once lived in turn-of-the-century luxury in the big white mansion on the hill where the Chateau Victoria now stands. Louis was a gift to Miss Victoria Jane Wilson from her father. After Miss Wilson died, her parrot was very well cared for via a stipulation in Miss Wilson's will. The mansion in which he lived was eventually destroyed, but the Chateau Victoria contains a rooftop residence dedicated to him. It is even said that Louis is still alive, although no one seems to be able to say where he is.

WEST VANCOUVER

Tudor Room

Park Royal Hotel
440 Clyde Avenue
West Vancouver
British Columbia
Canada
Telephone: 604–926–5511

All major credit cards
Breakfast, lunch, and dinner
Reservations necessary
Jacket required
Liquor served
Dinner: entrée only—$15 to $30
Lunch: $9 to $22
Chef: Hans Shaub
Maitre d': Guy Easter

The Park Royal Hotel is a charming, ivy-covered Tudor building with only 30 rooms; in these days of multistoried high-tech hotels, you'll find a different kind of luxury here. Situated beside the beautiful Capilano River, the hotel is an oasis of tranquility just minutes away from the bustle of downtown Vancouver.

The Tudor Room is an elegant place to dine and the recipient of such awards as Best Place in the Northwest to Dine and four stars from the *Mobil Travel Guide.* Among the highlights of the cuisine are Roast Venison, British Columbia Salmon, pheasant, local fresh fish, and the hotel's own bakery products made by an award-winning pâtissier.

ONTARIO
NIAGARA FALLS

Skylon

5200 Robinson Street
Niagara Falls
Ontario L2G 2A3
Canada
Telephone: 416–356–2651

All major credit cards
Lunch and dinner
Reservations recommended
Dress: casual
Liquor served
Dinner: $15 to $30
    full 3 courses, without wine
Lunch: $7 to $20
Chef: Maurice Olaizola
Maitre d's: Peter Warren and
    Mario Ferrentali

The Skylon is 775 feet above the base of Niagara Falls; it has three levels, including an indoor and outdoor Observation Deck, the famous Revolving Dining Room, and the Skylon Dining Lounge, all of which are reached by three external glass-enclosed "Yellow Bug" elevators taking 52 seconds from top to bottom.

The Revolving Dining Room offers gourmet cuisine and a view of the majestic Horseshoe and American Falls. The view changes during the year, and the Skylon is open year-round. It is particularly delightful from November through February during the Niagara Falls Winter Festival of Lights, which is a four-mile million-dollar lighting display going into its fourth year (in November 1986). The Skylon itself, when aglow, resembles a giant Christmas Tree, and everything else in the area, including the Falls, is magnificently lighted in colors of the rainbow, all beautifully reflected in the snow.

Among the recommended dishes in the Revolving Dining Room are Rack of Lamb and the Roast Prime Rib of Beef. Lunch is served at noon, and dinner begins at 5 P.M.

Top of the Rainbow Dining Room

Minolta Tower
6732 Oakes Drive
Niagara Falls
Ontario L2G 3W6
Canada
Telephone: 416–356–1501

All major credit cards
Lunch and dinner
Reservations not necessary
Dress: informal
Liquor served
Dinner: $20 to $40
    full 3 courses, without wine
Lunch: $10 to $20
Chef: Kevin McGann
Maitre d': Dino Pozzobon

Top of the Rainbow provides another revolving view of Niagara Falls and the 5,000 square miles of beautiful countryside surrounding them. It is a favorite of the many thousands of tourists who visit the Falls on the Canadian side. Particularly beautiful is the view at night.

Winner of several awards for its cuisine, the restaurant features Canadian specialties such as venison, pheasant, and fresh fish from Canadian waters.

The Victoria Park Restaurant
Queen Victoria Park

Niagara Falls
Ontario L2E 6T2
Canada
Telephone: 416–356–2217

All major credit cards
Breakfast, lunch, and dinner
Reservations not required
Jacket not required
Liquor served
Dinner: $9 to $17
full 3 courses, without wine
Lunch: $6 to $17
Chef: Alexander DeVries
Maitre d': Harry Webb

The Victoria Park Restaurant is located midway between the Horseshoe and the American Falls, offering a superb view of both cataracts of Niagara Falls. Resembling a Swiss chalet and once called the Refectory, this restaurant has been catering to visitors since 1904. There is a second-floor dining room and outdoor dining on a covered balcony.

Among the specialties is the local Niagara wine—a product of the famous Niagara Fruit Belt. Meals are served with fresh rolls, tasty desserts, and luscious French pastries baked on the premises.

A note about the falls—the Horseshoe Falls are 2,200 feet wide and 176 feet high, while the American Falls are 1,000 feet wide and 184 feet high, and both are named for obvious reasons. The word "Niagara" comes from the language of the Iroquois Indians, and it means "the thunder of the waters."

TORONTO

Top of Toronto

CN Tower
301 Front Street West
Toronto
Ontario M5V 2T6
Canada
Telephone: 416–362–5411

All major credit cards
Lunch and dinner
Reservations necessary
Jacket requested
Liquor served
Dinner: $20 to $26
full 3 courses, without wine
Lunch: $8 to $15
Chef: Nigel Shute
Maitre d': Franco Debe

This is Toronto's most visible and certainly its most famous landmark. Even the citizens of Toronto, who generally aren't given to boasting, find themselves telling visitors that the CN Tower is almost twice as tall as the Eiffel Tower.

The CN Tower was opened in 1976 as a combination communications tower, sightseeing platform, restaurant, and disco, with an elevator ride that would satisfy the most fearless thrill-seekers. The tower is the world's tallest freestanding structure, rising 1,815 feet from the surface of the pool at its base to the tip of its 130,000-ton needle-shaped transmission mast. On a clear day, from the indoor observation floor, at 1,136 feet, you can see for about 75 miles south to Rochester, New York, and north to the far shore of Lake Simcoe.

The observation platform and the restaurant are always packed with tourists. While the food—a variety of international cuisine—is certainly not the best in Toronto, the view is definitely the most comprehensive and exciting in town. It is not to be missed.

The Winter Palace

The Sheraton Centre of Toronto
K23 Queen Street West
Toronto
Ontario M5H 2M9
Canada
Telephone: 416–361–1000

All major credit cards
Lunch and dinner
Reservations recommended
Jacket necessary
Liquor served
Dinner: $25 to $30
    full 3 courses, without wine
Lunch: $10 to $15
Chef: P.C. Lee
Maitre d': Daniel Kadosh

The Winter Palace, a magnificent restaurant located on the 43rd floor of the Sheraton Centre of Toronto, overlooks the north side of the new City Hall (an architectural award-winning building) and the Nathan Philip Square.

The City Hall has a spaceship-like disc, which serves as the Council Chambers, surrounded by two semi-curved towers, approximately 20 stories tall; it is a modern structure that stands in brilliant contrast to the old City Hall and Osgoode Hall (which houses the courts) on either side, a salute to Toronto's heritage while at the same time setting the pace for the city's future. Nathan Philip Square, an open area in front of City Hall, contains a celebrated Peace Garden which was opened by former prime minister Pierre Trudeau and dedicated this past year by Pope John Paul II. During the summer months, this is a popular meeting place, and there are concerts and other free programs everyday. A fountain with massive arches curves over the water. In winter the fountain area is turned into an ice rink for skating (free of charge).

The south view from the Winter Palace overlooks the massive downtown financial center of the city, the CN Tower (the world's tallest freestanding structure) and Lake Ontario, which also has an island airport for small planes. Something is always happening, no matter the season, to create entertaining views from the Winter Palace.

The Winter Palace decor takes its cue from the lifestyle of the Tsars of pre-revolutionary Russia. The elegant double-headed eagle which was used as a symbol of the Russian Empire is used as the logo of the restaurant, and tapestries depicting the styles and important events of the times hang on the inside walls of the room. Other artifacts of the period, such as painted eggs, books, and a ceramic baking oven, are displayed discreetly throughout the restaurant. The staff uniforms also reflect the old Russian theme.

Such regal splendor has been appropriate at times: the Russian ambassador has been a guest here, while the queen of England, during a visit to Toronto, asked that the Palace's truffles be sent to her yacht. The floor-to-ceiling view is available from all spots, including the last stall in both the men's and ladies' restrooms!

The cuisine has won recognition from the National Restaurant Association, Ford

Fine Dining, and others. Popular specialties include *Zakuski, Salmon Kulebiaka,* Duck with Champagne Sauce, Charlotte Russe, and Capuccino Parfait.

The Winter Palace was named after the Winter Palace in St. Petersburg, now Leningrad. Since opening four years ago, the Winter Palace has been a huge success. With food beautifully prepared and presented, and graceful service, the diners are transported into the extravagant world of Tsarist Russia. We suggest you ask for the *Zakuska Plate,* a hot or cold sampler of such items as sweetbreads, stroganoff, and pastry-wrapped poached salmon. Another interesting dish is Venison Grand Duke Serge—medallions of wild deer with fresh chanterelles.

QUEBEC
LAC BEAUPORT

Manoir St. Castin

99, Chemin Tour du Lac
Lac Beauport
Quebec G0A 2C0
Canada
Telephone: 418–849–4461

All major credit cards
Breakfast, lunch, and dinner
Reservations suggested
Jacket required at dinner
Liquor served
Dinner: $15 to $38
  full 3 courses, without wine
Brunch: $10
Chef: Alfred Sioui
Maitre d': Jean Hainaut

The Manoir St. Castin, situated in a house dating from 1938, offers a view from every window table that is delightful in any season. You can see the shimmering (or frozen) *Lac Beauport* as well as the surrounding slopes of the Laurentians.

The food, classical French cuisine, is said to be excellent. The chef follows the "honored customs of the famous *relais gastronomiques* of old France."

The favorites are the Grilled Steak, the lamb, and, for dessert, the Black Forest Cake and the Napoleons.

MONTREAL

Le Cafe de Paris
and Le Jardin du Ritz

Ritz-Carlton
1228, rue Sherbrooke Ouest
Montreal
Quebec H3G 1H6
Canada
Telephone: 514–842–4212

All major credit cards
Breakfast, lunch, and dinner
Afternoon tea in the garden
Reservations required
Jacket required
Liquor served
Dinner: $25 to $51
  full 3 courses, without wine
Lunch: $11.75 to $15.50
Chef: Jean Saliou

Entering the Cafe de Paris means discovering a blend of the old and new worlds of elegance—subtle tones, soft lights, and cordial, unobtrusive attention given to even an unspoken wish. The view offers a glimpse of the garden beyond.

When the garden opens, all Montreal knows that summer has arrived. Guests are invited to "breakfast as the dew disappears from the rosebuds" . . . "where the scent of fresh blossoms mingles with the aroma of over twenty varieties of tea [at tea time]." The Cafe de Paris serves lunch and dinner in the true Ritz tradition of elegance. During the summer months, Le Jardin du Ritz, with its charming duckling pond, provides a cool and picturesque haven for lunch, tea, or dinner al fresco, and is a favorite breakfast spot as well.

The cuisine has garnered a good deal of recognition, including, since 1974, the *Travel/Holiday* Magazine Award. Highlights of the menu include hors d'oeuvres such as marble of lobster and calf's sweetbread with seaweed, *Le Feuillete de Saumon a la Ritz* as an entrée, and, for dessert, *Coupe.* Other specialties *de la jardin* include *Le Pithiviers de Langoustines aux Pleurotes, Les Bouchles de Sol de Douvres au Beurre de Morilles, Les Picattas de Veau aux Noix de Petoncles,* and *Les Escalopes de Ris de Veau aux Perles de la Foret.*

In the summer, most guests feel they *must* dine in the garden, so garden dining spots must be reserved well in advance.

Le Castillon

Hotel Bonaventure Hilton International
1, Place Bonaventure
Montreal
Quebec H5A 1E4
Canada
Telephone: 514-878-2332

All major credit cards
Lunch and dinner
Reservations required
Jacket required
Liquor served
Dinner: $25 to $35
 full 3 courses, without wine
Lunch: $9 to $15
Chef: Wahed Naja
Maitre d': Pierre Margueron

Le Castillon, the restaurant of the Hotel Bonaventure Hilton International, is located on the main floor of the Bonaventure, which is actually the 17th floor of the building in which it is located (the hotel begins on this floor). On the sixteen floors below is one of the largest commercial and exhibition centers in Canada.

The view from Le Castillon, with its floor to ceiling windows, is not, as one might suspect, a panorama of the city of Montreal. Rather, it is a unique view of the two-and-one-half acres of plush rooftop gardens surrounding it, not only with flowers and plants, but also streams, tiny waterfalls, and an outdoor dining terrace in the midst of all. It is most popular for lunch and dinner in the warmer months.

The decor of Le Castillon is of baronial splendor, enhanced by antique chandeliers, Renaissance wall tapestries, and deep plush burgundy velvet armchairs, all combined to give the room a 17th century French castle decor.

Among the many *haute cuisine* dishes served from gleaming silver trays and trolleys by the very stylish waiters (who dress in 17th century attire) are Rack of Lamb Castillon, Turbot stuffed with Smoked Salmon Mousse, and Roasted Quails with grapes and Port Wine sauce. The desserts include Brazilian *Crêpes Flambées, La Mousse aux Deux Chocolats* (dark and white chocolate mousse), Hazelnut Parfait, Pear in Pastry Shell with Cream Custard and Raspberry Sauce, and assorted pastries from a plentiful pastry wagon.

Helene de Champlain Restaurant

200, Tour de l'Isle
Ile Ste-Helene
Montreal
Quebec
Canada
Telephone: 514–395–2424

All major credit cards
Lunch and dinner
Reservations requested
Jacket required at dinner
Liquor served
Dinner: $14 to $25
full 3 courses, without wine
Lunch: $6.95 to $10.95
Chef: George Geropoulos
Maitre d': Shirley Duhaime

This lovely restaurant with a view also has an interesting history. It was built as a Sports Chalet in 1937 by the government of Quebec. In 1942, it was given by Quebec to the City of Montreal and soon became a favorite spot for government-sponsored functions, located as it is on picturesque Ste-Helene's Island in the St. Lawrence River. In 1954, the Sports Chalet was renamed for the island's honoree, Helene de Champlain.

During Expo '67 this restaurant—temporarily called the *Pavillon d'Honneur de l'Expo '67*—was used by the commissioner general of the Expo, Pierre Dupuy, to host dignitaries and guests of the great international exposition. In 1983, it became a restaurant open to the public under the management of Les Entreprises Marcotte, Inc.

The view of its own gardens, set up like a miniature palace garden, of the river, and of some of the buildings that have remained in use since the Expo, is pleasant, making the restaurant a continued favorite of business people, dignitaries, and others. Among the dishes on a fine menu are Feuillete of Snails, Roast Prime Rib of Beef, and the house specialty, *Crepes Helene de Champlain*. The cuisine has received awards from the *Societe des Chefs de Cuisine et Patissiers de la P.Q.* and *Commanderie des Costes du Rhone*. Helene de Champlain Restaurant is reached from downtown Montreal via the Concord Bridge.

Helene de Champlain

Tour de Ville

Le Grand Hotel
777 University Street
Montreal
Quebec H3C 3Z7
Canada
Telephone: 514–879–1370

All major credit cards
Dinner and Sunday brunch
Reservations recommended
Jacket required
Liquor served
Sunday Brunch: $13.50
Chef: Pierre Pedeches

The Tour de Ville, the only revolving restaurant in Montreal, atop Le Grand Hotel, offers views of the Notre Dame Church, *Chateau de Ramezay* (where early Montreal's governors lived), the Bank of Montreal, and other sights. The restaurant is so arranged that every table has a magnificent view of the city. At night, the city is awash with twinkling and multicolored lights, so the view is sheer delight. Le Grand Hotel is in the heart of Montreal, close to Old Montreal. The Tour de Ville is large, seating 220.

Favorites from a menu featuring French cuisine include Lobster in Cream Sauce and Puff Pastry and Poached Sole in Riesling wine stuffed with Mousseline of Trout in Cream Sauce. The two most popular desserts are Chocolate Cheesecake and Bavarian Cake flavored with coffee liqueur.

PERCÉ

La Normandie Dining Room

2210 Route 132
Percé
Quebec G0C 2L0
Canada
Telephone: 418–782–2112

All major credit cards
Breakfast and dinner
Reservations recommended
Jacket not required
Liquor served
Dinner: $9.50 to $24
    full 3 courses, without wine
Chef: F. Letourneau
Maitre d': M. Boudreau

The Hotel La Normandie opened in 1937 but was destroyed by a fire in 1977. A beautiful new hotel, offering the same fine hospitality and food, and the same view of the famous Percé Rock and Bonaventure Island, was built on the same site. Percé, the lovely site of La Normandie, is on the popular and beautiful Gaspé Peninsula, where the southern shore of the St. Lawrence River meets the Gulf. This peninsula is hundreds of millions of years old, one of the oldest land masses on earth, but one of the most recently populated. Its coastline is rugged as well as beautiful, a fitting attraction for explorers such as Jacques Cartier, who set up a wooden cross here in 1534 and claimed the land for the King of France, and Samuel de Champlain, who in 1603 gave the place the name of Gachape, from the Indian word *gespeg,* which means the "end of land" in the language of the Micmac Indians.

The dining room of La Normandie is noted for its fine food—the government of Quebec has awarded it three forks. Among the favorites are Crabmeat Crepe, Frog Legs with Raspberry Vinegar, Scallops in Leek Sauce, Tenderloin Beef with Seafood Sauce, and Sole with Apple Butter Sauce. For dessert, try Peppered Fresh Strawberries or Maple Syrup Pie. The annual fall and spring buffet tables are also quite a treat. Most of the diners here come from the surrounding area, though the occasional prime minister or celebrity has been seen here as well. La Normandie is located at the center of Percé, directly on the water, about 500 feet from the town wharf.

POINTE AU PIC

L'Auberge des Trois Canards

49, Cote Bellevue
Point-au-Pic
Quebec
Canada
Telephone: 418–665–3761

All major credit cards
Dinner
Reservations required
Jacket requested
Liquor served
Dinner: $16
full 3 courses, without wine
Chef: Jocelyne Girard
Maitre d': Michel St-Pierre

This is the dining room of a small 1920s country inn which overlooks the St. Lawrence River. The food is prepared Continental style. Among the specialties are Veal Picatta *à la Creme* and *Filet Mignon Brochette.* The favorite dessert here is the homemade cheesecake. The menu offers a wide range of choices, from seafood to veal, beef, and steak.

QUEBEC CITY

L'Astral

Hotel Loews Le Concorde
1225, place Montcalm
Quebec City
Quebec G1R 4W6
Canada
Telephone: 418–647–2222

All major credit cards
Dinner and Sunday brunch
Reservations recommended
Jacket required
Liquor served
Dinner: $16
Buffet: $18
Sunday Brunch: $10
Chef: Pierre Majois
Maitre d': Rene Duchesne

One of the oldest cities in North America, 377-year old Quebec City, capital of the Province of Quebec, is one of the most beautiful urban areas on the continent. Samuel de Champlain founded the colony of New France in 1608 on the banks high above the St. Lawrence River, and it was here in 1763 that the British won Canada from the French.

Nonetheless, Quebec City, with its narrow streets, open public squares, and imposing fortifications, looks as French today as it did before the British took over. It is the only walled city in North America, and within those walls are some delightful old sights—among them the majestic Chateau Frontenac and Rue Sainte-Anne, a street occupied by bistros, boutiques, cafés, art galleries, and street entertainers. Many of the homes and other buildings date to the 17th and 18th centuries, and the grand promenade in the Upper Town has a magnificent overview of the busy St. Lawrence River.

The best place to see almost all of this at once is from Quebec City's only revolving restaurant, situated on the 29th floor of the Hotel Loews Le Concorde. The highlights of the view from here are the Grand Allee, which is called Quebec City's Champs-Elysées, Battlefield Park, the city fortifications, the Laurentian Mountains, the Parliament building, and, of course, the St. Lawrence River.

The cuisine at *L'Astral,* which features French and Continental specialties, is superb. The favorites are Breast of Pheasant in Mustard Sauce, Scallops Casserole with Cream of Leeks, and Sautéed Snails in Chartreuse Sauce. The desserts include assorted cakes and Maple Syrup Soufflé, or you might ask to try the pastry chef's specialty of the day.

ST-MARC-SUR-LE-RICHELIEU

Auberge Handfield

555, rue Richelieu
St-Marc-sur-Richelieu
Quebec
Canada
Telephone: 514–584–2226

All major credit cards
Breakfast, lunch, and dinner
Reservations suggested
Jacket suggested at dinner
Liquor served
Dinner: $14
     full 3 courses, without wine
Sunday brunch: $8
Sunday buffet: $8
Chef: André Morizot
Maitre d': Pierre Handfield

This is a 200-year-old country inn on the shores of the beautiful Richelieu River that has been carefully refurbished and which serves, as you might expect from an age-old establishment, classic, venerable dishes that have withstood the test of time. Two such favorites are Dover Sole and rabbit sautéed in white wine.

The view from the windows of the cozy dining room is, of course, of the river and the countryside. Not all seats have views, but the Handfields will try to seat you, if you ask, so you can enjoy the view while you dine.

PORTILLO

Terrace Dining Room

Hotel Portillo
International Road
Portillo
Chile
Telephones: 231–3411/2/3

All major credit cards
Breakfast, lunch, and dinner
Reservations recommended
Jacket required for dinner
Liquor served
Dinner: $5 to $25
  full 3 courses, without wine
Lunch: the same
Proprietor: Henry C. Purcell

The dining room of the Hotel Portillo looks upon *Laguna del Inca* from an altitude of 9,400 feet. The Lake of the Incas is over two miles long and of such incredible depth that the water reflects the most brilliant of blues and other colors. Rising around the entire area are some of the highest and most beautiful mountains in the Western Hemisphere, including Mt. Aconcogua, the highest of them all.

The dining room offers international and Chilean cuisine. Most of the guests are from Argentina and Brazil, as well as from Chile. Those from the United States are usually ski enthusiasts.

Portillo is easy to find, located as it is on the International Road between Los Andes (Chile) and Mendoza (Argentina).

GUANGZHOU (CANTON)

The Roof and the Four Seasons restaurants at the China Hotel

Liu Hua Lu
Guangzhou (Canton)
China
Telephone: 66888

All major credit cards
Lunch and dinner
Reservations necessary
Jacket recommended
Liquor served
Dinner: payment is in Foreign
*   Exchange Certificates*
Chef: Chinese—Y.Y. Ho
*   Western—Robert Kogler*
General Manager: Joachim E. Burger

There are several restaurants in the new China Hotel, but for the best view of the pretty Liu Hua Lane to the west and, around it, one of Guangzhou's most scenic parks, try the Roof Restaurant on the China Hotel's 18th floor. Part of the pleasure of the view is the trip to the dining room in an outdoor elevator.

The Roof serves gourmet and standard Continental cuisine. Although not yet competitive with the cuisine of Europe, the main problem being that, owing to import restrictions, all of the meat and some of the seafood, such as salmon, has to be imported frozen, the food here is still good, thanks to the high standards and imagination of Chef Kogler.

About 60 percent of all ingredients used are imported, but local fresh produce and seafood are used where possible.

A true effort is made to offer a full Continental menu. Hot and cold appetizers, for example, include French Vineyard Snails, Frog Legs *Provencal,* Quenelles Cantonese (tiny dumplings made of fish and shrimp farce, individually wrapped in lettuce leaves, poached, and served in Chablis sauce), Smoked Canadian Salmon, Air-Dried Beef and Pork in the Swiss tradition, and Salad of Duck Confit. For the soup course, you can try Crab Bisque Creole.

Main dishes at the Roof include Beef Tenderloin in Bourdeaux Sauce, Supreme of Chicken with Ginger, Roast Young Pigeon, Pork Medallions in Paprika Sauce, Veal Steak *Vigneron,* Beef Fillet with Black or Green Pepper, and Tiger Prawns Piccadilly. A Caesar Salad is served with the meal.

Among the desserts are French Apple Tart, Chocolate Mousse *Suchard,* Crêpes Madagascar, and Ice Biscuit "Reverie," which is a combination of frozen cherry and pistachio parfait. Sherbets and ice cream are made fresh every day.

The Roof is a long but cozy dining room that seats about 100 people. It has chandeliers and candles at the tables, along with fresh flowers. Its 18th-century drawing room decor features pale green carpeting and silk draperies, peach paneling, and peach and green floral wallpaper, all of which provide a suitable background for replicas of Louis XV chairs. The dining room and its lounge are considered one of the most attractive of its kind in China.

There are other restaurants in the hotel. The Four Seasons Restaurant offers 140 different kinds of *dim sum,* which are typical Cantonese small snacks, both sweet and savory, such as steamed shrimp dumplings, egg rolls, spare ribs, and tiny pastries which are served at breakfast or lunch. The Four Seasons' menu changes with the seasons to feature the province's abundant natural produce. In spring, fresh vegetables are utilized; in summer, squashes and melons are featured along with fresh luchees, a nut with a fruity taste; in autumn, the menu offers casseroles and snake soups, a local Cantonese delicacy; and in winter, wild game dishes and rich winter vegetables are highlighted.

Curaçao, N.A.

WILLEMSTAD

Belle Terrace

Avila Beach Hotel
Penstraat 130
Willemstad,
Curaçao, N.A.
Telephone: 614377

All major credit cards
Breakfast, lunch, and dinner
Reservations recommended
Jackets not required
Liquor served
Dinner: $18 to $25
  full 3 courses, without wine
Lunch: $12 to $18
Proprietor: F. N. Moller
Maitre d's: Rob v. Kouwen
  and Lucy Rubiano

The Avila Beach Hotel was originally a governor's mansion. In a book on Curaçao by Dutch historian Dr. Johan Hartog, we learn that in 1812, during the occupation of the island by the British at the time of the Napoleonic wars, the English Governor Hodgson moved from the old government house to the *Belle Alliance* mansion, presumably named to commemorate the alliance against Napoleon. The mansion had a pen for animals and a pleasure garden, as it was called, which was said to have been extremely beautiful. Today, the building houses the Avila Hotel, with 45 modern guest rooms, its own private beach, and an open-air restaurant called Belle Terrace.

This romantic restaurant by the sea has all the old-world charm you'd expect in a 200-year-old mansion. The split-level restaurant extends to the beach with a bar and patio. At lunchtime the Danish chef serves a delicious smorgasbord platter. On Saturday night, a tenderloin beef barbecue is enhanced by a scrumptious salad bar. Every evening except Saturday and Monday there is an à la carte menu featuring specialties of Scandinavia and Curaçao, with emphasis on fresh fish, grilled, poached, or otherwise. For dessert, try Coco Sherbet.

Denmark

AALBORG

Kilden Restaurant

Hotel Hvide Hus
Vesterbro 2
DK-9000 Aalborg
Denmark
Telephone: 08–13–84–00

All major credit cards
Breakfast, lunch, and dinner
Reservations requested
Jacket required for dinner
Liquor served
Dinner: $17
    full 3 courses, without wine
Lunch: $7 to $12
Chef: Kaj Hoff
Maitre d': Aron Steffensen

Things have changed considerably since we first wrote about the Kilden Restaurant. In the 1960s it was a fine old three-floor dining establishment situated in a lovely park, facing a fountain, in the heart of Aalborg. Well, the Kilden is still in the same spot, but it is now on the 15th floor of a smart new skyscraper hotel of the Danish Golf Hotel Group, the Hotel Hvide Hus, the largest city hotel in the Danish provinces.

Kilden means "the spring"; the restaurant was given that name in reference to the park, containing a small lake with a spring, in which it lies. The park is well-known for its beautiful flower arrangements and its many sculptures—one of which is *The Merman Group,* made of porcelain by the Danish sculptor Jean Gauguin, which is the largest single piece of porcelain to go through the famous Bing and Grøndahl Porcelain Factory in Copenhagen.

The new Kilden, depending upon where you sit, has added to its view of the park a panoramic view of the town, the surrounding countryside, and the beautiful fjord. Obviously, the view has improved.

There is piano music with lunch and dinner on most weekdays. The food is excellent, offering first class international and French cuisine, along with an excellent selection of wines.

If you can possibly arrange it, be here on the fourth of July. Most people are surprised to learn that Denmark celebrates America's independence day. In the national park south of Aaalborg there are speeches, parades, and, of course, fireworks. In fact, you can most likely see the fireworks from the dining room. In addition, the young people of the city join in a torchlight parade, affording both Americans and Danes a happy time.

COPENHAGEN

Belle Terrasse and Fajance Bar

Tivoli Gardens
1620 Copenhagen
Denmark
Telephone: 1–12–11–36

All major credit cards
Lunch and dinner
Reservations recommended
Jacket requested
Liquor served
Dinner: $25 to $45
    full 3 courses, without wine
Lunch: $10 to $24
Chef: Finn Lytje
Maitre d': Gert Bentzen

There are twenty-three restaurants in Copenhagen's Tivoli Gardens, making it extremely difficult to select the one with the most beautiful view. So we let others do our work for us—people like David Niven, Earl Warren, Walt Disney, and John Gielgud. They and many other well-known people among the nearly 5,000,000 visitors a year to the celebrated Tivoli Gardens picked their favorite restaurant with a view: Belle Terrasse.

Belle Terrasse offers a panorama about which Eleanor Roosevelt said, as she paused on the porch and looked into the gardens and the lake surrounding the restaurant, "I simply adore this view." Kurt E. Christensen and his wife Pylle reacted the same way when they first took a similar gaze some forty years ago. As Kurt told us: "I did not hesitate one second in establishing the restaurant in a summerly, gay nineties style, with plenty of flower decorations and green plants everywhere; at night carbon filament bulbs add that mellow light that makes beautiful ladies even more beautiful."

As rapt as the Christensens are with their restaurant so are people in general in love with the Tivoli Gardens. Founded on August 15, 1843, by Georg Carstensen, the gardens on that day had 3,615 visitors. Today, many times that number visit these gardens daily, by all counts making this a steady love affair between people and place.

Belle Terrasse is situated in the Glass Hall in the middle of Tivoli Gardens, with a beautiful view overlooking the lake (which was part of the ancient rampart around pre-1843 Copenhagen). In the background is a reminder that this park is in the center of the city—the tall green-copper top of the city hall clock tower.

The Glass Hall was built in 1843 and used as a concert hall. It has been rebuilt several times, most recently in 1945 and 1946, to repair the damage done by Nazi bombings. The famous Danish architect Poul Henningsen and his son, Simon, reproduced it to be exactly like the original hall.

As is the practice in many famed European restaurants, there is a Golden Book where thousands of guests have registered. Among the famous names you'll find are President Dwight D. Eisenhower, Igor Stravinsky, Leslie White, Janet Leigh, Olivia de Havilland, Bertil, the Prince of Sweden, Duff Cooper, Golda Meir (who had been there the same day we were years ago), Ernest Borgnine, and many of the members of the royal families of

Denmark, Sweden, and Holland. Less known but in greater numbers are many American, Danish, and European business people.

A hobby of the Christensens ended up making a contribution to Belle Terrasse some years ago. In a small, cozy room, they have established the Fajance Bar. *Fajance* means pottery. Kurt and Pylle, in their trips around Europe, have collected many interesting specimens—some actually dating from ancient times—and used them prominently in the bar's decor, creating a rather unique ambience. The bar has room for about 40 people ("sixty when it is packed like sardines, which very often happens," according to Kurt) and the restaurant and its lively terrace can seat about 230 people.

The Belle Terrasse is one of those international restaurants requiring a Danish, French, and Italian corps of chefs to cater to a discriminating palate. Rave reviews in publications around the world are commonplace. Other champions of Belle Terrasse cuisine, we are told, are the 75 percent of all Americans who visit Copenhagen and have one or more meals at Belle Terrasse.

Kurt, now 75, and his son Jan, 39, have both been in the business for most of their lives. Kurt has spent time at the Carlton Hotel in London, the International Hotel School at Lausanne, the Hotel Scribe, and Prunier, the famous fish restaurant in Paris.

Jan Christensen is proud of having taken over the running of Belle Terrasse, and of maintaining the high quality of its cuisine. Some of the specialties he has added are *Filets de Sole, Sauce au Foie Gras D'oie,* and *Filet de Veau Sauce aux Conquillages.* And be sure to try the *Crepes de Framboise.* The shrimp sandwiches are also among our favorites—who can resist sweet-tasting shrimp, maybe hundreds of tiny ones, pyramided on fresh bread? Though it comes as an appetizer, we have been tempted to make a meal of the shrimp alone.

Terrace of the Restaurant Reine Pédauque

Hotel d'Angleterre
34 Kongens Nytorv
DK-1050 Copenhagen K
Denmark
Telephone: 1-12-00-95

All major credit cards
Breakfast, lunch, and dinner
Reservations suggested
Jacket required for lunch and dinner
Liquor served
Dinner: $30 to $50
     full 3 courses, without wine
Lunch: $10 to $25
Chef: Ole Grønvang
Maitre d': Kurt Vangaa

Restaurant Reine Pédauque is part of the widely known Hotel d'Angleterre in Copenhagen, a grand hotel located on the fashionable Kongens Nytorv (The King's New Square) in the center of the city. Just around the corner is the famous shopping street called the *Strøget.*

From the restaurant and its terrace there is a great view overlooking the most beautiful square in Copenhagen and the Royal Theatre (home of the Royal Danish Ballet). This is Copenhagen's equivalent of Paris's Café de la Paix, a place to enjoy a quiet cup of coffee, a quick lunch, or the dish of the day, while the hustle and bustle of city life takes place on the square.

The food in both is excellent; in fact, the choices are so numerous that it is difficult to make a selection. The favorites are the tasty *Gravad Lax* (Smoked Salmon), the Danish *Smørrebrød* Breast of Duck, the fresh fish specialties, and the world-famous pastries.

It is customary for the big stars at the Royal Theatre to visit the d'Angleterre. The Reine Pédauque is one of Victor Borge's favorite restaurants in Copenhagen. Danny Kaye is also a regular guest—he has often wound up in the kitchen cooking for himself and the cooks! You might also sight members of the Danish Royal Family.

The first thing you notice when you enter the Restaurant Reine Pédauque is the magnificent and elegant interior setting. First you see the arrangements of fresh flowers. Then you notice the walls covered with rosewood paneling and decorated with ancient porcelain plates, paintings, and collages of labels from fine French wines. It is all part of the old-world charm that offers one a welcome respite from the new world outside. What a delightful place to dine and to view.

CAIRO

Jewel of the Nile and
Belvedere Restaurants

Nile Hilton
Tahrir Square
Cairo
Egypt
Telephones: 740777 or 750666

All major credit cards
Lunch and dinner
Reservations recommended
Jacket requested
Liquor served

The Nile Hilton is a large hotel with 462 rooms, 46 suites, six restaurants, a supper club, a discotheque, and three bar lounges. It is in the heart of Cairo, within walking distance of the main business and shopping areas. The best views to dine by here are from the main dining room, the Jewel of the Nile, and from the delightful Belvedere and its Belvedere bar.

The Belvedere is built like a bilevel amphitheater and has a panoramic view of the city and the Nile. The Jewel of the Nile is an unusual dining room because it was built so that nearly everyone can enjoy the expansive view of Cairo, the Nile, the Old Citadel, the Mokataam Hills, and the Pyramids. It, too, has bilevel seating and its decorations—in cool blue and turquoise—feature the hieroglyphic symbols of the Nile and an armada of Nile barges.

To complement the view, the Nile Hilton offers the best Continental cuisine in Cairo.

England

BROADWAY

The Great Hall

The Lygon Arms
Broadway
Worcestershire WR12 7OU
England
Telephone: 0386–852255

All major credit cards
Breakfast, lunch, and dinner
Reservations required
Jacket and tie required for dinner
Liquor served
Dinner: $22 to $42
full 3 courses, without wine
Lunch: $14 to $22
Chef: Alain Dubois
Maitre d': Isi Salcedo

This ancient inn has always won the praises of its guests, even as far back as 1787, when Lord Torrington wrote of it, "There could not be a clenlier, civiller Inn than this, which bears the mark of old gentility, and of having been a manor house. The hay is so good and everything so neat—and the dogs so fat."

The Lygon Arms is the centerpiece of a Cotswold village said to be the most beautiful in England. Unfortunately, this means the inevitable hordes of tourists crowding most of the town's shops and restaurants, particularly during the summer months. While this deluge might make your stay in Broadway less than ideal, the Lygon Arms is a calm and beautiful oasis, preserving its dignity and beauty in the midst of a sightseeing storm.

The Lygon Arms was built about 1530 and for the next 300 years was called the White Hart (the badge of Richard II). It was General Lygon, who settled at Springhill, Broadway, after the battle at Waterloo, who gave the place its name.

John Treavis, the landlord who reigned over the inn from 1604-1641, added a front doorway in 1620 which bore both his name and that of his wife Ursula. Remarkably, it's still there. Other features remaining from that era include the fine stone fireplace and the plaster ceiling and frieze in the Great Hall. Additional historical notes include the fact that Charles I met his local supporters at this inn in 1645 and that Oliver Cromwell slept in the room bearing his name in September, 1661, two days before the battle at Worcester.

The Lygon Arms was purchased in 1904 by the late S.B. Russell, who read about it in J.J. Hissey's *Across England in a Dig Cart* and then set out to make it the perfect English inn, combining his knowledge of architecture, old English furniture, and true English cooking to achieve his goal. The establishment remains in the family under the care of Douglas Barrington, O.B.E., who has maintained it well—restoring, where necessary, both the building and its fine collection of seventeenth- and eighteenth-century furnishings.

Broadway, since Elizabethan times, has been called "the Heart of England." Indeed, Stratford-upon-Avon, Warwick, Worcester, and Oxford are all within a short distance, and a day spent touring or antique shopping in the picturesque and quaintly named Cotswold villages is another rewarding experience.

The view comes upon you when you arrive and see the fine old building of the inn. At breakfast, if you glance out of the windows, you might see horses being readied for a hunt or a jaunt. During the rest of the day the view is of parts of the village and its almost overwhelming collection of visitors from nearly everywhere in the world. There is also excellent cuisine to enjoy, with such delights as Oyster Fuillete served warm with raspberries, Fresh Quail stuffed with Pine nuts, and Raisins Glazed with Orange. Our favorite dessert is the classically English Sticky Toffee Pudding.

EAST GRINSTEAD

Gravetye Manor

Near East Grinstead
West Sussex RH19 4LJ
England
Telephone: STDO342-810567

No credit cards
Breakfast, lunch, and dinner
Reservations necessary
Jacket required at dinner
Liquor served
Dinner: $26 to $41
   full 3 courses, without wine
Lunch: the same
Chef: Allan Garth
Maitre d': Malcolm Hamilton

The beauty of Gravetye Manor and the excellence of its cuisine has not changed in the nearly quarter century since we last visited. This is, of course, a tribute to its longtime owner, Peter Herbert; he has kept his pledge to create the best country house hotel possible.

It is no wonder that so many of the distinguished guests stay for several days or more, and that others are willing to drive down from London just for lunch or dinner.

Gravetye Manor lies in the midst of over 1,000 acres on the edge of old Ashdown Forest. Within it are the wild and formal gardens created by William Robinson, who acquired the property in 1884 and created his own memorial on 50 acres of land, surrounding the manor house. He brought to these grounds, both in the gardens and the woodland, a great variety of carefully selected and nurtured specimens of trees and plants.

The original Elizabethan manor was built in 1598, and it is still in splendid shape. The Virginia creeper, the clematis wisteria twine about it, and large magnolias flank it. The hall and drawing rooms are rich and comfortable with their fine paneling, paintings, furniture, flowers, and great log fires.

Peter Herbert's constant pride through the years has been in the cuisine. He has had excellent chefs, among them Karl Löderer (when we first visited), Michael Quinn (of the Ritz Hotel, London), and then the man who taught both of them and who is now in charge, Allan Garth. The restaurant has been well-honored. It has a Michelin star and two stars in the *Egon Ronay* guide.

One of our favorite three-course meals is Parfait of Chicken Livers as an appetizer, Best End of Lamb as the main course, marinated in herbs and served on aubergine with garlic sauce, and, for dessert, Pine Champagne Sorbet. Other delicious first courses include Smoked Scottish Salmon, Cream of Carrot Soup, Crayfish Consommé, and Mousseline of Chicken served with a Ragout of Crab. Main courses include Poached Turbot or Sea Bass, Fillets of Dover Sole, Medallions of Venison, Sautéed Guinea Fowl, and Veal Sweetbreads in Puff Pastry. Desserts include Dark Chocolate Mousse, Carrot and Hazelnut Cake, Almond Pastry Horn filled with fruit (in summer), Strudel layered with strawberries, and Poppy Seed Parfait.

The menu features both French cuisine and traditional English dishes; simpler dishes are also available. The bread is baked twice daily. Croissants and sorbets, as well as the conserves offered at breakfast, are made on the premises. The walled garden you see provides vegetables, fruits—and flowers—for the manor. The freshwater spring which has served the manor since 1598 supplies the water for the tank where fresh trout and crayfish are held until they are cooked. The wine list is superb, one of the more comprehensive we have seen, with some 350 wines in the cellar.

It is difficult to find your way to Gravetye Manor. Write Peter Herbert before you go, tell him you read about Gravetye Manor in this book and would like a map to guide you. With the map in hand, it is an easy trip from London, or from the airports.

HORNS CROSS

Hoops Inn

Horns Cross
Bideford
North Devon
England
Telephone: 023–75–222

No credit cards
Breakfast, lunch, and dinner
Reservations advised
Jacket not required
Liquor served
Dinner: $13 to $21.50
full 3 courses, without wine
Lunch: $2.50 to $14
Chef: David Malcolm
Proprietors: Mr. and Mrs. J. Malcolm

Sir Walter Raleigh and other high officials often stopped at this 13th-century Devonshire inn. It had long been a haunt of notorious smugglers as well, and later was renowned for its home-brewed ale. Today, it attracts guests from around the world.

Guests feel this Inn's heritage and enjoy basking in it. A tantalizing and elusive fragrance abounds—a blend of old oak beams, casks of wine, fresh flowers, and even of wax polish, all spiced with a whiff of some rich savory wafting out of the kitchen. The dining selections are bountiful. Local salmon, beef, lamb, pork, duck, sole, crab, and homemade soups which, we must warn you, can sometimes serve as a meal in and of themselves. Herbs from the garden are used generously. As for the desserts, the homemade fruit pies, trifles, cheesecakes, and other sweets are all served with fresh cream. There are also local cheeses and granary bread.

The restaurant at Hoops Inn is mellow with age. The aura is enhanced by oak paneling, candlelight in the evenings, and beautiful arrangements of fresh flowers. The latticed windows have rose pink velvet drapes and look out on the Hoops Garden—at its best in spring when the daffodils and narcissi are in bloom—and the rolling Devonshire hills.

LONDON

The Princes Room and The Carvery

The Tower Thistle Hotel
St. Katharine's Way
London E1 9LD
England
Telephone: 01–481–2575

All major credit cards
Breakfast, lunch, and dinner
Reservations advisable
Jacket required
Liquor served
Dinner: fixed price $21
*   3 courses, without wine*
*   à la carte menu entrées*
*   from $10 to $15*
Lunch: the same

London's 834-bedroom Tower Thistle Hotel is one of thirty-four hotels in the United Kingdom operated by the London-based Thistle group. This particular one on the bank of the River Thames was the first major hotel to be built during this century to serve the City of London.

The Tower Thistle Hotel stands on the north bank of the Thames next to the Tower Bridge and the Tower of London, and overlooks the St. Katharine Dock. It is next door to the World Trade Centre and is a short distance from the Barbican Centre for Arts and Conferences. Its two main restaurants both have views of the surroundings. The Princes

Room has a breathtaking view of the Tower Bridge and the very busy Thames, and offers international cuisine. The Carvery, with views of the St. Katharine Dock, offers a fixed price menu. Guests may help themselves to as much roast beef, lamb, or pork as they like, with all the traditional English trimmings. In addition, superb views of the Thames River can be had from the Thames Bar, another part of the hotel.

St. Katharine Dock is an interesting new attraction featuring yachts, boutiques, walkways, and bridges. But the view we love most is the more established one of the Tower Bridge. We all see the Tower Bridge in passing, usually while en route to someplace else. Here we have a chance to study, at relative leisure, a quintessentially British structure.

Among the items listed on the menu under the heading "To Commence" are Poached Pear with Cream Cheese, Mediterranean Prawns, Crab *Bavarois,* Smoked Scottish Salmon, Duck Liver Terrine, and Scampi Black Watch. Entrées include Grilled Dover Sole, Baked Turbot, Seafood Pancake, Supreme of Salmon, Province Style Best End of Lamb, Piccata of Veal Calvados, Fillet of Beef with Black Currants, Chicken Aunt Celestine (cooked with cream, Grand Marnier, toasted almonds, and apple), Supreme of Duckling Marco Polo (breast marinated in spices and herbs, grilled and served with aromatic sauce), and Peppered Veal Kidney.

To complete the meal there are selections of ice creams and fruit sorbets, as well as choices from a dessert trolley.

Roof Restaurant and the British Harvest Restaurant at the London Hilton on Park Lane

22 Park Lane
London W1A 2HH
England
Telephone: 01–493–8000 Ext. 4878

All major credit cards
Lunch, dinner, and
after-theater supper at 11 P.M.
Reservations necessary
Jacket required
Liquor served
Dinner: $44 to $68
full 3 courses, without wine
Lunch: $22 to $30 (incl. half bot. wine)
Chef: Michel Sram
Maitre d': John Obertelli

Situated atop the London Hilton, on its 28th floor, the Roof Restaurant has the best view of London we've ever seen. Not only can you see three of the parks (Green, St. James', and Hyde), but you can also see Piccadilly, a few of the bridges over the Thames, and most of the largest borough of the Greater London complex, the city of Westminster (including Parliament and Westminster Abbey), the West End, and Mayfair. But the best-kept secret around is that the London Hilton on Park Lane also affords a bird's-eye view of Buckingham Palace and its grounds. Some say they've even sighted the royal family out for a stroll in their lovely gardens!

The London Hilton is possibly the best known of the hotels on fashionable Park Lane. Its dramatic lobby is always a scene of international commingling, since its guests represent many nationalities.

The hotel is in the process of completing a $7 million remodeling effort. We first saw it shortly after it opened about twenty years ago and believed it to be an impressive modern hotel that could hardly be improved upon. Yet today it is more beautiful and functional than ever before.

The new Lobby Lounge is elegant, with a club-like atmosphere fostered by oil paintings on paneled walls, armchairs, and sofas. Flower arrangements are everywhere, and soft harp or trio music plays in the background during tea and supper. Go up a magnificent winding staircase to the first floor above and you find the new British Harvest Restaurant. Inspired by the American Harvest Restaurant in the Vista Hotel in New York, the British Harvest Restaurant features a different menu each season, offering the best of foods from all parts of the British Isles, plus wines from British vineyards.

The Roof Restaurant is our very favorite place at lunchtime. Here a splendid buffet lunch is served from 12:30 P.M. until 3 P.M. Not only is there plenty to select from, but it is all very good. Guests may start with fruit or vegetable juice, or one of many soups. Then, as a main course, there's a selection of salads, terrines, preserved meats, succulent cold roasts, fresh seafood, hot roast joints, and the daily specialty. A *table d'hote* menu is also available. While the cuisine is predominantly French, it is unfettered by rigid classicism. The dessert cart is overwhelming.

The à la carte menu during the dinner hours at the Roof Restaurant offers a grand selection. Among the starters are Cornish Lobster Salad, Scallops and Snow Peas, Raw Minced Salmon in Sour Cream with Dill, Beluga Caviar from the Caspian Sea, Goose Liver Mousse garnished with Truffles and Applesauce, and Duck Breast Salad with Lettuce Hearts in Tarragon Dressing. Entrées include Lightly Steamed Sea Bass (in a creamy sauce of Salmon Roe and Shallots), Dover Sole with Mild Mustard and Chive Sauce, Fillet of Turbot with Dublin Bay Prawns and Julienne of Cucumber, Fillet of Salmon in Puff Pastry with Sorrel Sauce, Panfried Fillet of Beef and Goose Liver in light Madeira Sabayon, Strips of Salmon with Crushed Peppercorns and Courgette Flan, Medallions of Veal Braised with Lettuce in Brown Ale Sauce, Roast Rack of Lamb with Lemon Balm Sauce and Macaire Potatoes, and Breast of Guinea Fowl on a Bed of Spinach with light Mango Sauce.

The desserts include a large selection from the trolley, Crêpes Suzette (for two), a choice of homemade sherbets, and Cointreau-flavored Sabayon with seasonal fruits.

A delightful after-theater supper is served at the Roof Restaurant. To start you have a choice of lightly smoked Scottish Salmon or clear Beef Consommé with Green Peppercorns. Main course offerings include a choice of Poached Fillet of Sole with Morecambe Bay Shrimps and Lamb with Mint Sauce. Cheeseboard and sweet-trolley selections are followed by coffee and petit fours.

Every Thursday, Friday, and Saturday night a cabaret is held in the Roof Restaurant. It was started on May 23, 1985, when Lon Statton, star of *Starlight Express,* began his nightly appearance for three months.

The Savoy Restaurant

The Savoy
The Strand
London WC2R OEU
England
Telephone: 01-836-4343

All major credit cards
Breakfast, lunch, and dinner
Reservations necessary
Jacket and tie required
Liquor served
Dinner: $32
  full 3 courses, without wine
Lunch: $25
Chef: Anton Edelmann
Manager: Luigi Zambon

It was in 1246 that Henry III presented to Peter, the Count of Savoy, the land between London and Westminster. Here the Palace of Savoy was built, and this great structure was called the "fayrest mannor" in all of Europe.

Savoy Restaurant

It was in 1884 that the famous producer Richard D'Oyly Carte showed a group of friends a dreary plot of land which had once been the site of the old Palace of Savoy and told them he would soon build a hotel for London that could compete with the finest hotels around the world. He succeeded, and in the process became something of a luminary himself. One of his more notable contributions to dining history was his establishing and promoting, in his flamboyant manner, the after-theater supper, served every weekday from 11 P.M. until half past midnight.

In December of 1889, César Ritz came to the Savoy to manage the hotel and the restaurant, bringing with him the enthusiasm and approach that gave it true Continental flavor and excitement. Among the things he brought to the Savoy was the idea that music was a perfect accompaniment to fine dining; the strains of Johann Strauss and others became de rigueur at any Ritz fete.

Dining at the Savoy is still an elegant experience, not only because the guests, mostly local people, enjoy dressing to dine here, but because the view features a beautiful bend in the River Thames and because the delicious cuisine is served with such flair. Put simply, the Savoy is one of the top-rated restaurants in a city with an abundance of fine restaurants.

REIGATE

Bridge House Restaurant

Bridge House Hotel
Reigate Hill
Reigate
Surrey RH2 9RP
England
Telephone: Reigate 07372–44821 or 46801

All major credit cards
Breakfast, lunch, and dinner
Reservations recommended
Jacket required
Dinner: $16 to $23
      full 3 courses, without wine
Lunch: $13 to $14
Chef: David Dunn
Maitre d': Gianni Codo

    To enjoy the view, it is vital that you sit at a table on the terrace or by a window of the dining room. The hotel and the restaurant accommodate mostly local people and an international clientele passing through nearby Gatwick Airport, so it is an easy drive on the M25 Motorway to A217 Road on which the Bridge House Restaurant is situated at Reigate. As you relax at your table you have a view of the beautiful Surrey countryside, looking toward the South Downs.

    Chef David Dunn, a native of Scotland, has received both national and international recognition, winning gold and silver medals in competitions such as the *Salon Culinaire Ecosse.* He has competed in the *Hotelympia,* receiving the *Conseil Culinaire Francaise de Grand Bretagne* Cup and Gold Medal. He has also won the Most Outstanding Craftsman award from the Restaurateurs Association of Great Britain. The daily menu offers gourmet English and Continental cuisine. Sunday lunch features roast beef carved from the trolley.

WORLESTON

Dining Room of Rookery Hall

Worleston
Cheshire CW5 6DQ
England
Telephone: Nantwich 0270–626866

All major credit cards
Breakfast, lunch, and dinner
Reservations necessary
Jacket and tie required at dinner
Liquor served
Dinner: $30
    full 6 courses, without wine
Lunch: $18
Owners: Audrey and Peters Marks
Chef: Brian Hamilton

Rookery Hall is a vast mansion, and its beautiful 28-acre estate includes a walled garden, a lake, and a park area with fine old oak trees. It was altered in the 1850s by its second owner, Baron von Schröder, who gave it an imposing Continental European appearance.

Most magnificent is the Dining Room, probably the finest Victorian Dining Room in England and most impressive when the candlelight from the beautifully set tables throws into shadowy relief the coats-of-arms on the fine plaster ceiling. The walls are beautiful, too, with polished mahogany and walnut paneling. The dining room looks out across the open fields of the estate and includes in its view an active fountain. As one dines here, it is difficult to feel anything less than regal.

The cuisine matches the magnificent setting. It has been recognized by many food critics and is one of the twelve Great Restaurants of Britain cited in the 1985 American Express calendar. Among the specialties to keep in mind are these: Spinach Soup with Lemon as an appetizer; lean, tender roast lamb with onion and mint jelly (featured on Sundays only), and bread and butter pudding. The *Crêpes à la Crème,* pancakes served with Peking duck, layered with ham and melted Grùyere cheese and served in a light cream sauce, are also delicious. Other main dishes include Panfried Trout with Capers, Supreme of Chicken with Tarragon, and Poached Fresh Salmon.

If the crisp bread and butter pudding isn't fancy enough for dessert, you may want to try the light *Mousse Brulee,* served chilled with a caramel topping, or perhaps you would prefer a plate of fresh fruit sorbets. The ultimate dessert for us was the Chocolate Roulade in Pistachio Sauce.

Europe

Venice Simplon Orient-Express

Contact:
Suite 2831
One World Trade Center
New York
New York 10048
Telephone: 212–938–1500

American Express
Breakfast, lunch, and dinner
Reservations necessary
Jacket required
Liquor served
Cost: $820 per person (including meals)
Chef: Christian Bodiguel

There is no better view of Europe than the one from this moving dining room. It's all there: the glorious tree-clad mountains and flower bedecked meadows of the Austrian Tyrol; Italian vineyards clinging to the terraced slopes of the Dolomites and spreading into the rich Po Valley; the fertile plains of northern France; the dizzy approaches to the awesome Arlberg pass, a route 6,000 feet high through the eastern Alps that was once the only crossing between Switzerland and the Tyrolean capital city of Innsbruck; and the grandeur of Switzerland's Alps, lakes, snow-capped peaks, cascading rivers, and stark and dramatic crags. There's more: the rolling green fields of Kent, the Garden of England; and the dramatic white cliffs of Dover; historic towns such as Zurich, with its lake like a necklace of lights along the water; and Verona, the pale terra-cotta town immortalized by *Romeo and Juliet,* lying at the gateway to the Venetian plain; age-old villages and ginger-bread chalets with fretted balconies overlooking the train's track; and historic towns where triumph and defeat are displayed in the variety of architecture.

This ever-changing view is the unique feature of the Venice Simplon Orient-Express which, in 1981, resumed what had started in 1883, when the Orient Express became the favorite of the rich, powerful, famous, and beautiful wanting to traverse the Continent. Now the legend lives again.

The journey on today's magnificent Orient Express takes two days and one night from

Victoria Station in London, across the English Channel on the Sealink Ferry to Boulogne, to Paris by nightfall, to Zurich by morning, to Innsbruck by lunchtime, and to your destination, Venice, in time for dinner. You can also travel from Venice to London.

Christian Bodiguel is the Chef de Cuisine for this prestigious hotel on wheels. The menu is as elegant as the train's luxury cars. For lunch, as a main dish, you may order Scallops in Puff Pastry with Avocado Butter, Piccata of Tender Veal with Julienne of Bitter Orange Rinds, Fresh-Vegetable Ravioli, or a light Spinach Flan. For dinner, you may select Fillets of Salmon and Sole with Sweet Pepper Creamed Sauce or Breast of Duckling *foie gras.* Among the desserts offered during the trip are Raspberry Mousse with Kiwi Sauce and Dark Chocolate Mousse with Curaçao Cream.

The first lunch is served on the train going southbound out of London. (If you are traveling to London, a cream tea is served shortly before your arrival.) On the Continental portion of the journey, from Paris to Zurich, through the Alps to Innsbruck and on to Venice, passengers are served dinners in two or three seatings, depending upon how many passengers are on board, as well as lunch, brunch, and tea. Black tie is not required, but jacket and tie are. Many passengers wear black tie anyway, and women often dress in the 1920s-style "flapper" outfits just for the fun of it.

France

BARBERAZ-CHAMBÉRY

Le Mont-Carmel Restaurant

1, Route de l'Église
Barberaz-Chambéry 73000
France
Telephone: 79–70–06–63

All major credit cards
Lunch and dinner
Reservations necessary on Sunday
Jacket not required
Liquor served
Dinner and lunch: $12 to $24
full 3 courses, without wine
Chefs: Robert and Jacques Blanc
Maitre d': Fabiene and Jamie Blanc

Here is a view of tranquility and strength. The restaurant sits high above the valley of Chambéry, with a view of the mountains surrounding that beautiful valley—particularly the *Massif du Mont-Revard,* which is part of the mountain group of Margèriaz—and, looking further, the mountains dominating the valley of Grésivaudan.

The restaurant is located in an ancient inn of Savoy, about a mile from Chambéry, of the Commune of Barberaz, next to Charmettes, a place known to be dear to the heart of Jean Jacques Rousseau. The Blanc family are the dedicated proprietors and staff of this beautiful and luxurious four-star restaurant.

Among the popular dishes are *Foie grad Frais, Petite Langouste Sauce Tourteaux,* and *Pigeon de Bresse au chou Vert.* For a delightful finish to the meal, carefully study the *Chariot de Patisseries!* You'll find few fellow Americans among the mostly Swiss and Italian visitors and local people who frequent this establishment.

BEAULIEU-SUR-MER

La Reserve de Beaulieu

5, Boulevard General-Leclerc
F 06310 Beaulieu-sur-Mer
France
Telephone: 93–01–00–01

No credit cards
Lunch and dinner
Reservations necessary
Jacket required
Liquor served
Dinner: $42 to $50
full 3 courses, without wine
Lunch: $30
Chef: Gilbert Picard
Maitre d': Barthelemy Lanteri

La Reserve de Beaulieu overlooks the Mediterranean and is on the quietest and best-situated part of Beaulieu Bay, halfway between Nice and Monte Carlo. It is an elegant restaurant as well as a four-star luxury hotel catering to a most discriminating clientele.

The restaurant was founded in 1894 by the Lottier family. As early as 1918, La Reserve had become known as one of the most famous restaurants on the French Riviera and was a point of rendezvous for kings, queens, and other luminaries of the day. It can hold 120 guests, and has views both front and back. In the back it overlooks a lovely flowered patio with a pretty fountain. In front it faces a large terrace directly over the swimming pool and offers a full view of the Mediterranean from Cap d'Ail to Cap Ferrat. During the summer months guests come to the restaurant, which is extended to the edge of the pool during this season, by boat, and they dock at the private harbor while they enjoy lunch.

Because of its cuisine, general elegance, and fine service, the restaurant is well known. Among the favorites of the guests, according to manager Henri Maria, are these specialties: *Brouillade aux Fruits de Mer au Basilic, Carre d'Agneau aux Fascis Nicois (saison), Loup "Reserve,"* and the famous dessert, *Soufflé Chaud aux Framboises.*

Gordon Bennett, the former owner of the New York *Herald Tribune,* was a regular guest of La Reserve; in fact, so often did he come here that he needed to establish a special telephone line into the hotel so he could continue to conduct his business. The line was given a special designation, Number 1, Beaulieu-sur-Mer, in 1891, and for years, to reach the hotel, you called, simply, Number 1.

CANNES

La Palme d'Or
Hotel Martinez
73, La Croisette
06406 Cannes
France
Telephone: 93–68–91–91

All major credit cards
Dinner
Reservations necessary
Jackets required
Liquor served
Dinner: $30 to $50
  full 3 courses, without wine
Chef: Christian Willer
Maitre d': Jacques Chavance

This is a brand new restaurant with a view, open since May 8, 1985 and located in the delightful Hotel Martinez. Its splendid art deco decor has been retained even though the hotel has undergone extensive modernization. Its name comes from the highest award given during the famous Cannes Film Festival.

Situated on the first floor of the hotel, La Palme d'Or and its terrace have a superb and commanding view of the beautiful Bay of Cannes. The view also encompasses the hotel's private beach and jetty, which has its own buffet restaurant and bar.

The Martinez itself dates from 1929; the recent renovation began in 1982 by Thierry Taittinger, nephew of Jean Taittinger of champagne fame. Pierre-Yves Rochon handled the interior decor and created an art-deco environment reflecting the original deco style of the hotel. Armchairs of the era were restored, painted in black varnish, and reupholstered in pearl gray and burgundy. The chest in the salon bar was made by London's Waring & Gillow in 1929. Richard Duvauchelle, the hotel's general manager, and his wife searched the area's antique shops in the area to find the restaurant's reception desk (made by Majorel) and the vases, all dating from the 1930s. The cutlery, silver clocks, and glasses were all selected from a 1930s catalog and were specially recreated for La Palme d'Or.

It should be no surprise, then, that the view to dine by inside the dining room is exciting. The walls are decorated in beige and rose and highlighted with black-and-white portraits of such famous movie stars as Greta Garbo, Marilyn Monroe, Clark Gable, Groucho Marx, Simone Signoret, Maurice Chevalier, Ingrid Bergman, Yves Montand, and Anthony Perkins. There are also photographs of a 1972 meeting held at the hotel between Arthur Rubinstein and Robert Redford.

On August 5, 1985, only three months after its opening, the restaurant received the *Gault Millau* guide award of the *Cle d'Or de la Gastronomie,* earning Chef Willer three red caps.

Among the recommended specialties are *Compote de Lapereau au Sabayon Froit de Poivrons Doux, Langoustines en Papillote de Celeri, Saute de Langouste aux Morilles, Foie de Veau Roti a la Sauge et aux Pommes Acidulées,* and *Crepinette de Pieds de Porc a la Moutarde a l'Ancienne.* For dessert, select from such wonders as *Gateau au Chocolat Sauce Pistaches Grillées, Soufflé Glace a l'anis, Pamplemousse Rose au Carmel et au Miel de Provence,* and *Fraises de Bois au Grand Marnier et a la Creme Glacée de Fromage Blanc.*

MAUSSANE

Oustau de Baumaniere

Les Baux de Provence
13520 Maussane
France
Telephone: 90–97–33–07

All major credit cards
Breakfast, lunch, and dinner
Reservations recommended
Jacket required
Liquor served
Dinner: $50 to $60
        full 3 courses, without wine
Lunch: $40 to $50
Owner: R. Thuilier

This restaurant is located in a 16th-century monastery that was restored by Monsieur R. Thuilier, the present proprietor, in 1946. In so doing he turned a certain ruin into a beautiful inn that retains much of its past charm and quaintness.

The view from here is of the flanks of the Alps, looking into what has been called the "valley of Dante's *Inferno.*" It is believed that this "Valley of Fire" is where Dante found his inspiration for his famed work. As you observe the jagged rocks of this valley, particularly as the sun begins to set, and your imagination is permitted free rein, you'll see, just as Dante probably did, the rocks beginning to take the forms of animals and human beings—a bird of prey, a Roman warrior, an old man.

Despite its sometime nickname, the valley offers peace and quiet, and the restaurant a distinguished, high quality cuisine in a magnificent setting with real Provence flavor. Try the lobster soufflé, leg of mutton pie with *gratin dauphinois,* or the mullet specialty. With your coffee, enjoy petit fours and other dainties in a delightful dining room with wall tapestries, flowered tablecloths, and rich French provincial furnishings.

NICE

Chantecler Restaurant

Hotel Negresco
37 Promenade des Anglais
BP 379 - 06007
Nice
France
Telephone: 93–88–39–51

All major credit cards
Lunch and dinner
Reservations requested
Jacket required
Liquor served
Dinner: $30 to $40
  full 3 courses, without wine
Lunch: $30 to $40
Chef: Jacques Maximim
Maitre d': Jean Max Haussy

The location of the Negresco, a fabulous Riviera hotel, and of its equally famous Chantecler Restaurant, was selected by its founder, Henri Negresco. He had been the manager of the Casino Municipal Restaurant in Nice, which had become the restaurant most frequented by affluent visitors to the coast—kings, princes, and important Americans like the Rockefellers, Vanderbilts, and Singers were all diners at his establishment. But Negresco's dream was to build a palace of his own on the fashionable seaside Promenade des Anglais. A rich industrialist, Alexandre Darracq, became interested in his plans. So the two took a world tour, visiting the big European and American hotels to discover what a wealthy client would wish to have in the way of comfort and luxury.

Negresco opened his hotel in 1913. It seemed the whole world was present and Negresco was thrilled. Unfortunately, his triumph was short-lived. After World War I started in 1914, the hotel was made into a hospital. In 1918, when the building was returned to him, Negresco found that his rich clients had disappeared. He died in 1920 in Paris, an unhappy and disappointed man.

Negresco's dream has since come true. The hotel and restaurant are once more the meeting places of choice for prominent personalities from the worlds of politics, industry, and art. Since 1957, the hotel has been owned by the family of Mr. and Mrs. Augier, and is now directed by Mme. Jeanne Augier. It was designated a Perpetual National Monument in October 1974. Its slow but determined march back to world renown surely would have pleased Monsieur Negresco.

The view from the Chantecler, if you can arrange to have a window table, or if you dine in summer on the terrace, is of the fashionable Promenade des Anglais, with the beautiful Baie des Anges on the right and the city of Nice to the left. Dining in this ornate palace, alongside the palm-tree lined boulevard and the shores of the Mediterranean, can't help but give you a feeling of affluence, importance, and serenity.

The food is supervised by the famous Jacques Maximim, winner of the *Meilleur Ouvrier de France* and other prestigious awards through the years. The *Gault Millau* guide awarded M. Maximim his fourth *"toque"* and 19 out of 20 points, describing his meal as *"meilleur repas de l'anee."* This is one of the few hotel restaurants to have earned two stars from the *Michelin* guide. Among those dishes that have received particular acclaim are *Courgettes a la Fleur et aux Truffes, Saumon au gros sel, Tian d'Agneau Nicois, Gratin de Fraises des dois au beurre d'Orange,* and Dover Sole. Maximim's most celebrated dish is said to be his steamed baby zucchini blossoms stuffed with a puree of zucchini flesh, cream, and basil; the tiny squashes, with flowers attached, are sliced into a fan-shaped form from the stem end and dished up with a butter sauce strewn with slivers of truffles.

PARIS

Les Ambassadeurs

Hotel de Crillon
10, Place de la Concorde
75008 Paris
France
Telephone: 42–65–24–24

All major credit cards
Breakfast, lunch, and dinner
Reservations required
Jacket required
Liquor served
Dinner: $35 to $80
*   full 3 courses, without wine*
Chef: J.P. Bonin
Maitre d': M. Dumont

The view to dine by from Les Ambassadeurs, one of the most beautiful dining rooms in Paris and one of only three hotel restaurants in Paris to receive the honor of two *Michelin* stars, is of what is definitely the most magnificent square in Paris (some say in the world), the Place de la Concorde.

It is a view of history as well as of artistry. The Place de la Concorde was designed for Louis XV in 1763, after whom it was then named. Thirty years later the statue of the king in the center was taken down, the name was changed to Place de la Revolution, and it was here that Louis XVI was guillotined. During the Reign of Terror this was the bloodiest part of Paris. It wasn't until the end of the revolution that the square received its present name. When it was being restored in 1836, King Louis-Philippe recalled a bit of history and firmly vetoed the idea of putting a royal statue in its center. Instead he opted for the Luxor Obelisk, a 3,300-year-old art treasure from Egypt.

Perhaps the greatness of the square lies most in the unmatched vistas which open up from every side. The twin mansions on its north are the work of Gabriel, the great architect of the 18th century; the one on the left is now occupied by the French Ministry of the Marine, while the other houses the luxurious Hotel Crillon, a bank, and the Automobile Club of France. The view of the square at night is enchanting. On Friday and Saturday it is spectacularly flood-lit and the lights play over the waters of the central fountain and the Obelisk.

Les Ambassadeurs is grand, as much a ballroom as a dining room. Yet its size is not overpowering, for the arrangement of the tables and its rich furnishings create a feeling

Les Ambassadeurs

of intimacy. The golden-rich marble walls and floors, enormous mirrors, glistening chandeliers, and colorful flowers make everyone feel beautiful.

The two Michelin stars are well deserved. Jean-Paul Bonin has been the hotel's executive chef since 1980, has won many awards, and was named a member of *l'Academie Culinaire de France* and *Chef de l'Année* in 1980. He and executive assistant chef Jean-Pierre Biffi command the team of forty which prepares the grand meals served here. Among their specialties: Truffle Omelet, Salad of Artichoke Hearts, Pheasant, *Langouste Rotie Scorsonere Gingembre Creme, Viennoise de Turbot aux Pignes, Coeur de Filet de Boeuf Grille, Cotes d'Agneau a la Fleur de Thym, Foie de Canard Poele aux Petites Cereales, Carre d'Agneau Roti "Vrai Jus" with Pomme Puree,* and *Saute de Boeuf Minute en Bourguignon, Pates a la Canelle. Velours de Cacao* is just one of the chocolate desserts which are available.

Lasserre Restaurant

17, Avenue Franklin-D.-Roosevelt
75008 Paris
France
Telephones: 43–59–53–43/67–45

No credit cards
Lunch and dinner
Reservations required
Jacket required
Liquor served
Dinner: $40 and up
  full 3 courses, without wine
Lunch: the same
Chef: Marc Daniel
Maitre d': Mr. Louis
Proprietor: Rene Lasserre

To enjoy this view at its best, you must look up. There are some who might say that this view does not properly belong in a book of views to dine by. Obviously, we disagree. Monsieur Rene Lasserre makes such beautiful use of the Paris sky that we felt it warranted not just mention, but appreciation too.

Through the years, M. Lasserre has done many wonderful things with that beautiful sky. Most beautiful of all, at night he allows the stars of the Paris sky to enter his restaurant merely by opening his sliding roof. During a beautiful day, the Parisian blue is just as pretty, enhanced by the lovely flowers which surround the window frame. Monsieur Lasserre also has a taste for the unconventional. Once, at a dinner during the hunting season, he presented a fashion show with mannequins in hunting outfits; at a signal, the

models pointed their rifles at the ceiling, shooting blanks. The roof slid open and down fluttered a batch of stuffed pheasants. On another occasion, the crest of the city of Paris was presented in a replica of a ship filled with flowers which floated down from above by virtue of invisible thread. From the ship flew half a dozen white doves.

Another trademark of Lasserre's is his copper pans, which had become so popular that patrons would very often take them for souvenirs. M. Lasserre has taken to presenting each lady with a beautiful china replica in miniature; after all, he must have something in which to cook! Meanwhile, for thousands of men throughout the world, all selected by M. Lasserre to be members of his *Club de la Casserole,* there are tiny silver pan key rings signifying membership in this gourmet society. One can become a member only upon recommendation of another member.

Another exceptional view at Lasserre's is that of the beautifully dressed women who seem to make veritable stage entrances from the elevator into the dining room. Dressing up by both sexes is part of the Lasserre way.

The food is beautiful both to look at and to eat. The skillful presentation is especially remarkable. You might get an ice cream dessert in a golden cage spun from carmelized sugar. The fillet of sole, lobster tails, and fruit pies are served in pastry shells with beautiful pastry handles. Vegetables such as turnips or radishes are fashioned into flower shapes. One specialty for which Lasserre is famous is *Steak Poele Dumas;* another is an exciting blue-flaming dessert, *Pannequet Soufflé Flambé.* And speaking of desserts, our choice is *Profiteroles,* tiny cream puffs filled with rich ice cream and covered in a thick hot fudge sauce.

There are window views, too. A large corner room with wide windows looks onto delightful summer gardens. With the flick of a switch a wall rises up from the floor and this area can be transformed into two comfortable private dining rooms. Each side of the wall is covered with oil paintings depicting typical 17th-century scenes done by the Parisian artist Francoise Estachy. This room is on the first floor; the main dining room, with the sliding ceiling, is on the floor above.

If you are fortunate, you might attend one of the candlelight evenings, usually an event held to launch a film, present fashions, or welcome the hunting or winter sports seasons. It is a tradition at these events to release doves during the serving of dessert, and sumptuous gifts are given to the guests who are lucky enough to have a dove land on their table. These gifts are offered by the famous major design and perfume houses of Paris.

Pavillon de la Grande Cascade

Allee de Longchamp
Bois de Boulogne
75016 Paris
France
Telephones: 47–72–66–00 or
    45–06–33–51 or
    47–72–78–49

All major credit cards
Lunch and dinner
Reservations recommended
Jacket required
Liquor served
Dinner: $50 to $60
    full 3 courses, without wine
Lunch: $40 to $50
Chef: Jean Sabine
Maitre d': George Lambert
Proprietor: André Menut

There are several lovely restaurants in Paris's famous park, the Bois de Boulogne. Best of all is to finish a wonderful day of strolling by having dinner at the Cascade.

Whether you dine inside, on the terrace in the front, or in the garden on the side, you have a tranquil view of the pretty green lawns, trees, and plants. It is fun and rewarding to find such a quiet, lovely, and secluded spot in the middle of a busy city like Paris.

André Menut, manager since 1964, doesn't know exactly when Napoleon III built his hunting pavilion on this spot, but it was the first building to occupy the space now occupied by La Cascade.

This restaurant is, gastronomically and architecturally, the best of the pavilions in this park. It was named after the forty-foot-high waterfall nearby. The building, built in the 1850s for Napoleon III as his private hunting lodge, is an authentic Second Empire gem, with its wrought-iron structure, glass roof, gilt paint, blue silk velvet curtains, candelabra-like lights, and large windows giving a fine view of the Bois. No one really knows what the Emperor hunted in the Bois; in fact, this was the subject of much chatter by the gossips of the day. Nonetheless, it was generally agreed among them that this lodge was indeed the right place for the Emperor's very private hunting activities, whatever they were. It was in 1900, the time of the Paris World's Fair, that the restaurant was established.

The Grande Cascade is open all year except from mid-December to mid-January, but only lunch is served in the winter. It is a favorite lunch spot on weekdays for the high level Parisian business executives who, according to M. Menut, "enjoy discussing their difficult business problems while surrounded by flowers and beauty, calmness, and superior cuisine."

Among the favorites from the generous menu are *Langoustines Roties aux Parfums de Provence, Delice des Landes aux Salades Tendres, Panache de Poissons a la Vapeur d'Algues au Basilic, Rosette de Boeuf aux Champignons des Bois, Filets Mignons et Abats Fins Forestiere, Marquise Fondante au Chocolat Amer Nougat Frais,* and *Dentelle aux Peches Carmalisees.*

Le Regence

The Dining Room of
Hotel Plaza-Athénée
25 Avenue Montaigne
75008 Paris
France
Telephone: 1–47–23–78–33

All major credit cards
Breakfast, lunch, and dinner
Reservations required
Jacket required
Liquor served
Dinner: $45 to $55
    full 3 courses, without wine
Lunch: $35 to $45
    Chef: Claude Barnier
    Directeur Restaurant:
        Roland Reverdi

Here the view is a matter of choice. It consists of the sumptuous decor of Le Regence restaurant and/or the magnificent courtyard panorama, which at times is full of exotic flowers, lush vegetation, and colorful sun umbrellas.

Le Regence is one of the great dining rooms of Paris, in or out of a hotel. One of the reasons for this is the commanding presence of Roland, the restaurant's director, who years ago had the same position at Tour d'Argent. His gentle concern for his guests is world renowned and rarely equalled.

The recently refurbished dining room has made this restaurant one of the world's most elegant dining settings. It even feels like being on the set of a Luigi Visconti film. The cream and peach tones are enhanced by gold stucco friezes; classical pillars border damasked walls; and stately portraits peer down upon the luxurious surroundings. Dominating the room is a magnificent fireplace of deep-toned marble topped by a gold-framed mirror. The crystal chandeliers, the wall lamps, and the candles on the tables provide a mesmerizing interplay of light. Rich, thick, pink linens on the tables are adorned with fine silver and crystal and small but graceful flower arrangements—just the setting for elegant cuisine.

Such opulence did not come easily. The redecoration effort required 1,200 hours of work by craftsmen and 25,000 gold leaves for the ceiling decoration, not to mention the best of practically everything else: Porthault linen, silver by Christofle, and china from Haviland in Limoges. The carpeting, which complements the table settings, was designed exclusively for this room in Aubusson.

The cuisine accepts and meets the challenge established by the setting. It is extremely difficult to make a choice; that is why you see Roland in conference at each table, guiding guests in their most important decision of the moment. Certainly he was right in recommending the *Soufflé de Homard Plaza* (lobster soufflé) to us, as well as the hot oysters with herbs, and the Saint Jacques julienne. For the end of the meal, we found the chiffonette of cherry crepes perfect, but almost any selection from the elegant Christofle dessert cart would do just fine. The wine selections are endless; a conference with Roland and/or the excellent wine waiter is usually necessary.

Franco Cozzo, the managing director of the Hotel Plaza-Athénée, feels that a top hotel such as his must have a restaurant that can stand on its own in maintaining traditional refinement and elegance. Not only the hotel guests, but also the terribly discriminating residents of Paris, agree that Le Regence has done just that.

The hotel and its restaurant are well located, within a few minutes of the Champs-Élysées and not too far from the Eiffel Tower, on the fashionable Avenue Montaigne, which also features the salons, boutiques, and elegant shops of some of the most famous designers in Paris. This hotel is their hotel, too, and you may see them, the models, and buyers from around the world among your fellow diners. They, too, are part of this extraordinary view to dine by.

Restaurant Jules Verne

2eme Etage de la Tour Eiffel
Champ de Mars
Paris
France
Telephone: 45–50–60–44

All major credit cards
Lunch and dinner
Reservations required
Jacket required
Liquor served
Dinner: $35 to $50
      full 3 courses, without wine
Chef: M. Grondard
Directeur: Pierre Ody

In the last edition of this book we wrote about the view from En Plein Ciel, the quality dining room that was then located in the middle of the Eiffel Tower. It has been replaced by the new and posh Jules Verne Restaurant, a strikingly modern place with floor-to-ceiling picture windows and a black and off-white decor that seems intended as a frame for the view of the city and the Seine below. The ceilings are much lower than the old En Plein Ciel, and the furnishings are not in the luxurious turn-of-the-century style.

This is all very deliberate, and perhaps more appropriate. The ornate decor of En Plein Ciel seemed out of place in the heart of the tower. The decor of the Jules Verne, on the other hand, is more in keeping with the mechanical style of the tower itself. In addition, the simplicity of the decor allows what is first and foremost—the view—to take center stage.

The view here at night hasn't changed in two decades, except that the lights on the river boats seem brighter. Most of the major buildings of Paris have undergone considerable steam-cleaning during the last few years, so they can be seen in sharper relief. And, as ever, the lights of Paris are bright and intriguing.

The food at the Jules Verne is magnificent. No wonder you need to make your reservation two-to-three weeks in advance. After an appetizer such as *Foie Gras,* paper-thin Sliced Smoked Salmon, or Sole Salad with Raspberry Vinegar, try the Sliced Veal with Fresh Pasta in Basil-Tomato Sauce or the *Pigeonneau* (roast squab in a casserole with a *confit* of onions).

The desserts are tantalizing, and you rarely leave having eaten only one. After you've selected something like a bitter chocolate cake with coffee sauce or a beautiful fruit pastry from the cart, and are relaxing after your meal, without warning you are served an accompaniment to your coffee—not sugar cookies or candies as is done in many places, but an enticing and nearly decadent item called *Tuiles.* These are lacy cookies shaped something like ice cream cones served with mounds of luscious pistachio chunks. We challenge anyone to leave without finishing the entire thing!

The cocktail lounge has a piano player in the early evening, when the view from the lounge is of the floodlighted Les Invalides.

The view at lunch time is beautiful but not as romantic as at night; however, lunch reservations, while necessary, are less difficult to make than dinnertime ones. There's a separate elevator for the guests of the restaurant; look for the Jules Verne awning at one of the legs of the Eiffel Tower.

The Summer Restaurant

Hotel Le Bristol
112 Rue du Fauborg St. Honoré
75008 Paris
France
Telephone: 266–91–45

All major credit cards
Breakfast, lunch, and dinner
Reservations required
Jacket required
Liquor served
Dinner: $35 to $50
full 3 courses, without wine
Lunch: the same
Chef: Emile Tabourdiau
Maitre d': Robert Chauland

The Bristol Hotel, established in 1924, is just a few steps from the Elysée Palace on the very fashionable Rue du Fauborg Saint-Honoré, a promenade where visitors and residents alike enjoy strolling to see and be seen. It is a charming, luxurious hotel, associated with one of the more flamboyant times of Parisian life.

Simply entering the hotel is a pleasure. Its lobby is more like the foyer of a mansion than a hotel reception area. Check-in and information desks and the like are off to the sides and are hardly noticeable. Lighted by 23 Baccarat crystal chandeliers, the lobby is much like it was when the hotel was originally built. The white marble is adorned with a large 19th-century Savonnerie tapestry. The chairs, armchairs, and Louis XVI sofas have been recovered in silk brocades woven in Lyon. Most of the furniture and *objets d'art* of the Hotel Bristol were acquired between 1924 and 1930 from the Louvre and most are priceless collector's items.

The Summer Restaurant is in business from May through October. Built as part of the hotel's 1975 construction program, it is another tranquil spot in the heart of busy Paris. The large floor-to-ceiling windows open onto the hotel's large landscaped French garden, also established in 1975.

When we dined at the Summer Restaurant, the menu was modest yet magnificent, with four hors d'oeuvres, four selections from the sea, four entrées, and three desserts. As appetizers, two delightful items were the *Savarin de Magret de Canard a la Mousse de Truffles* and the *Saumon Fenouillette et son Emince de Melon.* All the main courses were good, including *Escalope de Turbot au Sauternes, Sole Etuvée aux Carottes, Emince de Filet de Boeuf au Vin de Moëlle, Medaillon de Veau au Beurre d'Herbes,* and *Pot au Feu de Pigeon et Foie Gras au Fumet de Pomerol.* The desserts included *Peches caramelisées au Coulis de Framboises,* the *Tulipe de Fruits Rouges et Son Sorbet a la Menthe,* and *Les Guartiers de Poires Duchesse Anne.*

After your meal, what can be more pleasant than strolling in the fine gardens? From the gardens you will see the three buildings that make up the Le Bristol Hotel complex and that tell the history of one of Paris's finest residences. In 1924, near the Elysée, former residence of the Pompadour, Le Bristol was opened by Hypolite Jammet. It was a chic and discreet hotel catering mostly to diplomats and members of the aristocracy. After World War II the hotel was restored and again made one of the most beautiful in Paris. The owners acquired the adjacent property of the Convent of the Sisters of Good Hope when the Sisters left to go to Canada; this became the Bristol's left wing. In 1975 the French gardens were created and the newest wing of the Bristol, La Residence, was constructed.

You are welcomed in the spring and summer by Robert Chauland, who is pleased to offer guests his advice as to the best of the restaurant's nouvelle cuisine. The innovative menu was created by the chef, Emile Tarbourdiau, *Meilleur Ouvrier* of France in 1976. Because of its excellent cuisine and attention to detail, the Summer Restaurant was awarded its second Michelin star in 1984, one of only three in Paris to be so honored.

La Tour d'Argent

15–17 Quai de la Tournelle
75005 Paris
France
Telephone: 1–43–54–23–31

All major credit cards
Lunch and dinner
Reservation necessary
Jacket required
Liquor served
Dinner: $70 to $100
    full 3 courses, without wine
Lunch: $50 to $70
Proprietor: Claude Terrail
Chef: Dominique Bouchet
Maitre d': Monsieur Carlo

Legend has it that people have enjoyed the fantastic view from this restaurant as long ago as 1582, when a man called Rourteau opened an elegant inn between the Seine and the Cistercian Convent in order to entertain and lodge the lords and gentlemen of the Court of Henri III. These men were said to be tired of seeking their pleasures in "gaming houses and dens of thieves," and instead sought out a genteel place with a view. The place earned its name because it was built of silver-colored champagne stone; La Tour d'Argent means "the hostelry of the tower of silver."

Whether you are welcomed by La Tour d'Argent's owner, Claude Terrail (the son of Andre Terrail, the previous owner) or one of his captains, you will be seated, when in the Louis XVI Room, so that you may look toward Notre Dame, one of the most important buildings in Paris.

When the lights are dimmed in the dining room, images of French history may run through your mind as you look upon the flood-lighted old lady of Paris—Esmeralda dancing in the moonlight before the entranced eyes of the hunchback, Quasimodo, or the Protestant King, Henri IV, who paced outside of Notre Dame with his courtiers while his brand new wife, Marguerite de Valois, went inside to attend mass. (In fact, it may well have been then that Henri made his *bon mot* that "Paris is well worth a mass.")

Some of the most important episodes of Parisian and French history have occurred within the confines of your view from La Tour d'Argent. On her way to be beheaded, the Marquise de Brinvilliers stopped the cart which was taking her to the guillotine and knelt, barefoot, with a rope around her neck and a crucifix in her hand, to pray to God for forgiveness and help. It was here that Marie Antoinette gave thanks for the birth of a son. Saint Louis is buried here. And Napoleon the First was married here to Josephine de Beauharnais.

If you are as fortunate as we were, you may discover that you are seated at what, since

May 16, 1948, has been called the "Queen's Table"—for it was at this table that Claude Terrail entertained Queen Elizabeth and Prince Philip of England. And it was here that Prince Philip is said to have remarked, when the restaurant lights were dimmed so that the royal couple might enjoy the flood-lighted beauty of Notre Dame, "I have been here as a bachelor, but never in this room, and I never had the lights dimmed so that I might enjoy this wonderful room. I have gained so much by marriage."

It is not only France's political and social history that come to mind in this restaurant. It is claimed that three great gastronomical inventions were born here—the fork, coffee, and *Le Caneton Frederic* (the numbered pressed duck). You can learn more about this if you visit the wonderful *Petit Musee de Gastronomie* on the main floor.

Fittingly, Claude Terrail is as much a philosopher as he is a restaurateur. When he first inherited the restaurant from his father, he wasn't too happy with the idea of going into the business; he had never liked haughty waiters and demanding customers. Needless to say, he has changed his thinking quite significantly. In his book *Ma Tour d'Argent,* Terrail praises his restaurant by referring to it as "my most faithful mistress . . . my affair, my beloved."

Certainly if you like duckling, you will enjoy the food here. But we feel that there are many more fine items on the menu. We had the poached salmon as an appetizer (extraordinary), and the rack of lamb as our main course. A selection of soufflés and choices from the dessert cart followed.

ROQUEBRUNE CAP MARTIN

Vistaero
Grand Corniche
06190 Roquebrune Cap Martin
France
Telephone: 93–35–01–50

All major credit cards
Lunch and dinner
Reservations necessary
Jacket required at dinner
Liquor served
General Manager: H. Wegener
Chef: J. Zuccarelli

You'll have to postpone seeing this magnificent view until early 1987, since the restaurant closed on November 1, 1985, to undergo a complete renovation and refurbishing program.

When completed, according to the general manager, H. Wegener, the dining room will be much enlarged; a tea room and a piano bar will also be added. Chef J. Zuccarelli will continue to be in charge of the kitchen so that the same fine cuisine will be served.

We're glad that more people will be able to enjoy the view from Vistaero. Built on a high rock jutting out over the beach at Monte Carlo, its height of 1,033 feet gives guests a magnificent view of an extensive Mediterranean panorama—of Cap Martin, Menton, Monte Carlo, the Cote d'Azur, and the Italian Riviera as far as Bordighera.

BADENWEILER

Dining Room of the Hotel Römerbad

Black Forest
7847 Badenweiler
Germany
Telephone: (0 76 32) 700

American Express, Visa
Breakfast, lunch, and dinner
Reservations suggested
Jacket suggested
Liquor served
Dinner: $15 to $25
　　full 3 courses, without wine
Lunch: the same
Chef: Joachim Möhringer
Proprietor: The Fellmann-Lauer Family

　　Hotel Römerbad, the name of which translates, appropriately, into "Roman Bath," is in the Black Forest spa area of Germany, the charming, easy-to-reach region where Germany, France, and Switzerland meet. The legendary waters are readily available here.

　　The hotel has been family owned and managed since 1825 and has been maintained, according to *Vogue* magazine, as "one of Germany's last dream hotels." It is set in its own park with lawns that slope gently down to a wooded area. The view from the dining room is of this park, which is especially beautiful when it is lighted at night. There is a full view of a medieval fortress from the dining room as well. Next to the hotel grounds is the Kur-park, the town park that contains the 2,000-year-old ruins of Roman baths in the shade of towering sequoia trees. It is from these baths that the hotel was given its name.

　　The grounds are delightful for exploring. There are greenhouses and cutting gardens which furnish a constant display of vibrant flowers, such as the tulips (with two-feet-long stems) and lilacs that are displayed in vases throughout the hotel's corridors. These greenhouses and gardens also contribute fresh herbs and green vegetables that enrich the local fish, grilled veal or steak, and bountiful salads served here. Also from the grounds come some of the fresh fruits featured in the delightful desserts.

　　Frau Liessel Fellmann-Lauer and her son, Klaus Lauer, the director, work together with Chef Joachim Möhringer to create lighter, butter-free, low-calorie, yet tasty versions of standard dishes. The chef has been in charge of the dining room for 17 years. He uses only fresh ingredients, never any frozen or canned foods; he procures the fresh food—which may include lamb from Ireland or fish from the Paris fish market, the North Sea, or the Lake of Constance—everyday.

　　Among the specialties on the menu are Green Crepes (spinach and a vegetable sauce with ham from Parma), Tureen of Salmon with Avocado Cream, Poached Ray with Brown Butter, Norwegian Salmon with Mashed Leek, Deer Fillets with handmade *spätzle* (the special noodles of the region), Tournedos with Truffle Sauce, Roasted Barberie Duck with Rosemary, and Turbot. Among the desserts are freshly made ice cream with fruits of the season, a variety of *Mousse-au-Chocolat,* and all kinds of fancy and plain cakes, tarts, tortlets and biscuits.

　　Badenweiler is an interesting place to be. In one afternoon, it is possible to have your passport stamped three times by crossing the Rhine into Mulhouse, France, then driving back to Basel in Switzerland, then back to Badenweiler in Germany.

BERLIN

Blockhaus Nikolskoe

Nikolskoer Weg
1000 Berlin 39
Germany
Telephone: (0308) 05–29–14

American Express
Lunch and dinner
Reservations recommended
Jacket not required
Liquor served
Proprietor: Dietmar Schittkowski

By the time you read this, Nikolskoe—partly destroyed by fire in 1984—will have been restored to its original charming self.

Nikolskoe is a Russian-style loghouse that was built in 1819 and given by King Frederick William III as a present to his daughter, Charlotte. (Her husband was a Russian Prince who later became Czar Nicholas I.) Today the log cabin is a delightful restaurant.

The views are varied, but one worth noting is that of the Church of St. Peter and Paul, a Russian Orthodox Church that stands nearby, looking a bit out of place in a German woods.

As for the food, about a hundred years ago, the innkeeper at Nikolskoe was a Russian coachman who as an old age pensioner had been given the job as caretaker but just didn't have the talent to be an innkeeper—he did little to cater to the needs of his guests, and the cuisine was rarely more elaborate than bread and butter with ham or sausage, which is what he enjoyed. Today, however, the cuisine is much better and more varied, with the current favorites being Pig Knuckle, Roast Leg of Pork and, in winter, game. Another favorite is Eel in Dill Sauce. Guests are mostly local people, with lots of Berlin businessmen bringing guests. Business lunches are popular.

COLOGNE

Die Bastei (The Bulwark)

Konrad-Andenauer-Ufer 80
5000 Cologne 1
Germany
Telephone: (0221) 12 28 25

All major credit cards
Lunch and dinner
Reservations recommended
Jacket required
Dinner: $30 to $60
full 3 courses, without wine
Lunch: $20 to $40
Chef: F. Schlagowski
Maitre d': H. Niessen

Practically overhanging the west bank of the Rhine just north of Cologne, Die Bastei has a commanding view of the busy river traffic, the bridge, and most important of all, the famous Cologne Cathedral.

As proprietor Tochen Blatzheim says, it is not difficult to find this restaurant . . . "everybody in Cologne knows Die Bastei."

The restaurant offers diverse cuisine; among the favorite entrées are Breast of Chicken Stuffed with Fresh Lobster in Cream Sauce, Medallions of Lamb on Crouton with Fresh Goose Liver, Medallions of Veal on Crayfish Cream with Leaf Spinach, and Saddle of Venison with Mushrooms of the Season (served for two persons only). Among the tantalizing desserts are Vanilla Pancakes with Whisky Cream and Orange Ice, Cassis Tartlets with Candied Violets, and Walnut Ice with Mocca Cream. Scrumptious!

FRANKFURT

Museumstubb

Henninger Tower
Heinerweg, 60–64
Frankfurt
Germany
Telephone: 6063–500

No credit cards
Lunch and dinner
Reservations required
Jacket not required
Liquor served
Dinner: $8 to $10
    full 3 courses, without wine
Lunch: $6 to $9
Chef: Karl Funk
Maitre d': Gerhard Weykopf

On the outskirts of Frankfurt, atop the silo of a brewery, in a slowly revolving round basket-shaped sphere, is the restaurant of the Henninger Tower.

The Tower is 343 feet high; this means that from the restaurant you have a lovely view of the city of Frankfurt, the Taumus Heights, the Rhine and the Main rivers, and the rolling wine country of Rhine-Hesse and the Palatine. Two high-speed elevators take diners to the top of the tower in 30 seconds or less. The restaurant has two rooms, one seating 160 and another seating 40; both get all views as it revolves.

The menu features typical German specialties: *Hessische Kartoffelsuppe* (Potato Soup) to start, *Braumeisterpfanne, Sachsenhäuser Schweinebraten, Frankfurter Rote Grütze mit flüssiger Sahne,* and *Frankfurter Kranz.* As you may have guessed, Henninger beer is the drink of choice here.

HAMBURG

Bavaria Blick

Bernhard-Nicht-Strasse 99
2000 Hamburg 4
Germany
Telephone: (040) 31–48–00 or
31–44–53

All major credit cards
Lunch and dinner
Reservations recommended
Jacket not required
Liquor served
Dinner: $9 to $18
*   full 3 courses, without wine*
Lunch: $7 to $15
Chef: Günther Hoffmann

This restaurant was built in 1958 on the top floor of an eight-story wing of the famous Hamburg Brewery, Bavaria St. Pauli. The extensive view over the immense shipyards and docks of this port city makes it very popular among the city's leading citizens, particularly businessmen. Bavaria Blick also attracts tourists, many of them Americans.

The chef, Günther Hoffmann, is proud of the specialty of the restaurant, fresh salt-water fish. Here, too, international dishes are found, as are Hamburg specialties, plus good German and French wines, and, of course, that famous Hamburg beer.

MUNICH

Restaurant Königshof

Hotel Königshof
Karlsplatz 25
8000 Munich 2
Germany
Telephone: (089)–55 84 12

All major credit cards
Breakfast, lunch, and dinner
Reservations recommended
Jacket and tie required
Liquor served
Dinner: $25 to $40
*   full 3 courses, without wine*
Lunch: $20 to $35
Chef: Wolfgang Abrell
Maitre d': Manfred Friedel

In 1862 the residence of Baron von Sternbach was renovated and renamed the Hotel Bellevue. Fifty two years later it was redubbed the Hotel Königshof. Destroyed during World War II, the hotel was reopened by the Geisel family, owners of two other fine hotels in Germany, and over the past few years the Hotel Königshof has been renovated and redecorated so that it has finally regained its eminence. But despite its sense of luxury, the hotel/restaurant still has the intimacy which attracted well-known politicians, poets, movie, theater, and opera stars, and international business executives. Among the more famous guests have been Paul Anka, Mel Ferrer, and Peter Ustinov.

Before its improvement, the Restaurant Königshof already had one star from *Michelin*. It now features an elegant French decor and has become one of the favorite dining spots in Munich. The interior design by Count Pilati expresses the hotel's desire to combine luxury with traditional warmth. Among the favorites on the menu are Lasagna with Crayfish and Sole in Pistou Sauce, Stuffed Pike Dumplings with Sweetbreads in Nouilly-Prat Sauce, and Breast of Barbarie Duckling with Honey and Apple Juice Sauce.

The view was also enhanced by the refurbishing work: large soundproof glass windows keep the noise at bay while you view the famous Stachus and the surrounding old part of the city of Munich. In addition to the Karlsplatz square, the view includes a part of the ancient Old Town wall and the beautiful towers of the Munich Cathedral. At night, the lights are dimmed to avoid reflections on the glass which might distort the view.

OBERWESEL

Burghotel-Restaurant "Auf Schönburg"

6532 Oberwesel
Germany
Telephone: 0 67 44–70 27

American Express, Visa
Lunch and dinner
Reservations recommended
Dress: casual
Liquor served
Dinner: $16 to $25
    full 3 courses, without wine
Lunch: the same
Chef: Wolfgang Hüttl
Maitre d': Iris Marx

Built on the top of a hill high above everything else in Oberwesel is a five-towered 1,000-year-old castle aptly named Schönburg (beautiful castle). The great French writer, Victor Hugo, said that one would not expect to find such a magnificent and beautiful panorama anywhere except on the stage of the Paris Opera House.

The oldest parts of the castle date back to the year 951; it is thought that construction of the entire castle took over a hundred years. More recently, the town bought the castle from an American whose family was of Rhenish origin and in whose careful possession the castle—and its art treasures—had been preserved for more than seventy years. In 1983, almost $1 million was spent on restoration work.

The inn was opened 28 years ago by Hans and Ria Hüttle; Hans had been a maker and connoisseur of wines, and he and his wife simply decided to use the same patient skills and care that profession required to create a delightful inn. Their son Wolfgang has carried on the family tradition.

Wolfgang, who grew up in the castle, has as his major concern the mouth watering food he prepares for the three restaurants of the castle hotel. He is young, about the age most chefs are just entering their apprenticeships, but he has mastered the culinary arts and earned a red chef's hat in the *Varta* guide. He concentrates on the use of fresh products only, *cuisine legere,* with the menus changing every week. Wolfgang's wife, Barbara, is an ideal hostess who makes sure that her guests are comfortable and happy.

If *Kalbsmedaillon im Mandelrock,* which is a fillet of veal baked in an almond crust, is on the menu when you are there, you should by all means try it. Other interesting specialties include Whiskysteal of Veal in Fresh Mushroom Sauce, Lamb Chops in Morel Cream Sauce, and Roulade of Salmon and Sole. Among the desserts are Fresh Pear Ice Cream with Warm Fruitcake, Cinnamon Zabaglione, Bavarian Vanilla Ice Cream with Raspberry Sauce, and Peppermint Ice Soufflé.

The view from the restaurants of the Rhine Valley, overlooking the yard of the castle and the vineyards of the countryside, is magnificent; the view of the Rhine itself, unfortunately, is not as spectacular.

OESTRICH IM RHEINGAU

The Dining Terrace
Hotel Schwan

Rheinallee 5-7
6227 Oestrich Im Reingau
Germany
Telephone: 06723–3001

All major credit cards
Breakfast, lunch, and dinner
Reservations recommended
Jacket not required
Liquor served
Dinner: $12 to $32
 full 3 courses, without wine
Lunch: the same
Chef: Dr. Wenckstern

This is a modern hotel in an ancient setting; the year 1628 is clearly visible on its gable, signifying the year in which this place was erected. The dining rooms—there are a number of them, such as the *Erkerzimmer* (the Bay Room), the *Turmzimmer* (the Tower Room), the *Mainzer Zimmer, Rotes Zimmer, Neue Räume,* and the Pavillon—are all pleasant, but the spot we love most is the dining terrace overlooking the Rhine. The cuisine is typically German, with game featured as the house specialty.

RÜDESCHEIM-ASSMANNSHAUSEN AM RHEIN

Dining Room and Terrace of
Hotel Krone

Rheinuferstrasse 10
D-6220 Rüdescheim-Assmannshausen am Rhein
Germany
Telephone: 06722–2036

All major credit cards
Breakfast, lunch, and dinner
Reservations not necessary
Jacket required
Liquor served
Dinner: $20 to $45
 full 3 courses, without wine
Chef: Herbert Pucher
Proprietors: The Hufnagel Family

Dining Room and Terrace of Hotel Krone

The pleasant dining terrace here has a "roof" consisting of grapevines and wisteria on a trellis. It is a fitting canopy, under which you sit in comfortable wicker chairs and gaze upon the Rhine.

The little village of Assmannshausen is at the point where the Höllenback River joins the Rhine after it has traveled from the mountains of the Rheingau and cut deep passages down to the Rhine through the slate hills. On these hills of the lower slopes of the Höllental Valley the famous Assmannshausen red wine grapes are grown and the wine produced. Because of these precipitous slopes so close to the Rhine, the small town of Assmannshausen simply cannot grow any larger; therefore it has retained its small-scale beauty, making this a classic Rhine Valley setting.

To the north, on the opposite bank, are large and still-secluded forests. The castle of Rheinstein, rebuilt from a ruin into a romantic fortress by the Prussian Prince Friedrich in 1823, gives Hotel Krone guests a truly picturesque view.

Like the Krone red wine which has been exported since the early 19th century, the cuisine at the Krone is well known and enjoyed. It earned, long ago, the *Michelin* star. The kitchen, in the center of the hotel, is often visited by international gourmets. Some of the main dish delights are Fresh Poached Salmon with Hollandaise Sauce (or grilled with Bearnaise Sauce), Wiener Schnitzel, Veal Steak Cordon Bleu, and, served for two, such specialties as Fillet of Veal with Fresh Vegetables and Morel Sauce, and Saddle of Lamb Provencale. Among the great desserts are Ice Soufflé Grand Marnier, Mocca-Parfait Savana with Himbeersauce, and *Vanille-Frappee Asbach Uralt.*

Greece

ATHENS

Galaxy Bar and Supper Club

Athens Hilton
46, Vassilissis Sofias Avenue
Athens, 146
Greece
Telephone: 7220–201

All major credit cards
Dinner
Reservations advised
Jacket suggested
Liquor served
Dinner: $20 to $35
  full 3 courses, without wine

Like many of the fine Hilton International hotels, the Athens Hilton has four restaurants; the one we like best is the Galaxy Room on the top of the hotel. When we last dined there, the food was particularly great. Still, the view is what one comes here for. The hotel and its top restaurant face the great monument of Greek history, the Acropolis. The view is excellent during the day and even more magical at night when the floodlights are trained on the ancient structure.

The Galaxy is open for dinner only. Guests are served from 7:30 P.M. to 2 A.M.

CRETE
HERAKLION

Limeniko Periptero
(The Glass House)

behind the Xenia Hotel
Sofoklis Venizelous Street, 4
Heraklion
Crete
Telephone: 283–096

No credit cards
Breakfast, lunch, and dinner
Reservations preferred
Jacket not required
Liquor served
Dinner: $5
  without wine
Proprietor: Georgios Kalomiris

Situated by the sea and overlooking the ancient harbor of Heraklion, this delightful restaurant is called the Glass House because it has walls of glass ten feet high so that diners may get a full view of the ocean and the harbor.

Heraklion is the main point of entry for visitors to this wonderful island of scenic splendor and fascinating archaeological wealth. It was here that Hellenic civilization flourished over 2,000 years ago.

A plain restaurant, the Glass House serves Cretan food fresh from the sea and the land. At night Cretan music adds a native touch to the proceedings.

AMSTERDAM

La Rive
Amstel Hotel
Prof. Tulpplein 1
1018 GX Amsterdam
Holland
Telephone: 020–79–31–42

All major credit cards
Breakfast and dinner
Reservations required
Jacket not required
Liquor served
Dinner: $20 to $35
full 3 courses, without wine
Chef: Paul van der Mey
Maitre d': Hans Engel and Fred Nees

Dining at the Amstel is a very pleasant experience. La Rive, situated in the garden of the hotel on the banks of the Amstel River, offers guests classic European atmosphere and grandeur and a view of the river that gave Amsterdam its name.

The interior of what was once called the Silver Room, which now seats 55 people, gives the impression of being a large private library. It still contains a rich collection of handcrafted ancient Dutch silverware, varying from simple tea spoons to large and magnificently decorated silver trays.

Looking out the windows, you may see the same river where centuries ago majestic galleons started their long journeys to the coasts of India and beyond in search of the spices that made Holland famous in world trade markets.

In summer, all this can be seen from the delightful Amstel Terras, where you feel almost as if you are dining on the Amstel River itself. In the winter, from the dining room, you can see ice skaters on the river while you listen to the piano music of the Amstel Hotel pianist, Theo Wijnen.

About 60 percent of the guests are local people, sometimes including members of the Dutch Royal Family or other celebrities. About 20 percent of the guests are Americans.

Hong Kong

The Bauhinia Room

The Hongkong Hotel
3 Canton Road
Kowloon
Hong Kong
Telephone: 3–676011

All major credit cards
Breakfast, lunch, and dinner
Reservations recommended
Jacket not required
Liquor served
Dinner: $13 to $26
full 3 courses, without wine
Lunch: the same
buffet lunch: $10
Chef: Max Liechti
Maitre d': Clement Wong

This restaurant—named for Hong Kong's national flower—is on the sixth floor of the Hongkong Hotel and has a panoramic view of Hong Kong Island and the harbor. The distinctive, subdued atmosphere of understated elegance which pervades the Bauhinia Room was achieved through meticulous attention to the color scheme and the selection of furnishings. The delicate colors and stylized motifs of the Bauhinia flower—pink, white, and purple—are all neatly blended into the upholstery, and the total effect is very pleasing to the eye. Paintings on the walls depicting the flower in a variety of moods and angles are the work of a local artist.

Among the favorites on the menu are Tenderloin Beef Bauhinia, Rack of New Zealand Lamb, Grilled Tiger Prawns, and Steamed Garoupa. Other unusual dishes include Goose Liver Terrine with Celeriac Salad, Boula Boula (green pea and turtle soup with champagne), and Avocado and Crabmeat Gratin—tasty fresh crabmeat refined with Armagnac and baked with Parmesan cheese. White Chocolate Mousse is a favorite dessert.

This is a split level restaurant, built that way so more guests can enjoy the view to dine by.

Carlton Grill

Carlton Hotel
Taipo Road
Kowloon
Hong Kong
Telephone: 3–866222

All major credit cards
Lunch and dinner
Reservations not necessary
Jacket not required
Liquor served
Dinner: $18 to $25
  full 3 courses, without wine
Lunch: $18 to $25
Chef: Leung Kwan

Since it's open for both lunch and dinner, the Carlton Grill offers two Hong Kong views, one during the day and one at night, both overpowering and both a challenge to absorb. To us, the view of the millions of varicolored lights at night is the more exciting.

The Carlton attracts many Australians and Americans, as well as European and English tourists, because although it boasts fine European cuisine it specializes in Roast Prime Rib of American Beef (the best in Hong Kong, or so they claim) and Boston Oysters, which are flown in weekly.

The Carlton Hotel was built in October 1957 by Cheung Koon-sing, a Hong Kong construction man. He had started to build his home on this spot when a friend wanted to rent the property from him, intending to change it to a hotel and a restaurant with a view to dine by. Mr. Cheung liked the idea so much he decided to do it himself.

Ian Fleming, author of *Thrilling Cities,* wrote: "Dinner at the Carlton unfolds one of the world's most memorable panoramas: the jeweled lights of Kowloon, the harbour, and the island."

Eagle's Nest

Hong Kong Hilton
2 Queen's Road C.
G.P.O. 42
Hong Kong
Telephone: 5–233111 Ext. 2501

All major credit cards
Lunch and dinner
Reservations not necessary
Jacket not required
Liquor served
Dinner: $20 to $25
  full 3 courses, without wine
Lunch: $8.75 to $11.25
Chef: K.K. Leung
Maitre d': Richard Li

From the Eagle's Nest on the 25th floor of the Hong Kong Hilton is a breathtaking panoramic view across the harbor to the kills of Kowloon, behind which are the New Territories of Hong Kong and China. It is also possible to get a glimpse of Lion Rock—a natural formation resembling a lion, located on one of the nine hills in the distance. The view takes in the whole of the Kowloon peninsula and the Central District on the island of Hong Kong, where the hotel is situated, and encompasses the business and financial center, where it seems a new building is being erected at every glance! Right now one can see the foundations for the new Bank of China building, designed by I.M. Pei, which, when completed, will be 70 stories high—the tallest building in Hong Kong.

The Hilton was built in 1963 and its Eagle's Nest has always been very popular. While all of the hotel and its 800 guest rooms have recently undergone substantial renovation, this beautiful restaurant has not been touched.

The Eagle's Nest serves specialties from both Canton and northern China. In the evening, music is provided by Bading Tuason and his orchestra. There is a special dinner menu for $24 per person which entitles the diner to select as many delicious dishes as he or she wishes.

At both lunch and dinner Chinese *dim sum* is offered with at least ten varieties of Northern and Southern Chinese desserts. Lotus seed paste and red bean paste are quite popularly used in Cantonese desserts, and the deep-fried or steamed red bean paste dumpling, coated with sesame seeds and called *chin tuio chai,* is worth trying. More distinctive and unusual Szechuan desserts are Toffee Apple or Banana Fritters. The sizzling hot caramelized fruit in these desserts must be put into ice-cold water to harden and crackle before serving; this is done at the last minute right at your table.

Another specialty here is, of course, Peking Duck, a dish for which each chef has his own little secret (which makes for a great variety in what you might be served). The basic principle similar to all preparations is the filling of the duck with air and water to make the skin lift away from the body. This enables the skin to cook to a crispy brown and the meat to simmer to a delightful tenderness. The meat is eaten with special thin pancakes, rich plum sauce, spring onions, and cucumbers.

A popular alternative to Peking Duck is Beggar's Chicken. This exotic dish is named because of its origin; the story goes that one day a beggar having nothing to eat stole a chicken. But since he had no cooking utensils, he wrapped the chicken in lotus leaves, packed mud around it, and placed it into a fire in the ground. Chefs use more modern materials with their lotus leaves and mud, yet the general method used to cook this dish is still the same. Most dramatic is the ceremony by which the chicken is released from its mud casing—with a hammer!

Your maitre d' will help you select the wonderful Chinese specialties.

The Excelsior Grill

The Excelsior
Causeway Bay
Hong Kong
Telephone: 5-767365

All major credit cards
Breakfast, lunch, and dinner
Reservations preferred
Dress: smart casual
Liquor served
Dinner: $20 to $30
  full 3 courses, without wine
Lunch: $15 to $25
Chef: Kurt Binggeli
Maitre d': Howard Chow

The exciting view from the Excelsior Grill on the third floor of Hong Kong's Excelsior Hotel takes in Causeway Bay, a picturesque typhoon shelter, the Royal Hong Kong Yacht Club, and the famous Noon Day Gun. The Excelsior's cocktail lounge, "Noon Gun Bar," is named after the historic Jardine's Gun, fired daily at noon from the waterfront opposite the Excelsior to signal the opening of the bar. In 1968, when he was visiting Hong Kong, Noel Coward fired the Noon Day Gun and later wrote a song immortalizing this colorful tradition.

The Excelsior Grill has an elaborate salad bar and a wide selection of jet-fresh meats—including prime cuts of juicy steaks—displayed on a marble counter. Guests may enjoy as many helpings as they please and complement them with a wide selection of condiments and homemade dressings. Seafood such as Grilled Fresh King Prawns is also available. In addition to the buffet, the Grill has a selective à la carte menu which specializes in grilled and French dishes. The Scottish Salmon is specially smoked in-house and is one of the starters, along with Deep-Fried Medallions of Brie with Port- and Champagne-Flavored Grape Cream Sauce. Soups include Cream of Watercress and Cream of Chicken with Shark's Fin. Among the main course are the North Sea Trio, which is grilled sole, turbot, and salmon with a ginger cream sauce, Poached Fillet of Lamb in Saffron Sauce with Carrots and Turnips, and Roast Pigeon with Mushrooms, Celery, Onion, and Chicken-Liver Stuffing. There's a sumptuous dessert trolley and a dessert special each day.

The Excelsior has seven restaurants and bars, and dining options range from Continental cuisine to *dim sum.* The hotel is next door to the World Trade Centre; the two are linked by an air-conditioned walkway. It is less than a five-minute walk from the downtown business center, ten minutes away from the Hung Hom Railway Station, and fifteen minutes away from the Kai Tak International Airport.

The Grandstand Grill at the
Sheraton Hong Kong

29 Nathan Road
Kowloon
Hong Kong
Telephone: 3-691111

All major credit cards
Breakfast, lunch, and dinner
Reservations required
Jacket not required;
*   dress: casual but elegant*
Liquor served
Dinner: $18 to $25
*   full 3 courses, without wine*
Lunch: $11 to $18
Chef: Joseph Bruegger
Maitre d': Samuel Cheung

Nathan Road, where the Sheraton Hong Kong is situated, is one of the busiest and most fun-filled shopping boulevards in the Kowloon area. But on the fourth floor of the hotel, all is elegant peace and quiet in the Grandstand Grill, the hotel's gourmet restaurant.

Here the view through the large windows provides a dining backdrop of skyscrapers and, at night, the lights of the buildings on Hong Kong Island.

The cuisine is elegant. Among the favorites served here are Prime Rib of Beef, Roasted Rack of Lamb, Roasted Quail, Sans Fancise Ciobbino Lobster and Prawn Salad, and Veal Sweetbread and Ham. Desserts include Chocolate Mousse and Apple Tart.

For the grand view from the 18th floor in this hotel, see the listing for the Pink Giraffe.

Margaux

Restaurant of the
Shangri-La Hong Kong
64 Mody Road
Kowloon
Hong Kong
Telephone: 3-7212111

All major credit cards
Lunch and dinner
Reservations preferred
Jacket required
Liquor served
Dinner: $30 to $45
*   full 3 courses,*
*   without wine*
Lunch: $11 to $19
Chef: Mark Hellbach
Maitre d': Jean Fleisch

Margaux is considered one of the top dining rooms of Hong Kong. Not only does it afford spectacular views of Victoria Harbour, but the seating is wonderfully comfortable, with a lot of space between tables so you can enjoy the view and have an unusual degree of privacy. Margaux seats as many as 100 people, but the feeling is of a smaller place, of an intimate club, perhaps. The wood-paneled room is decorated in cool colors of dusty peach and powder blue, with velvet patchwork design for the seats of the dining chairs. The heavy curtains, held back with large elegant brass clips, match the chairs. Brass is the major decorative theme throughout, set off by the teak wood of the walls. Berndorf silver, Wedgwood china, and Waterford crystal are used for the table settings.

Superb Continental cuisine is served. Among the favorite entrées are Crabmeat Ravioli, Turbot in Olive Oil, and Lamb with Thyme Sauce. The wine list is good, especially strong on Bordeaux, and in this room, Chateau Margaux is, of course, the featured item. One of the favorite—and most expensive—dishes is Navarin of Boston Lobster on a Bed of Leeks with Sauterne Wine Sauce; there is also Lobster Sautéed in Orange Sauce with Green Peppercorns. This dining room has received the Westin Silver Spoon Award. Dinner served from 7 P.M. until 11:30 P.M. Lunch from noon until 3 P.M. (closed Sunday).

Pierrot

The Mandarin
5 Connaught Road, Central
GPO Box 2623
Hong Kong
Telephone: 5–220111 Ext. 4028

All major credit cards
Lunch and dinner
Reservations required
Jacket and tie required at dinner
Liquor served
Dinner: $50
    full 3 courses, without wine
Lunch: About $37
Chef: Michel Hendler
Maitre d': Philippe Requin

Pierrot is acclaimed for its panoramic view over the most fabled harbor in the world, Hong Kong's Victoria Harbour, and of the bustling Kowloon Peninsula across the harbor, bound by a range of hills in the north called the Nine Dragons.

Chinese junks in full sail mingle with the ships of the U.S. Seventh Fleet and the jetfoils gliding smoothly to Macau. The luxury liner *Queen Elizabeth II* docks at the Ocean Terminal, oil tankers and container ships enter the harbor, while the famous Star Ferry boats make one of their many crossings of the day between the island and the mainland. All of these and more are scenes that diners at window tables of Pierrot may view.

Located on the 25th floor of the Mandarin, Pierrot is the hotel's exclusive French restaurant, and certainly one of the best of its kind in Asia. The elegant decor takes its theme from Pablo Picasso's portrait of his son Paul, Pierrot, as interpreted by the international designer Don Ashton. Luxurious red velvet furnishings and prints by Picasso and other masters set the mood for the classical French cuisine served both at luncheon and dinner.

Under the supervision of Executive Chef Hendler is Hans Wismer, who has been in charge of Pierrot's kitchen since 1983, when he arrived here after several years spent working with Anton Mosimann, the executive chef of the Dorcester in London.

We recommend the *Chartreuse de Homard aux Endives sur Navarin de Poivrons* (Fresh Lobster and Endive Timbale served with a Seafood and Sweet Pepper Sauce); *Tian de Saint-Jacques aux Fleurs de Broccoli, Sauce Bouzy* (Sautéed Scallops with a Broccoli Flan accompanied by Bouzy Red Wine Sauce); *Filet de Boeuf á la Fricassée de Champig-*

nons des Bois, Nouilles á la Sauge (Pan-fried Beef Tenderloin with Sage Ravioli and Wild Mushroom Sauce); and *Eventail de Canard Sauvage au Citron Vert et son Riz á l'estragon* (Roast Breast of Wild Duck presented with a Tarragon Rice and Lime Sauce). We took our French pastries from the trolley for dessert. Perhaps you should be more adventurous.

Pierrot is but one of eight restaurants and bars located in the Mandarin Hotel. We think it is the best, not only because of the fantastic view, but because its food is wonderful too. The restaurant is very well located, in that it shares a luxurious shopping arcade with three lower floors of the hotel, and it is connected by a footbridge over the street to five other shopping galleries in the Prince's Building, the Alexandra House, Swire House, Connaught Centre, and the magnificent new shopping complex, the Landmark. Together they make up the most comprehensive shopping complex in all of Hong Kong.

Pink Giraffe

18th floor
Sheraton Hong Kong Hotel
29 Nathan Road
Kowloon
Hong Kong
Telephone: 3–691111 Ext. 1818

All major credit cards
Dinner
Reservations necessary
Jacket required
Liquor served
Dinner: $27 to $35
full 3 courses, without wine
Chef: Richard Stuttler
Maitre d': Paul Kwok

This is the highest view to dine by in Kowloon—the eighteenth floor of the Sheraton Hong Kong. And the magnificent view is made all the more exciting by its reflection in the restaurant's ceiling. Only dinner is served here, so the view is mostly of the lights of Hong Kong and the harbor boats.

The Pink Giraffe is an elegant place to dine. Among the fine cuisine on the bill of fare are Marinated Salmon, Oyster Muscovite, Prime U.S. Sirloin Steak in Pink, Green, and Black Pepper Sauce, salmon and grouper. For dessert, try the Floating Island with Vanilla Sauce.

Le Plume

The Regent
Salisbury Road
Kowloon
Hong Kong
Telephone: 3–7211211

All major credit cards
Dinner
Reservations required
Jacket required
Liquor served
Dinner: $30 to $50
full 3 courses,
without wine
Manager: Aldrin Leung

If ever there was a hotel dedicated to a great view, this is it. The Regent, which sits on top of 127 pylons sunk into the undersoil of Victoria Harbour, is not only on the waterfront, it is actually part of it. Those who think that the Regent looks, from the outside, like a very unspectacular skyscraper, are right. But the real fun of the Regent starts when you enter the lobby, a vast and seemingly endless stretch of highly polished reddish Portuguese granite. In the center of this immense space is a freestanding reception center built from burled wood. Behind the lobby is one of the largest cocktail lounges you have ever seen, and behind that are fantastic sheets of glass, about four stories high, giving a breathtaking view of the harbor and of Hong Kong across the water. The most delightful time of day to be in this popular cocktail lounge is at twilight, when, as the sun sets, the lights of Hong Kong begin to flicker on.

One of the world's great pleasures is dining at the Regent's Le Plume, one of Asia's most unusual restaurants. It offers dining on two levels so that as many people as possible can absorb the spectacular panorama. When we dined there our Hong Kong hosts sat with their backs to the view so we would not miss it—we were thankful for this display of hospitality; at the same time we could not imagine anyone becoming used to such splendor. It came as a jolt when we were asked to order. Who needs food with such a majestic view?

In case you do feel hungry, Le Plume doesn't depend solely upon the view to satisfy its guests' appetites. It is, in our opinion, one of the four best dining rooms in Asia; the other three are Gatti's at the Peninsula (a neighbor of Le Plume), Pierrot, at the Mandarin across the harbor, and the Normandie, at the Oriental in Bangkok.

When you are seated you are served a champagne-Mir, which is the house drink. Fresh Indian na'an bread baked in clay tandoor ovens is then placed on your table for you to nibble on while you decide. The cuisine is *nouvelle*, with a few exceptions. One of the delicious dishes we tried was the Artichoke Soup, flavored with Beluga caviar.

Rooftop Restaurant at the Park Lane Hotel

310 Gloucester Road
Causeway Bay
Hong Kong
Telephone: 5–7901021 Ext. 1915

All major credit cards
Breakfast, lunch, and dinner
Reservations necessary
Jacket required at dinner;
* casual elegant dress required at lunch*
Liquor served
Dinner: $15
* full 3 courses, without wine*
Lunch: $7
Chef: Lothar Andrias Becht

One of the newest places to dine with a view is at the Rooftop Restaurant of the Park Lane Hotel in Hong Kong. Reopened in April 1986, the Park Lane Hotel has a 270-degree panorama overlooking the spectacular Hong Kong harbor and beautiful Victoria Park.

The newly redecorated restaurant is now a split level dining room with floor-to-ceiling windows. Lavish use of marble and plants dominate the elegant decor.

A new feature here is the international Asian buffet at breakfast; Chinese à la carte and *dim sum* luncheons are also offered. In the evening Chinese cuisine is served and soft music for dancing is played. Dinner is served from 7 P.M. until 1 A.M. The generous buffet is available at lunch and dinner as well.

The Spice Market
Deck 2
Ocean Terminal
Kowloon
Hong Kong
Telephone: 3–676238

All major credit cards
Breakfast, lunch, and dinner
Reservations recommended
Jacket not required
Liquor served
Dinner: $8 to $12
    full 3 courses, without wine
Lunch: the same
Lunch/dinner buffet: $7 to $8
Chef: Max Liechti
Maitre d': Anthony Wong

One of the exciting delights of Hong Kong is visiting the Kowloon side for its gigantic shopping complexes—Ocean Centre, the Harbour City, and the Ocean Terminal. There are more than 40 restaurants here, and many of them have harbor views.

We felt we should tell you about one of these, the Spice Market on the second deck of the immense Ocean Terminal. It is located near the shopping arcade of the Hong Kong Hotel, which also runs this restaurant. It is the perfect luncheon spot, a respite from a busy day of shopping.

The Spice Market's view is of the harbor and of Hong Kong Island across the way. The restaurant has a tropical decor—plenty of bamboo, wicker, and palm trees. It offers a regional epicurean potpourri in an extravagant buffet among exotic fruits beneath shade roofs of palm leaves.

The chef is from Indonesia, but from time to time he is joined, for a week or two, by guest chefs from other parts of Southeast Asia and the East, who bring with them their recipes for specially designated weeks that feature the foods of their countries. Therefore,

at times you may find in the buffet selections authentic Philippine Lamb Stew, Shanghainese Drunken Chicken, Korean Kimchee, Indonesian Gado Gado, Indian Chili Crab, Singapore Rendang Beef, the curries of several countries, and dozens of other regional dishes and condiments.

This restaurant, with its delightful food and reasonable prices, is actually better known to residents than to visitors. So expect to see fewer Americans and Western faces than you might see at other Hong Kong dining spots. Tables with views are usually not available if you just walk in. Ask for yours when you call for a reservation.

The Verandah

The Peninsula
Salisbury Road
Kowloon
Hong Kong
Telephone: 3–666251 Ext. 1190

All major credit cards
Breakfast, lunch, and dinner
Reservations recommended
Dress: casual, no jeans
Liquor served
Dinner: $15 to $50
*   full 3 courses, without wine*
Lunch: $9 to $50
Chef: Erich Schaeli
Maitre d': E. Di Marco

The Verandah, spanning the entire front of the elegant Peninsula Hotel, offers its guests magnificent views of the harbor and of the Hong Kong skyline.

During the Peninsula's first 22 years of operation, the Verandah was an open-air terrace where guests of the hotel would take afternoon tea. It was covered over in 1950 to become a new restaurant for the hotel called the Playpen, which proved to be very successful. In the early 1960s, the Playpen was renovated to become what is now known as the Verandah.

The elegant tone of the hotel is retained in this fine restaurant, which has an old-world quality both in decor and service. The famous and beautiful Marco Polo lunchtime buffet is served here everyday. Offering an elaborate display of hot and cold, Western and Oriental dishes, the Marco Polo buffet is a favorite of travelers who are guests at the hotel and of local business people and residents. It is not only lavish in the number of items featured, but it is truly an artistic accomplishment.

The Verandah also has an extensive à la carte menu with a choice of Continental and Chinese cuisines. National food festivals are a regular event in this restaurant, which is usually one of the highest rated in Hong Kong.

Among the favorite appetizers are Salmon Tartare and Crab Salad with Grapefruit. Main dishes include Lobster Play Pan and Veal Steak Peninsula. For dessert you might try the Soufflé Rothschild or any of the homemade ice creams.

Ever since the Peninsula opened in 1928 it has been the top place for top people, where anybody who was anybody in Hong Kong went to see and be seen. VIPs of all kinds have always stayed here. The British selected this as the place to surrender the Colony to the Japanese in 1941.

Rumors persist that this grand hotel will be removed to make way for some modern skyscraper or shopping complex. If any serious intentions to demolish the hotel were to surface, there would probably be a cry heard around the world, just as there was in 1975 when it was announced that the Peninsula would be torn down and a more modern structure put in its place. Five months later the announcement was withdrawn and it was said, "The Peninsula will be with us for a long time." We hope so.

BUDAPEST

Bellevue Supper Club

Hotel Duna Inter-Continental
Apáczai Csere János utca 4
P.O. Box 100
Budapest 1364
Hungary
Telephone: 175–122/175

All major credit cards
Dinner
Reservations required
Jacket not required
Liquor served
Dinner: $20 to $50
full 3 courses, without wine
Chef: Imre Fazekas
Maitre d': Sandor Baja

Situated in downtown Budapest, between the Chain and Elizabeth bridges, on the Danube, the Bellevue Supper Club is the only rooftop restaurant in the city, offering spectacular views not only of the Danube but of the Buda hills and the former Royal Castle.

It is considered the most elegant and fashionable dining spot in Budapest, and features entertainment, music, and dancing in a joyous Hungarian setting.

The great Hungarian food is also a prime attraction; some of the main dish delights are Browned Chicken Breast Hungarian Style, Braised Rumpsteak Budapest, Stuffed Cabbage *Kolozsvár*, Cutlets of Pork with Gnocchi, Leg of Goose Hungarian Style, Gratinated Veal Steak in Spinach Salad, Filled Puff Paste Tartlets with Tongue and Calf's Brains, Saddle of Veal Orloff, Scallops of Veal *Nivernaise*, Rolled Roastbeef *Csáky* with Gnocchi, and Sirloin of Beef *Eszterházy*.

This is a deluxe restaurant in a deluxe hotel, with a great view. While you dine, not only do you see the former Royal Palace, the Danube, and the Buda Hills, but also the Fisherman's Bastion, Mount Gellert, the Matthias Church, and the Castle Hill Palace. Not to be missed.

NEWMARKET ON FERGUS

Dromoland Castle Dining Room

Newmarket on Fergus
County Clare
Ireland
Telephone: 061–71144

All major credit cards
Breakfast, lunch, and dinner
Reservations recommended
Jacket and tie required
Liquor served
Dinner: $37
　　　　full 3 courses, without wine
Lunch: $18
Chef: Noel Rooney
Maitre d': Catherine White

　　You may become so enamored of this castle that you want to live here! Dromoland Castle was a gift in 1570 to Donough O'Brien, after which it became the home of the royal O'Brien clan (descended in an unbroken line from King Brian Boru, victor over the Danes at Clontarf in 1014).

　　The view, of course, is the castle, its grounds, and the sumptuous dining room. Meals are served in the classic Continental manner, flavored to zestiness with Irish specialties— Dublin Bay prawns, native salmon, sea and brook trout, Irish bacon, tender spring lamb, magnificent steaks, and a small miracle called Irish Soda Bread, very different from its American version.

　　Most of the guests are American tourists. Watching and enjoying the guests are a few local people, usually celebrating an important family event.

HAIFA

Rondo Room

Dan Carmel Hotel
P.O. Box 6055
87 Hanassi Avenue
Haifa
Israel

All major credit cards
Dinner
Reservations requested
Jacket not required
Liquor served
Dinner: $28, à la carte
Chef: Miho Ucovic
Maitre d': Avi Dahan

On the edge of a Mount Carmel slope is a building which looks like a flying saucer sitting on top of a pedestal. This is the Rondo Room, a circular glass restaurant with a nighttime view of all of Haifa, which has been called "Little San Francisco" and the "Naples of the Middle East" because its views take in the Mediterranean, the wooded Mount Carmel, and the vista of a busy harbor.

The Rondo Room is a happy restaurant, with tableside cooking, lilting music, and a dream-like atmosphere blending well together. The view/dining room attracts both local people and tourists from all over the world. It is reached by a long glassed-in elevator from the Dan Carmel Hotel below it.

The hotel itself has views in every direction. Like the restaurant, it overlooks historic and magnificent Haifa Bay, and also commands a view of the green fields of the Valley of Jezreel and the hills of Galilee.

JERUSALEM

Mishkenot Sha'ananim

Yemin Moshe
Jerusalem
Israel
Telephone: 02–244696 or 225110

No credit cards
Lunch and dinner
Reservations necessary
Jacket advised
Liquor served
Dinner: fixed menu $32
  full 3 courses, without wine
Lunch: $15 "business special"
Chef/Maitre d'/Owner: Moihe Pe'er

This restaurant is situated in Yemin Moshe, a small area of Jerusalem named for Sir Moses Montefiore, founder of New Jerusalem, the first settlement outside the walls of the Old City. Yemin Moshe is now restored and is populated mostly by artists, who live and work here.

From Mishkenot Sha'ananim is a magnificent view of one of the holiest of Jewish sites, a relic of the Western Wall that surrounded the Temple Court centuries ago. The tiers of large stones date from the Second Temple, completed 520 B.C. by King Herod.

This excellent restaurant features Sha'ananim Duckling, the house specialty, with a choice of orange, cherry, peach, pineapple, olive, or mushroom sauce. The first course is a fun platter of mixed hors d'oeuvres, another popular specialty.

The cuisine at Mishkenot Sha'ananim has been honored with the highest grade awarded by a very tough Ministry of Tourism. It has also been recognized in the *Bazak* guide and the *Michelin* guide. This is a popular place for a lot of American visitors.

Italy

AMALFI
Hotel Santa Caterina

Via Nazionale, 9
84011 Amalfi
Italy
Telephones: 089–871012 or 871387

All major credit cards
Lunch and dinner
Reservations suggested
Jacket required at dinner
Liquor served
Dinner: $18 to $40
    full 3 courses, without wine
Lunch: the same
Proprietor: Giuseppina Gambardella

Since we last wrote about the Hotel Santa Caterina it has been upgraded from First Class (four stars) to Superior First Class (five stars). As a result the cuisine and the restaurant standards have been upgraded as well, so that a *grande carte* is offered featuring a large choice of regional and international specialties.

The view is as spectacular as ever. The restaurant has large windows offering views of the sea, the gardens, and the magnificent coastline along the Amalfi Drive, considered by many to be the most scenic drive in Europe.

There are two glass elevators now, built against the steep cliff, which take guests down to sea level, where there is a sea-water swimming pool. Above the pool there is an open air restaurant where buffet luncheon is served everyday during the summer. Twice a week in summer there is an evening buffet, accompanied by music.

Before lunch or dinner, we recommend lingering over an aperitif or an "Amalfi-Sea" (the exciting blue cocktail of the house) in the elegant bar on the large terrace. An awning of many-colored bougainvillea hangs overhead.

The most popular specialties include *Cannelloni All'Amalfitana, Spaghetti Primavera, Linguine con Scampi, Risotto al Radicchio, Penne al Limone, Aragosta o Scampi alla Griglia, Chateaubriand,* and *Crepes Flambees All'Aranica.* Your fellow guests will be a mixture of Europeans and Americans.

ANACAPRI
Hotel-Restaurant Caesar Augustus

Via G. Orlandi 4
80071 Anacapri
Italy
Telephone: 081–837–1421/44

All major credit cards
Breakfast, lunch, and dinner
Reservations recommended
Jacket not required
Liquor served
Dinner and lunch: $5 to $15
    full 3 courses, without wine
Chef: Mike
Maitre d': Ciro

As you sit on the dining terrace of the Caesar Augustus, situated atop a cliff some 850 feet directly above the Mediterranean, you will be so overwhelmed by the beauty that you will find it hard to believe you're not dreaming.

The view is almost too much to take in; it includes the sparkling Bay of Naples, the island of Ischia, the majestic and slumbering Mount Vesuvius, the flowered coast of Sorrento, and the charming nearby villa of San Michele.

You may enjoy the view at breakfast from 7:30 A.M. until 10 A.M., at lunch from noon until 4:30 P.M., or dinner from 7:30 P.M. until 9:30 P.M. The cuisine is classic Italian, featuring Ravioli Caesar Augustus, *Crespelli al Formaggio, Zuppa di Pesce Frutta Flambé,* and more.

FIESOLE
The Loggia
Il Ristorante
Villa San Michele
Via di Doccia
Fiesole
Italy
Telephone: 055–59451

American Express
Breakfast, lunch, and dinner
Reservations necessary
Jacket required at dinner
Liquor served
Manager: M. Saccani
Managing Director: Natale Rusconi

At this spot, one of our favorites, one can look out over the ancient city of Florence and the River Arno while enjoying a drink and meal. There are gardens sloping down from the hotel, all part of the view, where after lunch or dinner guests may wander past cypresses and olive trees and see two small solitary stone chapels, reminders of just how ancient this place is.

The Loggia is the dining porch of a restaurant in a hotel situated on the hill of Fiesole, a small town outside of Florence. San Michele a Doccia takes its name from the 15th century church dedicated to St. Michael the Archangel. The internal courtyard, with its nests of swallows, has the crest of the Davanzati family, attributed to Donatello, which dates back to 1416.

You enter this lovely inn through a facade designed by Michelangelo into an atmosphere of elegance recreated by Gerard Gallet with full respect for Florentine history and art. The present building was built toward the end of the 15th century when an earlier monastery was considerably enlarged; many of the works of art that were originally there are now in galleries and churches in Florence.

The Franciscans retained possession of this building until forced out by Napoleon. It was then that the property was taken over by a religious order led by sister Nicoletta Cipriani. At the beginning of this century, San Michele a Doccia was purchased by an American financier, Henry White Cannon. He restored the gardens, repaired the building, and built a roof on the 15th century courtyard. The building was hit by shellfire during World War II. In 1950, a Parisian, Lucien Tessier, bought the building and decided to repair it and make it into a private home. His objective of restoring the original design was achieved; he also added several 20th century amenities. As the work progressed the project took on such huge dimensions that Tessier realized it made more sense to turn the place into a hotel.

Now, after 200 years, the villa is back in the hands of a Cipriani. The new owner is the Hotel Cipriani of Venice, which also has a splendid view to dine by and appears further on in this book.

Known for its fine cuisine, San Michele a Doccia puts on a major gastronomic event every year, usually in August. In 1985, it was "Open-Air Cooking with Marcella Hazen," a world-renowned authority on Italian food, who demonstrated for the hotel's guests how meats, seafood, vegetables, and fruits could be transformed by the simplest and oldest of cooking techniques—such as a natural wood charcoal fire and an open-air grill—into appetizers, pasta sauces, entrées, and desserts of dazzling purity and matchless flavor.

FLORENCE
Roof Garden Restaurant
Grand Hotel Baglioni
Piazza Unita Italiana 6
50123 Florence
Italy
Telephone: 055–218441

All major credit cards
Breakfast, lunch, and dinner
Reservations not necessary
Jacket required
Liquor served
Dinner: $18 to $28
  full 3 courses, without wine
Lunch: the same
Chef: D. Dispensieri
Maitre d': A. Salvadori

When you dine in the Roof Garden Restaurant of the Hotel Baglioni, it's like dining in a garden in the sky. When we first saw the gardens more than twenty years ago, they had just been started and, while attractive, were hardly as lush and beautiful as they are today. The gardens even compete with the architectural beauty of other Florentine treasures such as the Cathedral and the Palazzo Vecchio. The view takes in almost all of the ancient buildings of note in Florence, and it can be experienced from almost any table—except for the purposely secluded ones for those who want to dine very much alone.

At night the Roof Garden is particularly lovely. The dim, colorful garden lights add charm to the star-studded Italian sky and the twinkling lights of Florence.

What to order? We suggest *Linguine al Limone,* Florentine Steak, and *Torta della Nonna.*

LAKE COMO

The Villa d'Este Verandah

Villa d'Este Hotel
22010 Cernobbio
Lake Como
Italy
Telephones: 031–511471 or 512471

American Express, Visa
Breakfast, lunch, and dinner
Reservations required
Jacket required
Liquor served
Dinner: $30 to $50
    full 3 courses, without wine
Lunch: the same
Chef: Luciano Parolari
Maitre d': Giordano Rizzi

Here in the basin of Lake Como are the villas that belonged to aristocrats of another, perhaps grander age. Most celebrated among all of these is the delightful Villa d'Este and its breathtaking view of formal gardens, ancient trees, and the lovely lakes.

The Villa d'Este has an ancient history, going back to 1442, when the Bishop of Como raised to the dignity of a cloister an unassuming retreat for nuns at the mouth of the River Garrovo. Today it is the celebrated resort hotel, the favorite and most elegant on the shores of Lake Como.

An Italian writer, Nino Podenzani, wrote a beautiful book for and about the Villa d'Este. We quote: "The aristocratic cypresses point skywards the double rows of their elegant arrows, leading down the steps towards the lake or gathering in groups as if to converse with the cedars of Lebanon, the plane trees, the beeches, and the ancient elms. The maritime pines, the fanlike palm trees, and the poplars all stretched towards the sun."

During the past twenty years, Villa d'Este has undergone a complete streamlining in order to provide up-to-date service. Luckily, this renovation has left the ancient facade and the impressive aura of its noble past intact. You'll inevitably notice some fascinating, fortress-like structures in the gardens; these were built in the 1780s. It seems that the Marquis who then resided at the villa passed away, his widow, Donna Vittoria Calderara, a much younger woman, wasted no time in remarrying a young, handsome Napoleonic General, Count Domenico Pino. Because she feared he might suffer from war nostalgia, she had a series of simulated fortresses and towers built on the slopes overlooking the gardens; today they are part of our view to dine by.

In addition to lovely private dining rooms, the Villa d'Este has a modern dining terrace—perhaps one of the most modern in the world (it is soundproof, weatherproof, and features giant windows). It is called the Verandah of the Villa d'Este.

The cuisine is well prepared, with offerings for a diversity of tastes. In addition to the Verandah, the formal dining room, and the rustic and informal grill, in the summer there are outdoor lunches and dinners in the garden. Among the favorites on the menu are Sturgeon with Coriander, Pumpkin Ravioli with Cheese Fondue, Sweet-Sour Duck, and, for dessert, Iced Fruit Cassata.

MILAN

Antica Osteria del Ponte
Piazza Negri 9
Cassinetta di Lugagnano
(near Milan)
Italy
Telephone: 02–942–0034

American Express
Lunch and dinner
Reservations necessary
Jacket required
Liquor served
Dinner: $40 to $60
   full 3 courses, without wine
Lunch: $35
Chef/Owner: Ezio Santin
Maitre d'/Owner: Renata Santin

This small Lombardy restaurant is a gem. Located just 23 kilometers from Milan by Lorenteggio Road and three kilometers outside the village of Abbiategraso, Antica Osteria del Ponte has been hailed by restaurant critics as "the best in Italy" and "the best in Europe." It may well be.

The restaurant is situated in a 600-year-old building at the foot of an equally ancient bridge (thus its name) in the picturesque little village of Cassinetta di Lugagnano Milano. The interior is alluringly cozy: white walls and heavy beamed ceilings delineating two pleasant rooms with just eleven tables. Soft pink Pratesi linens, antique Italian furniture, and beautiful flower arrangements on the tables and elsewhere complete the scene.

Ezio Santin is the chef-owner and his wife, Renata, is the charming red-headed hostess who makes sure that you are beautifully served with artistically displayed seafood, lamb, or tenderly prepared local vegetables.

Antica Osteria del Ponte has earned its two *Michelin* stars with main dishes such as homemade Ravioli with Lobster and Baby *Courgettes* and Fresh Sea Bass with Cream of Artichokes. For dessert, try the White and Dark Chocolate Mousse. New items are always being added, as the menu is changed daily.

NAPLES

Casanova Grill Bar

Hotel Excelsior
Via Partenope 48
80121 Naples
Italy
Telephone: 081–417111

All major credit cards
Breakfast, lunch, and dinner
Reservations recommended
Jacket not required
Liquor served
Dinner: $46 to $52
 full 3 courses, without wine
 2-course business dinner with
 wine and coffee for $29
Lunch: the same
Chef: Francesco Settembrini
Maitre d': Franco Cinquegrano

The Casanova Grill Bar of the Hotel Excelsior faces the Santa Lucia area, which encompasses the Bay of Naples and, in the distance, Mount Vesuvius.

The Hotel Excelsior, built by the Swiss in 1906 and since ranked among the finest deluxe hotels in Italy, has been under the management of the CIGA group of fine hotels since 1935. It is by far the best in the Naples area, combining modern facilities and service with the grandeur of a luxurious palace.

The food is very good. Among the specialties are Seafood Salad, Sea Bass in Paper Bag, Spaghetti *Posillipo* (with clams), Stuffed Squids *Isola Verde,* Sautéed Shrimps with Salmon, Carpaccio, and, for a special dessert, Crepes Casanova. The guests include many Italian businessmen, British visitors, and lots of Americans. While the menu changes with the seasons, Mediterranean cuisine is always featured.

PORTOFINO

La Terrazza

Hotel Splendido
Viale Baratta 13
Portofino
Italy
Telephone: 0185–69551 or 552

All major credit cards
Breakfast, lunch, and dinner
Reservations recommended
Jacket required for dinner only
Liquor served
Dinner: $35 to $45
    full 3 courses, without wine
Lunch: $25 to $45
Chef: Gilberto Pizzi
Maitre d': Giorgio Tognazzi

The view from the Splendido has been acclaimed by many as the most beautiful in the world. The hotel's terrace, where most guests dine, and its elegant dining room, which has large picture windows along one side, both look down upon a tiny cliff-lined fishing harbor with clusters of pretty fishing boats and colorful buildings grouped closely together, forming a collar around the cove. It is easy to pass several hours here in pleasant contemplation of the scene.

The Splendido is one of two imposing buildings perched high on the mountainside overlooking Portofino; the other was once the castle of the Countess Mumm. We love the terrace and particularly the flower-lined paths in the hotel's hillside garden. We suggest you reserve a table by a window in the beautiful dining room, if the days are cool. On nice days, the terrace is the place to be. Meals feature typical Ligurian cuisine of the region and classic Italian dishes.

RIMINI

The Dining Room of
Il Grand Hotel di Rimini

Parco Indipendenza
47037 Rimini
Italy
Telephone: 0541–24211

All major credit cards
Lunch and dinner
Reservations required
Jacket required at dinner
Liquor served
Dinner: $24 to $30
    full 3 courses, without wine
Lunch: the same
Chef: Valerio Tosseri

Rimini is both an old-time grand resort on the Adriatic Sea and a still-fashionable beach town. The view from this hotel's elegant main dining room encompasses the hotel's beautiful pool, the beach, and the sea.

The hotel itself is something of an attraction, with its luxurious and ornate furnishings. Federico Fellini, Rimini's most famous son, wrote in *La Mia Rimini* that, " . . . The Grand Hotel used to be a fable of riches, luxury, and oriental splendour. . . . When descriptions in the novels I used to read were not stimulating enough to arouse suggestive sceneries, in my imagination, we would pull out the Grand Hotel. . . . "

The hotel has not lost its powers to inspire. The views are magnificent from the main dining room as well as from the lovely beach restaurant, which features a buffet of the hotel's specialties. Or perhaps the fantasies are best summoned in the small, romantic Ristorantino, small and refined, open all night for those who love to dine and linger in a lush setting.

ROME

Charles Penthouse Restaurant

Hotel Eden
Via Ludovisi, 49
00187 Rome
Italy
Telephone: 06–474–3551

No credit cards
Breakfast, lunch, and dinner
Reservations suggested
Jacket required at dinner
Liquor served
Dinner: $35
  full 3 courses, without wine
Maitre d': Charles (Giancarlo Castrucci)

Charles Penthouse

The rooftop Panoramico restaurant is named for Charles, the veteran maitre d' of the Hotel Eden. It has one of the finest views in Rome: you can see the Seven Hills for which the Eternal City is famous and so much else that you must be sure to ask for the full-color "HER" folder, which opens up three feet across and clearly indicates the important buildings you can see from your luxurious perch.

Giafrancesco and Giuseppe Ciaceri, the two brothers who own the hotel, were born in the hotel (which has been in the family for 97 years), so even though they and their families live in homes just around the corner it is natural that they care for the Hotel Eden like a home. Located on a hilltop above the Spanish Steps, and next to a famous neighbor, the Hassler, the Penthouse Restaurant of the Hotel Eden is one of Rome's most popular dining spots. Each sitting provides dining space for about 80 guests and a 180-degree view of half of the inner part of Rome. The hotel itself is a small one, with 110 exquisitely furnished rooms, and has a five star, or deluxe, rating. The Ciaceris are always making improvements so their guests can enjoy themselves even more.

Giuseppe, in commenting on the cuisine, told us the following: "All of the dishes we serve are well-prepared, and, as is generally done with Italian cooking, the dishes are made to order and served to the taste of our patrons—Charles knows his clients! One of the dishes Italians like most, which we serve at the Penthouse, is made with flat homemade noodles we call *pappardelle* plus garlic, oil, and turnip leaves we call *broccoletti*. Of course, we have many other dishes as well." These include Fillets of Sole with Almonds, Fried Prawns with Tartar Sauce, *Tonnarelli alla "Charles,"* *Carpaccio* (Sliced Raw Fillet), and Shredded Fillet Venice Style. For dessert, a few suggestions are Charleston Ice Sundae, Crepes Suzette, and *Troika* Sherbet (with vodka).

The Hassler Roof

Hotel Hassler
Piazza Trinita dei Monti, 6
00187 Rome
Italy
Telephone: 06–678–2651

No credit cards
Lunch and dinner
Reservations requested
Jacket and tie required
Liquor served
Dinner: $40 to $80
 full 3 courses, without wine
Lunch: $30 to $40
Chef: Gildo Concari
Maitre d': Vincenzo Sabatini

There is very little of Rome that you cannot see from the rooftop restaurant of the luxurious Hassler. And to make sure you don't miss a thing, the restaurant gives a yard-wide folder with fine sketches identifying all the buildings you see.

The hotel is located at the top of the Spanish Steps, at the Piazza Trinita dei Monti, one of the many beautiful parts of Rome. In fact, in the library of the neighboring Convent of the Trinity, built in the 15th century, an inscription reads: *"Non est in tota laetior Urbe locus,"* which means that "in all Rome there is no more delightful spot." The church and its two bell towers are a characteristic part of the Roman skyline.

The Piazza de Spagna and its environs have always fascinated artists, poets, and lovers from all countries. They lived, found inspiration, and worked here—usually by the side of the Spanish Steps, or not too far away. Among the greats lured to this part of Rome have been Göethe, Byron, Keats, Shelley, Dickens, Ruskin, Gogol, and Hawthorne. Fernand Gregh, who had a house nearby, wrote, "Here on Trinita I drink in the Roman sunshine to stay me during the future Parisian winters starved of light."

The Roof Restaurant offers superb cuisine with the best of international dishes and typical Italian and Roman specialties. In the summer, favorites include Ribs of Veal Gypsy Style, Wild Duck Breast *Taormina,* and Beef Filet Wellington. Some of the regular special entrées include Veal Scallops *Caterina de' Medici,* Chicken Breasts *Bolognese,* Sirloin Steak *Fiorentina* (for two), Tournedos of Beef *Rossini,* Scampi *Veronica,* Poached Sea Bass with Hollandaise Sauce, and pastas such as Finger Maccheroni with Vodka, Noodles with Cream and Ham, and Noodles *Bosvaiola.* Among the desserts, try the Sicilian Cassate and Parfait, the Peaches with Macaroons Flambé, the Crepes Suzette, or something from the sweets trolley. Piano music is played in the evening.

Hassler Roof

La Pergola Roof Cordon Bleu Restaurant

Cavalieri Hilton International
Via Cadolo 101
Monte Mario
00136 Rome
Italy

All major credit cards
Dinner
Reservations requested
Jacket required
Liquor served
Dinner: $25 to $50
full 3 courses, without wine

As you dine atop the Cavalieri Hilton, you find that the quintessence of present-day Rome can blend beautifully with this spectacular ancient city.

This new hotel, designed by Rome's top architects, is the largest and most modern in the city. Among the sights of Rome easily distinguished while dining in the Cavalieri Hilton's rooftop restaurant are St. Peter's Church, the Vatican, the Victor Emmanuel II monument (the "wedding cake"), Villa Borghese, Trinita dei Monti, and more.

Monte Mario, the hill upon which the Cavalieri Hilton is built, is one of the highest in Rome and is also the location of an observatory and a fashionable residential/business section.

La Pergola is a favorite Rome meeting place, not only for its breathtaking view but for its fine food as well. The beautifully planned menu features food from around the world, including, of course, excellent Italian specialties.

SALERNO

Buca di Bacco

Buca Residence
Via Rampa Ieglia N.8
84017 Positano
Salerno
Italy
Telephones: 089–875699

All major credit cards
Breakfast, lunch, and dinner
Reservations required
Jacket not required
Liquor served
Dinner: $16 to $23
full 3 courses, without wine
Lunch: the same
Chef/Owners: The Rispoli Family

This magnificent viewing spot on the Tyrrhenian Sea has in the past delighted such visitors as John Steinbeck, the prince and late princess of Monaco, Yehudi Menuhin, Jacqueline Kennedy Onassis, and others. The Tyrrhenian Sea is that part of the western Mediterranean Sea between the west coast of Italy, the north coast of Sicily, and the east coast of Sardinia and Corsica. From here you can see Capri sitting like a gem on the bright blue sea.

This small, family-run hotel is situated right on the beach, which is also part of the view. The dining room is known for its local and international cuisine, especially the fresh seafood. Also among the favorites are all sorts of pastas, and such items as *Canelloni alla Bacco, Riso alla Pescatore, Insalata Frutta Mare,* and *Melenzane all Parmigiana.* For dessert we suggest the freshly peeled oranges soaked in caramel syrup!

Another joy here is the international mix of clientele. At any one time it is possible to have as fellow patrons people from France, Germany, Switzerland, England, South America, and Australia, as well as from the United States and Italy.

The Dining Room of Lloyd's Baia Hotel

84019 Vietri sul Mare
Salerno
Italy
Telephone: 089–210145

All major credit cards
Breakfast, lunch, and dinner
Reservations suggested
Jacket requested at dinner
Liquor served
Dinner: $6
full 3 courses, without wine
Lunch: the same
Manager: Luigi Lodi

The dining room of Lloyd's Baia Hotel is a great vantage point from which to view the beaches and the Tyrrhenian Sea. The dining room is in the center of the hotel, which gives its diners views of the Bay of Salerno and the Cilento coastline on its left side and the famous Amalfi Coast on the right.

Lloyd's Baia is one of the better-known hotels on the coast. It is 28 years old and has a large Italian clientele. A typical meal starts with Ham Rolls with Russian Salad, and then broth with beaten eggs and Parmesan cheese or Potato Soup with Noodles. Then you can sample the *Fettucine alla Carbonara* (noodles with eggs, bacon, and Parmesan cheese) or Ravioli with Meat Sauce. Among the seven different main dishes are Crayfish in Curry Sauce, Grilled Sirloin Steak, *Mozzarella en Brochette* with Anchovy Sauce, Veal Roulades Neapolitan style, and mixed Fried Fish with Tartar Sauce. The meal is followed by the Italian cheese tray, seasonal fruit, sweets from the buffet, and a choice of freshly made ice creams.

SANTA MARGHERITA LIGURE

La Terrasse

Grand Hotel Miramare
16038 Santa Margherita Ligure
Italy
Telephone: 0198–287013 or 287463

American Express, Visa
Breakfast, lunch, and dinner
Reservations necessary in
* high season*
Jacket required
Liquor served
Dinner: $40 to $50
* full 3 courses, without wine*
Lunch: the same
Chef: Pierantonio Bacchetta
Maitre d': Salvatore Mantelli

The village of Santa Margherita Ligure is enchantingly situated in a recess of the Tigullio Gulf, undisturbed by winds and providing the only access to the world-famous Portofino promontory. Here the mild winter climate and the sunny days from May through October attract guests from around the world to beaches and to fine hotels such as the Grand Hotel Miramare, which overlooks the sea and is surrounded by beautiful tropical gardens.

La Terrasse is well located. It has five large picture windows bringing into the room the picturesque Portofino Gulf; the other main sight is the luxurious and aristocratic Villa Durazzo, which is set on a hill dominating the village of Santa Margherita and is also surrounded by tropical gardens.

The fine Italian cuisine includes Miramare Fish Soup and Mussels au Gratin, Ligurian style. The chef calls his offerings nouvelle cuisine, with French and Italian specialties.

VENICE

Five Stars Restaurant

Above Harry's Bar
San Marco 1323
Venice
Italy
Telephone: 41–523–6797 or 41–85331

All major credit cards
Lunch and dinner
Jacket not required
Liquor served
Dinner: $40 to $60
* full 3 courses, without wine*
Lunch: $20 to $35
Chef: Alfredo del Precina
Maitre d': Gianni Tannon

Above the famous Harry's Bar, just off San Marco Square, is another sophisticated yet cozy restaurant that has been open since 1961. Known as the Five Stars Restaurant, it is operated by Arribo Cipriani, whose name is well known because his family originally owned the delightful Cipriani Hotel across the canal.

From each of the windows—you should call ahead to reserve a window seat—you have a magnificent view of the Grand Basin of Venice, with its gondolas and ships from all over the world, part of San Marco itself, the island of San Giorgio, and the Church of the Salute. In addition, this might be the only restaurant in Venice which includes the Ducal Palace in its view.

Specialties of the house include *Scampi a la Carlina,* Rice *a la Valenzia,* and Filet of Sole Casanova. All the pastas are great, and so are the desserts. Try the chocolate cake—*Michelin* gave it two stars.

The Gritti Restaurant

Hotel Gritti Palace
Campo S. Maria del Giglio 2467
30124 Venice
Italy
Telephone: 041-794611

All major credit cards
Breakfast, lunch, and dinner
Reservations recommended
Jacket required for dinner
Liquor served
Dinner: $40
    full 3 courses, without wine
Lunch: $30
Chef: C. Ciccarelli
Maitre d': G. Gava

N. Passante, one of the fine CIGA hotel directors who is in charge of the grand old Gritti, has given us permission to quote what one of the hotel's many famous guests once wrote about this jewel on the Grand Canal:

"There are few things in life more pleasant than to sit on the terrace of the Gritti when the sun about to set bathes in lovely colour the Salute which almost faces you. You see that noble building at its best and the sight adds to your satisfaction. For at the Gritti you are . . . a friend who has been welcomed as he stepped out of his motor boat, and when you sit down to dinner at the very same table you sat the year before, and the year before that, when you see that your bottle of Soave is in the ice-pail, waiting for you, as it has been year after year, you cannot but feel very much at home."

Those words were written on June 18, 1960, but serve just as well today. There are few places in the world I would trade for the Gritti Terrace on a summer's evening. As you dine, you may see a flotilla of gaily lighted gondolas drift by, with the central larger gondola carrying an orchestra and singers who treat passersby to operatic duets or solos.

The Gritti restaurant features classical Italian cuisine (learned from Escoffier and other experts) enriched with regional and local specialties. Dishes from other countries are served as well. Some of our favorites include *Gran Maestro Soppressa alla Maugham, I Risotti del Gritti,* and *Scampi in Erbaria.*

There is also a "natural" concept in the cuisine served here that is different from the *grande cuisine* which features rich, elaborate dishes. It is called *cucina verita,* which means using age-old recipes which call for produce in season, simple cooking methods, short cooking times (to avoid destroying the fresh flavor of the ingredients), very little fat, and absolutely no preserved goods. Some of the dishes made this way include *Bresavola Gritti Palace* (thinly sliced smoked beef, grapefruit quarters, rugola leaves, olive oil, and pepper), *Shrimp Salad Malamocco* (broiled small shrimps from the Adriatic Sea, thinly sliced radishes or artichokes, olive oil, and lemon juice), *Risi in Rosa* (boiled rice dried in oven, seasoned minced raw ham, quickly sautéed in its own fat, with plenty of parmesan cheese on top), and *Fillets of fish Mirandolina* (stewed with onion, garlic, basil, potatoes, and a laurel leaf).

In recent years, the Gritti has been the setting for some interesting gastronomic events, with special days given over to Indian cuisine, the aristocratic cuisine of the Kingdom of the two Sicilies, the Kingdom of Sardinia and the Duchy of Parma, and Japanese cuisine, to name just a few.

The Gritti restaurant is a favorite meeting place for the Venetian gourmets and the members of the "Doge's Club," which includes discerning connoisseurs of Venetian cuisine.

Palladio Room
and Poolside Restaurant

Hotel Cipriani
Giudecca, 10
30100 Venice
Italy
Telephone: 041-707744

American Express
Breakfast, lunch, and dinner
Reservations required
Jacket required
Liquor served
Dinner: $35 to $50
  full 3 courses,
  without wine
Lunch: the same
Chef: Giovanni Spaventa
Maitre d': Antonio Pandin

Palladio Room

You can find a beautiful view from almost anywhere in Venice, but here, on Giudecca, you have a special vantage point: you can look across the Venetian harbor where the Grand Canal begins and take in the majesty and excitement of San Marco.

The Cipriani is set on a tranquil three-acre estate at the tip of this island, with most of its rooms overlooking the blue lagoon that stretches for miles. The Cipriani's gardens have the only swimming pool in central Venice; along with the loggias and the terraces there is an unmistakable atmosphere of being on a private country estate. Thus it is especially nice to realize that the hotel is directly opposite the Piazza San Marco; in a matter of minutes, then, the hotel's launches can speed you across the water to any point in central Venice.

Recently some subtle improvements have been made at the Cipriani. Additional dining facilities have been added under the supervision of the Parisian architect, Gerard Gallet. The main dining room has been lavishly redecorated using Fortuny fabrics throughout. Above this, the Palladio Room has been constructed with floor-to-ceiling windows, providing an uninterrupted view over the lagoon toward the Lido. A new bar has been opened at the pool, where you can have a light lunch and also enjoy a grand view.

Compared to many other buildings in Venice, the Cipriani is fairly new. It was built in the middle of the 1950s by Commendatore Cipriani, who has been called "the last Doge of Venice" and who is best known for founding the famous Harry's Bar, the meeting place of society, royal and otherwise. Under his management the Cipriani built a reputation for quality and elegance but did not attract enough business to succeed. In the past ten years or so, this has changed. Robert Sherwood, the American sea-container magnate and owner of the magnificent Venice Simplon Orient-Express, decided to take over this modern Venetian Palace and make it even grander than it was. (That's why it is fitting that the swimming pool is Europe's largest; however, it got that way purely by accident—Comm. Cipriani misread meters for feet on the architect's plan!)

Natale Rusconi, who has managed other fine hotels in Italy, is the managing director. Says he: "This is a hotel in a grand style. . . . It means that the table is set with Limoges china and the best of Venetian glass on the finest of linens. It means that we have more staff than we have guests, and that means constant attention to every detail of their needs for their pleasure and their comfort."

Food is an event here at the Cipriani. In fact, there are annual food preparation seminars and meetings. The specialties include *Carpaccio Bresavola con Rucola e Pompelmo, Sfogi* in *Saor, Taglierini Verdi Gratinati al Prosciutto, Risotto Primavera, Filetti di S. Pietro Ca' d'Oro con Peperoni, Rombo alle Zucchine con Salsa Ciboulette,* and *Tournedos alle Due Sale.* For dessert, try the *Soufflé al Cioccolato Talmone.* There are also fabulous pastries.

The Restaurant of
Hotel Bauer Grünwald and Grand Hotel

30124 Venice
Italy
Telephone: 707022

All major credit cards
Lunch and dinner
Reservations recommended
Jacket required
Liquor served
Dinner: $30
    full 3 courses, without wine
Lunch: the same
Chef: Angelo Sorzio

Another of Venice's grand views is to be found at the fine old Hotel Bauer Grünwald, located in an enchanting corner of the Grand Canal, between the Church of the Salute and the Island of St. George, and just a stone's throw from Piazza San Marco.

From the restaurant of the hotel and its terrace on the Grand Canal there are excellent views across the canal, particularly of the Santa Maria of the Church of the Salute; you can also see ocean liners or naval ships maneuvering about the San Marcos Basin. From Seventh Heaven, the piano-bar on the hotel's roof, there's another magnificent view to be had.

At lunch, as an appetizer, you have your choice of an assortment of hors d'oeuvres, spaghetti with clam sauce, or fried eggs with shrimp. The main dishes include Baked Sea-Angler, Grilled Thin Veal Steak, and Sliced Calf's Liver Venetian Style, all served with roast potatoes and eggplant with oregano. There's also a cheese tray and a choice of fruits.

For dinner you have, for your choice of appetizers, Pennette with Tomato Sauce and Ham Strips, Cream of Leek Soup, or Vegetable Soup. For the main dish your choices are Adriatic Grilled Sole, Veal Medallions with Vegetable Goulash, and Fillet of Beef with Green Pepper, all with roast potatoes and peas. Assorted cheeses are available and desserts can be chosen from the trolley. These fixed price menus are typical; keep in mind that choices change daily.À la carte specialties include Rice *a la Vecia Dogana,* Giant Shrimp *a la Grünwald* served with Creole rice, Roasted Gilthead of the Adriatic, *Filet Mignon a la Gondoliera,* and, to top it all off, coffee *crêpes à la flame,* prepared and served at the table.

Roof Restaurant of
Hotel Danieli Royal Excelsior

Venice
Italy
Telephone: 26–480

All major credit cards
Lunch and dinner
Reservations recommended
Jacket required for dinner
Liquor served
Dinner: $40
  full 3 courses, without wine
Lunch: $30

From the deck of the terrace of the Roof Restaurant of the Hotel Danieli Royal Excelsior is a view of the whole Grand Basin of Venice, from the Grand Canal through the Giudecca, St. George's Island, and the Lido. Overwhelming! Certainly this is the most comprehensive view of Venice to be found.

The Danieli Royal Excelsior is really a trio of palaces. The center one is the 14th century Dandolo-Mocenigo Palace; to its right, as you enter, is a white and radiantly noble empire palace; and to the left is the new "palace" built in the 1950s.

Be sure to ask for the specialties of the house—*Scampi e Riso Flamingo Fettucina alla Buranella, Pollo in Tecia con Polenta,* and *Fegato alla Veneziana.*

The Excelsior is one of several CIGA hotels in Venice.

Jamaica

HANOVER

Dining Room and Terrace of the Tryall Golf & Beach Club

Hanover Parish (near Montego Bay)
Jamaica
Telephone: 809–952–5111

All major credit cards
Breakfast, lunch, and dinner
Reservations required
Jacket required in evening
Liquor served
Dinner: $35
　　full 3 courses, without wine
Lunch: $4 to $15
Chef: Paul Redihan
Maitre d': Barrington Gordon

The view from the dining room and terrace of this elegant and popular golf and beach club is of the hotel's own attractions: the pool with its swim-up bar in the center, the surrounding golf course, and, most beautiful of all, the Caribbean Sea.

The Tryall Golf & Beach Club, situated on a 2,200-acre estate of rolling hills, has been the recipient of many honors, the most recent of which is the AAA Four-Diamond Award for 1986. In receiving this award, Tryall has exceeded the American Automobile Association's criteria in most physical and operational categories.

Most noticeable in the view while dining is the well-manicured 6,680-yard, par 71 golf course. Sweeping along the sea and through the resort's inland hills, the course features palm-lined water holes, exotic fruit trees, and breathtaking vistas. It draws top pros and was the site for Shell's Wonderful World of Golf.

The Great House, where the dining room is located, was built in 1834 as the hub of a sugar plantation. The menu features Carribbean Veal Panpiettes and delightful desserts like Jamaican Pineapple Pie, Coconut Cream Pie, and Banana Rum Ice Cream.

Japan

OSAKA

Le Rendezvous

The Plaza
2–49, Oyodo-Minami 2-chome
Oyodo-ku
Osaka
Japan
Telephone: 06–453–1111

All major credit cards
Lunch and dinner
Reservations necessary
Jacket required
Liquor served
Dinner: $50 to $80
*   full 3 courses, without wine*
Lunch: $30 to $80
Chef: Stephane Raimbault
Maitre d': Toshio Goto

This restaurant on the 23d floor of the Plaza has two views. The one to north is especially splendid at sunset, when the cosmopolitan city of Osaka turns into a magical wonderland of lights. Golden light is reflected from the Yodo River, which leisurely runs east and west across the Osaka plains. Nearby neon lights come on one by one, forming a mystical rainbow of sorts. Every few minutes airplanes can be seen coming in for a landing at the Osaka International Airport near the foot of the distant mountains. Pretty!

Looking to the south after dusk falls, the scenario is quite different. From left to right you see Umeda Terminal, towering skyscrapers, the Nakanoshima business district and

Osaka Bay. It is another stunning symphony of lights, this one much more urban in character.

Inside, the pianist begins playing pieces from Ravel and Debussy, an aperitif is served, the menu scanned. It's time to sample what this city of *kuidaore,* or gourmet paradise, has to offer. Among the specialties are Rack of Lamb in its own juice and Fresh Lobster, boiled, roasted, or done as a soufflé. This restaurant is a favorite of local people and of French gourmets.

TOKYO

Chinzan-So

10–8 Sekiguchi 2-Chome
Bunkyo-ku
Tokyo 112
Japan
Telephone: 03–943–1111

All major credit cards
Lunch and dinner
Reservations necessary
Jacket required
Dinner: $20
Lunch: $13

Chinzan-So is a collection of restaurant gems, surrounded by an ancient, picturesque Japanese garden. The site was generally called *Tsubaki Yama,* which means Camellia Mountain, after Prince Yamagata, a veteran statesman who was active at the beginning of the Meiji Era and who was fond of this region. He purchased land for a residence here which he called Chinzan-So, or Mansion on the Camellia Mountain. The Emperor Meiji and dignitaries held important meetings here. Later, Baron Heitaro Fujita worked at making this famous garden even more distinguished. As a result, today Chinzan-So is a garden restaurant representing the best of Japan.

The food here features authentic French cuisine and other western dishes as well as traditional Japanese items. The Western-style restaurant is called Camellia, where you may enjoy French cuisine or beefsteak while watching a waterfall. Kaizan-Do stands beside a beautiful pond in the midst of trees and features barbecued specialties. Miyuki is the Japanese-style restaurant which includes Kaiseki cuisine and the more familiar tempura, sukiyaki, and Shabu.

It is so beautiful here that every year about 3,000 couples are married in the beautiful gardens, where many of the trees are 1,000 years old. The three-story pagoda in the garden was erected more than 1,100 years ago.

Shimizo

Next to Westin Akasaka Prince Hotel
1–2, Kioi-cho
Chiyoda-ku
Tokyo 102
Japan
Telephones: 03–261–4226/7

No credit cards
Lunch and dinner
Reservations preferred
Liquor served
Dinner: $50
   full 3 courses, without wine
Chef: Hideo Tachibana

Originally built as a quiet Ryokan Inn, Shimizo features traditional Japanese cuisine served in traditional Japanese style.

Set in a legendary Benkei Bashi Garden, with seasonal flowers in 70 varieties, blossoming trees, an ancient stone bridge, maple trees, and the king of the garden trees known as *mokkoku,* Shimizo is a sheer delight.

The famous old stone bridge in the middle of the garden has been designated a cultural treasure by the Tokyo city government. Moved to the garden from the Joshoin Temple northeast of the Imperial Palace grounds, the bridge is said to have been built in the mid-17th century by Princess Chio, daughter of the third Tokugawa Shogun.

Shimizo

The restaurant's structure, ornaments, room settings, and ambience work together in the Japanese style called *ryotei*. Sounds of cicadas and turtledoves drift into each of its radiating arms. The wind gently rustles wind chimes hung from its eaves. The rooms all face the garden, allowing sunlight in through *shoji* (Japanese screened walls). The decor includes ancient and modern art—lacquered boxes, incense burners, vases, and other antique furnishings commingle with gold and silver inlaid wild ducks crafted by Katsura Mitsuharu.

Shimizo's experienced chefs prepare food that is an adaptation of traditional Kyoto cuisine into a unique Edo style. Courses include appetizers, soup, sashimi, broiled fish, a variety of simmered foods, and a Kyoto-style *hassun* dish. *Hassun* refers to the presentation of the dish in a cedar bark platter; served on the platter are bite-sized dishes to accompany *sake* (a Japanese liquor made from rice). The delicate size of the portions is reminiscent of the meal's origin in traditional *kaiseki*—a light meal served prior to a ceremonial tea. Ingredients such as fresh fish from Kansai, vegetables from Kyoto, and sake from Nara are air-freighted to the restaurant, then meticulously prepared and served.

The restaurant opens at 11 A.M. It is situated two minutes from the Mitsuke station. You enter after crossing a wooden bridge over the palace moat.

Yamazato

Hotel Okura
2–10–4 Toranomon 2-chome
Minato-ku
Tokyo 105
Japan
Telephone: 03–582–0111

All major credit cards
Breakfast, lunch, and dinner
Reservations necessary
Jacket required
Liquor served
Dinner: $33 to $75
    full 3 courses, without wine
Lunch: $17 to $69
Chef: Kanichi Takahashi

The Hotel Okura always appears on lists of people's favorite hotels. In a survey taken by *Euromoney* magazine, it was selected as number one in the world, while an *Institutional Investor* magazine's poll awarded it second place. These publications represent not just an international business readership but a sophisticated clientele in general.

One of the reasons for Hotel Okura's acclaim is the quality of its eight fine restaurants, which offer an outstanding variety of cuisine and dining atmospheres. Only the Yamazato, the restaurant featuring Japanese cuisine, offers a view—of the hotel's magnificent Japanese garden and of the Tokyo Tower.

The Yamazato, under the direction of Chef Takahashi, is on the fifth floor of the hotel. It serves authentic Japanese dishes such as tempura, sukiyaki, teppanyaki, sashimi, shabu-shabu, and sushi. The *Japan Times* recommends "fresh seafood or sashimi and beef teppanyaki (beef roasted on a hot plate)" and also points out that "with the teppanyaki cooking, abalones and oysters have a special sweetness."

Although some 40 percent of this dining room's customers are foreigners, Chef Takahashi prefers to "preserve the Japanese flavor rather than Westernize" his cooking.

The view to dine by, the Japanese landscape garden, is worth seeing and exploring close up. You can climb a wooded path along a stream and waterfall to the Shinto Shrine hidden in the woods at the top of the hill. The grounds of the hotel are lighted in the evening. There is also a pond downstream filled with robust, filmly finned carp (cyprindae); they zip and whip through the water, flashing their colors and markings. All you need do is clap your hands and they'll come over to you to be fed. The site of the Okura was a Feudal Lord's residence in the Edo period (1603–1867). It had been called Ginko Manor because of the many venerable Ginko trees within the estate. It later became the home of the Okura family, from which the hotel got its name.

Kenya

BURA

The Dining Room of Salt Lick Lodge

of Hilton International
Taita Hills, Bura
Kenya
Telephone: Mwatate 44
Correspondence:
c/o Nairobi Hilton
P.O. Box 30624
Nairobi
Kenya

All major credit cards
Breakfast, lunch, and dinner
Reservations necessary
Jacket not required
Liquor served
Dinner: $8 to $10
*   full 4 courses, without wine*
Lunch: $7 to $8
Chef: Thomas Musiro Logos
Maitre d': Dufton Philips

Truly one of the most amazing views to dine by.

Imagine this. You are staying in one of a series of thatched-roof cottage towers, built on stilts (so as not to interfere with the African wildlife), all connected by walkways. In the center is a pavilion with an open terrace and a comfortable dining room. Here you may eat a 4-course dinner by candlelight. The grand view overlooks a broad and shallow fresh water hole surrounded by salty earth offering much in the way of minerals, a combination that attracts a steady flow of animals. Sitting there is like watching a dramatic pageant choreographed by Mother Nature herself. You may see a herd of elephants bathing and drinking. Then suddenly they leave (going off stage, as it were) and a herd of buffalo arrives and fills the water hole. All the while you can hear the roars of other animals, probably predators. Three or more lions appear and the buffalo depart in the opposite direction, with the lions in pursuit. Then the buffalo turn and chase the lions. This is the view to dine by from the dining room of Hilton International's Salt Lick Lodge.

It is a truly magnificent experience. Baboons, giraffes, zebras, gorillas, leopards, and many other wild animals are all part of the view here.

There is a bunker at ground level with special windows for close-up viewing and photographing of the animal visitors, and the area is flood-lighted at night. What you do not see of the animals (and birds) listed above, you can see on a tour of the 28,000-acre game sanctuary owned by the establishment.

While the temptation is to forget all about the food and concentrate on the view, Chef Logos would hear of no such thing. He provides a delightful buffet breakfast featuring the fresh fruits of Africa, while his lunch and dinner menus feature both local and international cuisines. Finally, the delicious desserts are all homemade.

SEOUL

The Ninth Gate

The Westin Chosun
87, Sokong-dong, Chung-ku
Seoul 100
Korea
Telephone: 771–05 Ext. 7366

All major credit cards
Breakfast, lunch, and dinner
Reservations required
Jacket required
Liquor served
Dinner: $22 to $30
    full 3 courses, without wine
Lunch: $14 to $22
Chef: Walter Neuhold
Maitre d': Kim Byung-gil

The ancient city of Seoul had eight gates, but we suspect that most visitors to Seoul are more likely to become familiar with its Ninth Gate.

This restaurant drew the inspiration for its name from a triple-arched gate that leads to the Temple of Heaven; both the gate and the shrine can easily be seen through the Ninth Gate's floor-to-ceiling windows.

The Temple of Heaven is an eight-sided, three-story pavilion with softly curving roof lines that stands as the centerpiece of the Westin Chosun garden. It was built in 1897 by King Kojong, the last king of the Yi Dynasty, and it was here that he prayed to the dynasty's founding ancestor just before proclaiming himself free of fealty to China and declaring himself "emperor" of an independent Korea.

The Ninth Gate has been the hotel's premier dining room since its opening in 1970. The restaurant is a favorite meeting place for business leaders, financiers, travelers, and journalists. In the evenings, the Ninth Gate attracts diners who enjoy the fine selection of wines and the excellent French and Continental cuisine. Favorite items from a varied Western menu include Gravd Lax, Smoked Salmon, Escargot, Veal Sweetbreads, French Onion Soup, Caesar Salad, Veal Ribeye, Prime Beef, and, for dessert, hot soufflés.

According to the maitre d' the name of the restaurant implies that it is "an entrance-way into the life of Seoul."

Luxembourg

CLERVAUX

Restaurant Hotel du Parc

Rue du Parc
9708 Clervaux
Luxembourg
Telephone: 91068 or 92650

All major credit cards
Breakfast, lunch, and dinner
Reservations not necessary
Jacket required
Liquor served
Dinner: $6 to $20
        full 3 courses, without wine
Lunch: $6 to $20
Chef/Owner: Simone Allard-Wilmes

From the dining room and the front porch of this castle-like hotel in a wooded area you see much of Clervaux, a small picturesque town in the Ardennes, one of the most fascinating spots in the Grand Duchy of Luxembourg. Its old castle, its Romanesque church, the Peasants' Memorial, and the Benedictine Abbey of St. Maurice overlook the valley of the Clerve. At night, all of these are illuminated.

The Grand Hotel du Parc occupies a spot of outstanding beauty, surrounded by a glorious park featuring century-old trees. Chef/Owner Simone Allard-Wilmes is proud of the hotel and of the cuisine in the beautiful dining room. View seating is very limited, so make arrangements in advance.

Among the specialties on the menu are Froglegs *a la Berlaymont, Scampis Grillées,* Peppersteak *Flambé, Truite* (trout) *aux Aromates,* and the picturesque *Tulipe de Sorbet au Coulis de Framboise.*

The dining room is open for breakfast at 8:30 A.M., for lunch at noon, and for dinner at 7 P.M. Guests are mostly local people, Belgian and Dutch visitors, and a few Americans.

One sad note: the medieval castle was heavily damaged during the German Ardennes offensive at the end of 1945 and hasn't been restored.

MANZANILLO

El Terral
Las Hadas Hotel
Rincon de Las Hadas
P.O. Box 158
28200 Manzanillo
Mexico
Telephone: 333-3-00-00

All major credit cards
Dinner only
Reservations required
Dress: casual but elegant
Liquor served
Dinner: $15 to $25
*   full 3 courses, without wine*
Chef: Josef Freudenthaler
Maitre d': Bruno Nadeaud

El Terral is a romantic open-air terrace restaurant with a breathtaking view of the Pacific coast. It overlooks the fascinating white towers of Las Hadas, a marina with luxurious yachts from around the world, and, at night, the sparkling lights of Manzanillo Bay.

El Terral was a private residence until the late 1960s, when Don Antenor Patino, the late Bolivian tin king, bought it as part of his dream to build the most beautiful resort in the world. He converted the house into a spectacular restaurant and bar with waterfalls and strolling musicians, and he left intact a unique tiled pool which is used by many of the hotel's guests during the day. *Terral* is the Spanish word for "land wind," a very pleasant breeze that starts at about 9 P.M.—another contribution from Mother Nature to a perfect dining experience. (If guests get too chilly late in the evening they are given thick, warming Mexican blankets.)

The popularity of El Terral skyrocketed when the restaurant was selected to be the dining spot for Bo Derek and Dudley Moore in Blake Edwards' hit movie *10,* which was filmed at Las Hadas. Six years later, guests are still asking to be seated at the table at which Derek and Moore sat.

The beauty of the surroundings has been known to have quite an impact on the guests. A Texas oil magnate was having dinner at El Terral with the restaurant's architect, Jose Luis Ezquerra. The Texan loved the look and feeling of Las Hadas, and as he talked about building a mansion overlooking the resort Ezquerra started drawing his idea of the new dream castle on the tablecloth. That castle is no longer a dream. It stands on the hill above Las Hadas and the tablecloth with the drawing is framed and hangs in one of the hotel suites.

Popular specialties on El Terral's menu include, as appetizers, Corn Mushroom Crepes and Chilled Avocado Cream Soup served in a half coconut. Two popular main dishes are Seabass Roll with Mexican Herb Mousse and Hot Pepper Stuffed with Lobster and Corn Mushrooms, served with sweet potatoes and fried bananas. For dessert, Caramel Crepes with Tequila is a good choice.

Morocco

TANGIER

El Erz and El Korsan

Hotel El Minzah
85 Rue de la Liberte
Tangier
Morocco
Telephones: 378–44 or 358–85

All major credit cards
Breakfast, lunch, and dinner
Reservations advised
Jacket required
Liquor served
Dinner: $15 à la carte
Lunch: the same
Chef: El Hmam
Maitre d': Mr. Aoujil

The El Minzah hotel has an attractive Moorish-style decor and sits in a subtropical garden. The view from almost the entire hotel overlooks the Straits of Gibraltar. The Bay of Tangiers, the *Fondak,* a typical Moroccan market, the port and old town of Medina, and the Spanish coastline across the Straits of Gibraltar are also visible.

There are two restaurants sharing this view. One is the main dining room, El Erz, which features international cuisine and has a capacity of 200 guests. The smaller dining room, El Korsan, seats 70 people and offers Moroccan specialties.

The El Minzah Hotel is a luxury establishment built by a British aristocrat, Lord Bute, and opened in 1930. It is situated on an expanse of land called Belevedere, which means "viewpoint," on the outer perimeter of what was considered the "old town" when the hotel was built. Over the years, a number of celebrity guests have come here, including Winston Churchill, Douglas Fairbanks, Rita Hayworth, Mary Pickford, Anthony Quinn, Gina Lollobrigida, Irene Papas, Rock Hudson, and Rex Harrison.

El Korsan is a refined restaurant where golds and greens blend harmoniously and delicately together. The food is prepared by local Moroccan women and is said to be the finest Moroccan cuisine in Tangier. Among the specialties are Harira Soup served with the "Delights of *Tafilalet,*" *Briouats El Minzah* (savory crisp pastries), Braised Sea Perch with Dates, Pigeon Tajine with Pears and Honey, and the famous *Couscous* with seven vegetables.

El Erz is Arabic for "cedarwood"; the ceiling of this restaurant is made from this fine material.

Norway

STAVANGER

Atlantic Restaurant

Atlantic Hotel
Vernbaneveien, 1
Stavanger
Norway
Telephone: 04–527520

All major credit cards
Dinner
Reservations recommended
Jacket not required
Liquor served
Dinner: $20 to $30
    full 3 courses, without wine
Chef: Klaus Posch
Maitre d': Roger Granum

The Atlantic Restaurant has a sweeping view of Lake Bredevannet, beautifully surrounded by the Stavanger Town Park. The Stavanger Cathedral, a Norwegian church dating back to the eleventh century, is located here.

Seafood and game are the highlights of the cuisine, including lobster, smoked salmon, venison, and partridge. Be sure to try the cloudberries and/or the blackberries—very fresh and abundantly tasty.

The Philippines

MANILA

Old Manila

The Manila Peninsula
Corner Ayala and Makati Avenues
Makati
Metro Manila
Philippines
Telephone: 819–3456

All major credit cards
Lunch and dinner
Reservations necessary
Jacket recommended
Liquor served
Dinner: $35 to $50
full 3 courses, without wine
Lunch: the same
Chef: Bruno Christen
Maitre d': Mario D'Amico

Manila, in the late 1800s, was in a period of quiet elegance. The women dressed in ornate Maria Clara gowns, with gold painetas adorning their hair, while the men were clad in hand-embroidered barongs. Life seemed deliciously languorous then, as time flowed easily and smoothly.

That ambience is recaptured in the nostalgic setting of Old Manila, the Manila Peninsula's main dining room.

Designed in the style of a 19th century residential interior, with wooden balusters, capiz inlaid panels, hanging antique lamps, and high-backed chairs with silk covers, Old Manila also evinces the distinct Fil-Hispanic character. A dozen large sepia photographs on the walls depict various Philippine scenes in Binondo, Escolta, Santa Cruz, and Bagumbayan at the height of the era's glory.

The cuisine features typical Filipino dishes such as *Kare-Kare, Calderetang Kambing,* and *Pancit Molo.* There is Continental cuisine as well, including home-smoked *Tanguingue* with Dill Sauce, Roast Rack of Lamb, and the very best cuts of top quality beef, flown in from Chicago. The Old Manila also serves several pasta dishes especially prepared at your tableside; these may be eaten as an appetizer or as a main course.

A favorite among the desserts is the Crêpes Old Manila with mango filling, flamed and served with vanilla ice cream.

Treasure Island

Philippine Plaza
Cultural Center Complex
Manila
Philippines
Telephone: 832–0701 Ext. 1594

All major credit cards
Breakfast, lunch, and dinner
Reservations preferred
Dress: casual
Liquor served
Dinner: $10 to $20
full 3 courses, without wine
Lunch: the same
Chef: Beat Burgi
Restaurant Manager: Larry Casas

Surrounded by lush tropical gardens and the Manila Bay, the Treasure Island of the Philippine Plaza is set on its own island in the center of a lagoon-shaped swimming pool; two picturesque bridges get you there. The hut-style restaurant bar, seating 81 people for any of the three daily meals, has a great view of the gardens dotted by tall palm trees swaying in the breeze from Manila Bay. Part of the fun, too, is watching the swimmers in the surrounding lake-sized pool.

Late afternoon is a favorite time here as diners have a front seat to a breathtaking Manila Bay sunset. After the sun sets, dining under the glittering stars and with the twinkling lights of ships in the bay and the city itself in the background is a most romantic setting.

Treasure Island

During the day, sandwiches and light meals are served informally by attendants wearing nautical uniforms; the tables all have colorful canvas umbrellas.

There's another fantastic view to dine by at the Philippine Plaza. Called the Pistahan Dinner and Cultural Show, it starts at 6 P.M. with cocktails and a torchlight ceremony. A sumptuous Filipino buffet dinner is served at 7 P.M. and, at 8 P.M., the show begins. The show traces the color and gaiety of the many Philippine festivals celebrated during the year with a spectacle of dances, songs, and costumes. This Pistahan event transforms the poolside into a nightly journey through the country's 7,000 islands. Sometimes happy, sometimes solemn, the dances celebrate marriage, victory, and bountiful harvests in a colorful mix of Christian, Muslim, and Pagan rites.

The start of the show—featuring a young man garbed as an Ati blowing a shellhorn from atop the hotel's waterfalls against a sunset-colored sky—is a spectacular sight indeed. The costumed Atis who dance-parade around the swimming pool and the gardens to the pulsating beat of native drums usher in the rest of the show.

Singapore

Top of the "M"

Mandarin Singapore
333 Orchard Road
Singapore 0923
Telephone: 737–4411

All major credit cards
Dinner
Reservations required
Dress: casual but neat
Liquor served
Dinner: $35 to $60
   full 3 courses, without wine
Chef: Charles Benz

The top attraction of the Mandarin Singapore's Top of the "M" restaurant is its spectacular view of Singapore and its neighbors, Malaysia and Indonesia. Situated on the 39th floor, 600 feet off the ground, and making a complete revolution every hour and a quarter, this unique rooftop restaurant is said to be the first of its kind in the world able to offer a sweeping panorama of three countries. The huge floor-to-ceiling windows give an uninterrupted view of the sea, distant islands, and the sky. Needless to say, sunset is a popular time of day here.

Ultramodern in design, the theme of this restaurant focuses on the signs of the zodiac, which adorn the dome-shaped ceiling. The overall effect gives one the feeling of being in space.

Just as international as the scene and its guests (about 40 percent are local, another 40 percent are Americans, and the remaining 20 percent have varied international backgrounds) is the menu. In addition to the different roasts from a silver trolley, Top of the Mandarin (which seats 160 people) has a select à la carte menu featuring favorites from both the Orient and the West. Among the selections are Avocado Balmoral, Filet Mignon Cardinal, Chili Prawns, and U.S. Prime Beef. A salad trolley allows guests to create their own salads.

MADRID

The Ritz Restaurant

Hotel Ritz
Plaza de la Lealtad, 5
28014 Madrid
Spain
Telephone: 91–221–28–57

All major credit cards
Breakfast, lunch, and dinner
Reservations requested
Jacket required
Liquor served
Dinner: $35 to $75
*   full 3 courses, without wine*
Lunch: $25 to $75
Chef: Patrick Buret

The Ritz in Madrid is one of the world's great hotels, now in the hands of John Macedo, its proud executive director. A Trust Forte hotel, it has been undergoing restoration work since Mr. Macedo took over a few years ago. The job has been magnificent, for after the death of his famous predecessor, Alfonso Font, the hotel started to decline, and my favorite view areas—the Ritz Terrace and Gardens—were neglected.

Now, not only are the Ritz Gardens open, more beautiful than ever, and available for lunch, dinner, and light refreshments from May until mid-October, the magnificent Ritz Restaurant, whose large windows face the gardens, has been restored to its original grandeur in both its decor and its cuisine.

The Ritz Restaurant was born at the same time as the Ritz Hotel, in 1910. The hotel

The Ritz

exists because King Alfonso XIII wanted Madrid to become a modern city with an elegant grand hotel and persuaded a group of Spanish aristocrats to build a magnificent establishment in the best area of the city, next to the Prado Museum and near the Stock Exchange and the fine residences of the area. In 1908 the group planning the hotel met and came to an agreement with the Swiss hotelier, Charles Ritz, and the project started.

The Ritz Restaurant embodies a world of dining tradition. Tables are set with shining napery, glistening silver, and crested glasses. Striped umbrellas shade the diners, and palm trees, flowers of the season, and climbing roses create a picturesque setting.

As you dine in the garden it is possible to glimpse some of the Ritz's superb surroundings. Among these are an exquisite fountain in the square, the mythological horses of Neptune's chariot, and the stupendous Prado Museum with its vast collections of Spain's greatest art treasures.

Another grand view is in the Ritz dining room. Not only is the decor magnificent, but so are the guests, some of whom, we felt, were the best dressed people we had ever seen. The last time we dined there, Mr. and Mrs. Placido Domingo were at a nearby table; ever since, I have told people I had lunch with them!

Some of the world's great chefs have served the Ritz. Chef Patrick Buret was appointed the *chef de cuisine* of the Ritz Restaurant in 1984. He started his professional career at the Auberge de la Cote (Berry au Bac) and then worked at Le Patin D'Or in Luxembourg. He perfected his culinary skills under Paul Bocuse's supervision in Lyon, France. In 1979, under his responsibility as *chef de cuisine,* a new restaurant, La Ferme Saint Simon, was opened in Paris where, after two years, it earned the famous *Michelin* guide stars and two from *Gault-Millau.*

Among the fantastic Ritz main dishes we've enjoyed are Papillotte of Sea Bass with Algae and Mint Butter, Spinney Lobster with Red Pepper, Roasted Milk Lamb with Thyme and Sweet Garlic Cake, Fillet Steak with Truffle and Wild Mushrooms, and Fricasse of Turbot with Crayfish and Parsley Sauce.

The dessert decision is the most difficult part of dining at the Ritz. You must choose from a beautiful display table in the center of the dining room or from the formidable dessert cart. We have never had the same thing twice; we believe that if we live long enough and come to the Ritz often enough we'll be able to try them all!

MARBELLA

El Puente
Hotel Puente Romano
Carretera de Cadiz km 177,6
Marbella
Spain
Telephone: 52-77-01-00

All major credit cards
Breakfast, lunch, and dinner
Reservations necessary
Dress: casual
Liquor served
Dinner: $25 to $50
    full 3 courses, without wine
Lunch: $20
Chef: Simon Padilla
Maitre d': Miguel Guillen

Puente Romano opened in 1979 in Marbella, long known as the international playground of European royalty and made famous by the efforts of Prince Alfonso Hollenlohe, president of the Marbella Club and the man in charge of Puente Romano.

The hotel is a unique resort complex which includes swimming pools, artificial lakes, and waterfalls surrounded by fabulously beautiful tropical gardens. The area that Puente Romano occupies was not planned as a hotel but rather was a section of an exclusive condominium apartment development. Puente Romano now occupies half the condominium estate, with guests living in suites decorated by some of Europe's foremost designers.

Puente Romano got its name from an ancient Roman bridge, still intact, but hardly noticed, dominated as it is by the splendor of the surrounding gardens and the modern

El Puente

whitewashed terraced structures. Near the bridge is a square, just as it might have been in a centuries-old Andalusian fishing village. Overlooking it is El Puente, the delightful dining room and dining terrace of the resort, affectionately called "the grill" by staff and guests. The cuisine is delightful, and much of the credit goes to Chef Padilla, formerly of the Ritz in Madrid. His concoctions make this a favorite Costa del Sol restaurant. The buffet spread at lunchtime is also exceptional.

Among the chef's specialties are Perch on Vegetables, Brochette of Solomillio and Crayfish, and Hot Spinach Mousse with Shrimp. In recent years, the raising of avocados has become a major industry on the Costa del Sol; so the finer restaurants take advantage of the fresh supply to create dishes ranging from Avocado Soup to Avocado Pie. The desserts at El Puente are all delightfully sophisticated and tasty.

The best view from the dining terrace is that of the richly pleasant gardens, equal to the famous gardens of the older Marbella Club and featuring many full bushes of bougain-villeas in a myriad of colors. The brilliant red geraniums in boxes on every terrace never seem more scarlet than from here. As you stroll in the gardens after lunch, the riot of colors includes those of roses from all parts of Europe, hibiscus from China, Birds of Paradise, cacti and rubber plants, and poinsettias; African hemp, jasmine, citrus blossoms, dragon trees, and Angel's Trumpet are among the many other botanical delights.

Sweden

STOCKHOLM

The French Dining Room and the Swedish Restaurant of The Grand Hotel

P.O. Box 16 424
S. Blaisholmshamnen 8
S-103 27 Stockholm
Sweden
Telephones: 08–22–10–20/17–20

All major credit cards
Breakfast, lunch, and dinner
Reservations advised
Jacket required
Liquor served
Chef: Wilhelm Ratzinger

One of the great views of Europe has always been the one from the dining room and the Grand Café of the Grand Hotel in Stockholm, overlooking the River Strömmen, where all the steamboats depart for trips to the archipelago. You see the best of Stockholm—the Royal Palace, the Legislature Building, the Old Town, and the Opera House, as well as many of the buildings from the turn of the century, like the Fersenska Palatset, which today holds the Handelsbanken, one of Sweden's largest commercial banks.

As this is being written, the dining room and the Grand Café are in the midst of substantial renovation. But don't worry. We have two pieces of good news for you. First, the new restaurants, more beautiful than ever, will still have that same grand view. Second, by the time you read this book, they should have re-opened.

The French Dining Room will be smaller than the Swedish Restaurant, with only 80 seats and a beautiful show kitchen. Appointed as the new chef for this restaurant is Wilhelm Ratzinger. He was formerly the chef at L'Escargot, one of the four restaurants in Stockholm with a star in the *Michelin* guide. The French Dining Room will keep the fine mahogany and stucco work on the ceiling that it had previously, but the carpet and furnishings will be new, as will the porcelain created just for this dining room.

What has been the Grand Café is to become a Swedish restaurant, unnamed at press time. It will feature seasonal Swedish specialties, and it will be the room in which breakfast is served.

Operakällaren

Operhuset
Box 1616
S-111 86 Stockholm
Sweden
Telephone: 08–24–27–00 or 11–11–25

All major credit cards
Lunch and dinner
Reservations required
Jacket required for dinner
Liquor served
Dinner: $30 to $50
    full 3 courses, without wine
Lunch: $10 to $20
Chef/Proprietor: Werner Vögeli
Maitre d': Maurice Chiera and Rikard Magnusson

Operakällaren was first opened in 1787 in the old Opera House built by King Gustav III. It was a typical cellar restaurant with fragrant juniper twigs strewn all over the floor. Patrons sat on benches around tables made of crude pine. From the start, the place became a popular haunt for people in the artistic and literary circles. And for two centuries it has been the home for many of Stockholm's cultural personalities and intellectuals.

In the beginning of the 19th century Operakällaren was known to its regular patrons by a pet name—*Nobis*. The word, of Greek origin, means Hell, and was coined by Opera House regulars and singers who, during intermissions, used to descend the steep winding staircase to the Opera Cellar for fortifying drinks. In a popular song of the time a regular patron described his love for the Royal Opera, ending his verse by stating that his love was still stronger for the "cellar below." The name Nobis has been restored to the present wine cellar, now a key club for the regular patrons of the restaurant.

In 1892, the old Gustav III Opera House was torn down to give way to a new, modern, and much larger Opera House. The characteristic terrace building in Baroque style was also to contain a much larger restaurant, typical of the time. In 1895, the new Operakällaren opened to praise from the press for its modern design, aesthetic values, and effective organization. However, the paintings in the main dining room by the artist Oscar Björck sparked a debate at the turn of the century, as they were condemned by the Parliament for their supposedly pornographic qualities. Many noted Swedish authors, such as Viktor Rydberg and August Strindberg joined in the dispute. The paintings remain and the debate is now regarded as an example of Victorian prudishness.

Decades later, Operakällaren was in need of great repair. Even though its public rooms had been declared a national monument, the restaurant was forced to close in 1955. The Royal Building Commission, which controls the Opera House and everything in it, set about doing a proper job of repair—perhaps not realizing the great expense which might be involved, particularly in the restoration of the fine woods and the art pieces in the dining room. The project caused a national scandal and almost daily headlines for a few years. It was even debated in Parliament, where Tore Wretman, the genius restaurateur of Stockholm, was given what turned out to be a blank check from Parliament to do the job right. The cost: nearly $7 million, most likely making it the most expensively refurbished restaurant in the world. Not only was the dining room costly, but the state-of-the-art facilities and kitchens built on four floors behind it are magnificent and still, today, may be the finest restaurant kitchens in the world.

The restoration and rebuilding required six years. The Opera House opened again in 1961. It now has the unique combination of a beautiful site and a most magnificent view of the Stockholm harbor and the Royal Palace, not only from the few window seats in the main dining room but also from the Opera Terrace and the Rotunda, the private dining rooms. The public rooms have faithfully restored the 19th century splendor and are

Operakällaren

wonderful views to dine by. The main dining room, with its oak-panelled walls and Oscar Björck's paintings, is one of the world's most beautiful. The glass enclosed terrace is open year-round.

Operakällaren's cuisine is superb, earning it membership in the famous French three-star restaurant association, Traditions and Qualité, which has among its members Tour d'Argent, Grand Vefour, and Maxim's in Paris, Lutece and the "21" Club in New York, and many great restaurants of the world. It features Smörgåsbord for lunch everyday (and for dinner in summer) as well as Swedish, French, and international cuisine of the highest standards. Some suggested dishes include *Salmon Mousseline* in Puff Pastry, Saddle of Young Reindeer with Game Sauce and Lingonberries, and, for dessert, Parfait of Cloud-berries.

Restaurant Gondolen

Stadsgarden 6
11645 Stockholm
Sweden
Telephone: 08–402021/2

All major credit cards
Lunch and dinner
Reservations recommended
Jacket requested
Liquor served
Dinner: $20
    full 3 courses, without wine
Lunch: $10
Chef: Gay Meyer-Hansen
Maitre d': Esa Karhu

In 1935 an elevator was built to make it possible to reach the top of Katerina, where there once had been a small cafe that was a favorite spot of the young Greta Garbo. The new elevator was intended to reach the Gondolen, a restaurant given its name because it seemed to float in the air, much like the gondola of a dirigible.

The view is fantastic, encompassing almost all of Stockholm. In fact, the restaurant has printed a four-foot-long color photograph showing the entire view with each of the major buildings identified; be sure to ask for a copy. This is a very good place to go when you first arrive in Stockholm, to orient yourself to the city and its attractions. The view is particularly interesting because the Gondolen is situated at the point where Lake Malar's outflow reaches the Baltic Sea. There are fifty window tables so you have a choice of views in both directions—over the water or over the Old City. In summer consider the open-air dining terrace, with refreshing harbor breezes. Swedish and French cuisine is served.

Wärdshuset Stallmästaregården

Norrtull
11347 Stockholm
Sweden
Telephone: 08/243910

All major credit cards
Lunch and dinner
Reservations requested
Jacket required
Liquor served
Dinner: $15 to $30
    full 3 courses, without wine
Lunch: $10 to $18
Chef: T. Dössegger
Maitre d': Magnus Wibjörn
Owner: Tore Wretman Restaurant AB

A tenderly nurtured garden, the result of 300 years of care, is the view from this garden restaurant on the outskirts of Stockholm. The old-fashioned flower gardens were the favorite of regent Queen Kristina, who had a little summer house built on the premises for her own use. It is said that she planted the four Linden trees which still shade the courtyard between the wings of the manor house.

Stallmästaregården was a gift to a servant. In 1620, Karl Karlson Gyllenhielm, the illegitimate son of Sweden's King Karl IX, had this little manor house built on one of the most beautiful spots of natural beauty on the shore of Brunnsviken, and later gave it to Ebbe Håkansson, his stablemaster. About 40 years later, it became an inn for travelers. From that time on it evolved into a favorite spot for people who enjoy tradition and culture and appreciate distinction in atmosphere and culinary art.

The Stallmästaregården is the only restaurant in Sweden with a charcoal grill, and its specialties include the charcoal-grilled fish. Before your meal, however, we suggest that you try *Lax Najad,* a salmon specialty which originated here; salted for two hours, smoked for 30 minutes, and cooked in white wine, it is very tasty and quite different from anything you've probably had before.

In the summertime, the Smörgåsbord is, of course, the favorite, and, for dessert, try the fresh Cloudberries.

Switzerland

BAD RAGAZ

Quellenhof Grill

Hotel Quellenhof
CH-7310 Bad Ragaz
Switzerland
Telephone: 085–901 11

American Express
Lunch and dinner
Reservations required
Jacket recommended for dinner
Liquor served
Dinner: from $30
*   full 3 courses, without wine*
Lunch: from $30
Chef: Hans Hediger
Maitre d': Giuseppe Mascoli
Manager: Pierre Barrelet

In 1874, when General Field Marshal von Moltke was a guest at the Quellenhof, he wrote to his brother, "This place is gorgeous. The view from Quellenhof is magnificent!" More than a century later, von Moltke's impressions still hold true.

Bad Ragaz has an excellent mild climate and practically no fog in the winter. It enjoys an excellent location, on the Munich-San Bernardino Tunnel/Lugano-Milan highway, and is only an hour by car or train from the Zürich-Kolten-International Airport. Trains go to Zürich every hour.

The Quellenhof Grill also has excellent cuisine. Fresh seasonal specialties, including live lobster, are featured every day, and there are a number of special gastronomical events held in the Grill Room every couple of months. The Quellenhof Grill is a member of *Chaine des Rotisseurs* and *Club Prosper Montagne*. U.S. Prime Beef, as well as a variety of lamb, veal, pork, and fowl dishes, are featured.

BASLE

Rotisserie des Rois

The Three Kings Hotel
(Hotel Drei Könige)
on the Rhine
Blumenrain 8
Basle
Switzerland
Telephone: 061–25–52–52

All major credit cards
Breakfast, lunch, and dinner
Reservations recommended
Jacket required
Liquor served
Dinner: $25 to $45
*   full 3 courses, without wine*
Lunch: $15 to $25
Chef: Bernard Muller
Maitre d': Giovanni Gelmi

The Three Kings Hotel has existed on the lovely banks of the Rhine since 1026 and therefore doesn't hesitate to call itself "the most ancient hostelry in Switzerland." It originally bore the name Zur Blume—At the Sign of the Flower—but soon after the inn was founded there was a historical meeting between Conrad II, Emperor of the Holy Roman Empire, his son (later Henry III), and Rudolf III, the last king of Burgundy. The purpose of this meeting was to draw up the treaty for the transfer of the territories which are now Western Switzerland and Southern France; their actions not only determined the fate of much of Europe but also gave the operators an excuse to rechristen the inn. Further, these kings were only the first of many luminaries to dine here—the Golden Book is signed by so many members of royalty and so many of the world's intellectual and political leaders that it would take many pages of this book to list them all.

The cuisine, too, is fit for kings; for example, the *Rotisserie des Rois* has won the coveted *La Fourchette d'Or de la Gastronomie Francaise* award. Among the entrées we suggest are *La belle Alliance de Saumon Fumé et Marine* and *L'aiguilette de Canette Fumée;* for dessert, *L'assiette de Fruits et Sorbets Floralie* is a good choice.

BERNE

Les Quatre Saisons and the
Bellevue Grill

Hotel Bellevue Palace
Kochergasse 3–5
3001 Berne
Switzerland
Telephone: 031–22–45–81

All major credit cards
Lunch and dinner
Reservations recommended
Jacket required
Liquor served
Dinner: $30 to $40
  full 3 courses, without wine
Lunch: $15 to $20
Chef: Heinrich Lauber
Maitre d': Kurt Aeberhard

The view from Berne's grand hotel of distinction is most magnificent. Constructed on a big bluff overlooking the Aare River, the hotel is set on the left-hand wing of the Swiss Parliament building, and commands an unforgettable view of the beautiful Aare Valley, the Embassy District, and the whole Alpine chain in the background.

Les Quatre Saisons is set on the ground floor, facing south. The dining rooms offer a five course dinner; the menu changes everyday. There is always an extraordinary variety of cheeses and desserts. Among the specialties are *Feuilleté d'Agneau* and *Epinards en Branches aux Raisins de Corinthe.* The dining rooms are popular with local residents and the many Americans who join them in the summer months.

BÜRGENSTOCK

Le Club Restaurant

Bürgenstock Center
Bürgenstock Hotel Estate
6366 Bürgenstock
Switzerland
Telephone: 041–23–43–37

All major credit cards
Dinner
Reservations required
Jacket and tie required
Liquor served
Dinner: table d'hote menu $25
    4 courses, without wine
      à la carte entrées $11 to $20
Chef: Franz-Josef Egli
Maitre d': Hans Schlunegger

The newest (1984) addition to the grand collection of hotels on the Bürgenstock Estate (the Palace, the Grand, and the Park) is the Bürgenstock Club. It is fantastic!

It has taken the owner, Fritz Frey, ten years to bring his dreams into being. Costing the Frey family some $7 million, the Club is unlike anything in the world.

You enter the club through a tunnel lined with marble walls and columns and crystal sconces. There are two elevators to take you to an antique-decorated foyer. From here you can go to a huge free-form swimming pool, rimmed with Carrara marble and surrounded by floor-to-ceiling walls of glass through which you can see one of the world's most dramatic views: Lake Lucerne and, beyond, the spread of Swiss Alps and forests.

The floor above the pool is the dining area, where you find Le Club and its equally magnificent view, plus magnificent furnishings and cuisine. The dining rooms are accented with massive oak beams across the ceiling and 300-year-old doors taken from an old Lucerne mansion. The elaborate sconces and lamps were made by hand in Florence and cost $10,000 each. They were meticulously designed by Frey and his daughter; Frey owns the largest lamp distribution company in Switzerland.

Franz-Josef Egli, only 37, is the executive chef; he supervises a staff of 30 chefs in the Bürgenstock kitchens. Egli arrived at Bürgenstock six years ago with ideas about how to make his cuisine, which he defines as neutral, classical, and modern. He has practiced his

Le Club

art at Raffles in Singapore, the Beverly Wilshire in Los Angeles, and the Dorchester in London, as well as at the Palace in nearby Lucerne. Among his favorites are *Escalope de Foie Gras, Tiedé, aux Reinettes et Raisins* (Goose-Liver Lukewarm with Grapes and Apples), *Carré d'agneau D'Ecosse Roti aux Aromates* (Ribs of Lamb with Breadcrumbs and Aromatic Herbs), and, for dessert, *Petit Panier aux Fraises de Bois et Leurs Sorbets* (Strawberries of the Forest and Strawberry Sherbet).

In summer, it is possible to dine on the terrace in a comfortable area beside the outdoor pool, with a gigantic cover of steel and canvas to protect you from the sun. This sunshade is so massive that it had to be brought up the steep mountain by helicopter.

There's something else you will enjoy viewing when you are in this grand resort. Bürgenstock owns one of the most distinguished art collections ever displayed in a hotel setting; it includes such masters as Frans Snyders, Antonis Van Dyck, Peter Paul Rubens, and Carlo Dolci. The unique paintings, tapestries, and furniture decorating the public rooms are all worth seeing.

GENEVA

Le Neptune

Hotel Du Rhone Geneve
Quai Turrettini 1
1211 Geneva 1
Switzerland
Telephone: 022–31–98–31

All major credit cards
Dinner
Reservations required
Jacket required
Liquor served
Dinner: $35 to $50
    full 3 courses, without wine
Chef: Francois Gillot
Manager: Eric E. Glattfelder

Le Neptune is the elegant rotisserie restaurant in Geneva's distinctive Hotel du Rhone. The decor and furnishings of this grand Swiss hotel are a delight; tapestries by Lurcat and Erni in the spacious lobby and beautifully furnished rooms and suites make this an exceptional place to be. It has been recently and richly refurbished and as a result looks the best it ever has since opening more than twenty-five years ago.

Le Neptune is beautifully located on the quiet bank of the Rhone River. It faces the

old town, has a lovely view of a 12th-century cathedral, and is within a few minutes of the famous high-water lake fountain, one of the landmarks of Geneva.

Le Neptune has been hailed by reviewers and critics as one of the top dining spots in Switzerland, and possibly all of Europe.

The French chef, Francois Gillot, had his training at many restaurants in Europe, including three years in Grenoble at the Restaurant l'Univers. He has been in charge of the Hotel du Rhone kitchen for more than ten years. The dining room specializes in true Perigord truffles (Truffle Mousse with Brioched Bread) and other truffle presentations, as well as in fish dishes—the fish arrives fresh every day from Roissy. In addition, there are high quality meat dishes prepared here on a charcoal spit.

Among the most popular selections are certainly the *Tressed Fillets of Sole and Salmon with Morels* and the paper-thin Apple Tart. We suggest that you try the *Croute Landais* (Warm Goose Liver with Chafed Cream Sauce), or perhaps the Lamb Kidney in Basil. Even the grilled chicken is perfectly and tastefully prepared.

Restaurant La Perle du Lac

128, rue de Lausanne
1202 Geneva
Switzerland
022–31–79–35

All major credit cards
Lunch and dinner
Reservations recommended
Jacket required
Liquor served
Dinner: $40 to $50
full 3 courses, without wine
Lunch: $30 to $40
Chef: Christian Grenard
Manager: Delfino Causin

At the beginning of the 19th century, the spot where La Perle du Lac now stands was a barren stretch of land outside of the city gates. H. Wilsdorf, founder of the Rolex Watch Company, bought a portion of this land; his wife became so enamored of one of the several buildings that stood at the very edge of the lake that she called it "the pearl of the lake." This same building, some years later, became the restaurant that we too enjoy.

Set in a peaceful and eternally fresh haven on lovely Lake Geneva, the view is thrilling even to the most blasé among us. It takes in an unforgettable panorama of Geneva and the lake, which hardly ever seems to be the same, ranging from mirror calmness to stormy. All is dominated by a view in the distance of the majestic Mont Blanc.

The quality of the cuisine is equal to the panorama. Delfino Causin, the manager, takes pride in his restaurant and it shows. This is, by the way, the only restaurant in Geneva with a garden terrace on the shore of the lake.

Fish and local specialties are served, in addition to Continental and international dishes. Among the favorite main courses are *Gratin de Queues de Langoustines et de Homard Fernand-Point,* Mixed Grill *de Poissons de mer Sauce Corail, Filet Mignon de Veau au Citron, Carre d'agneau Roti au Poivre Vert,* and *Filet Mignon de Boeuf Bordelaise et aux Pieds de Veau.* The dessert wagon is a view to behold, and choosing just one item from it is always difficult.

INTERLAKEN

French Restaurant

Hotel Beatus
3658 Merligen
Interlaken
Switzerland
Telephone: 033–51–21–21

All major credit cards
Breakfast, lunch, and dinner
Reservations required
Jacket required
Liquor served
Dinner: $20 to $30
full 3 courses, without wine
Lunch: the same
Chef: Willi Elsener
Maitre d': Luigi Botrugno

When this hotel was built a quarter of a century ago, it was done well: no rooms were placed on the road side of the hotel, while all of the rooms, plus the French Restaurant located in the hotel, were given views of the lovely lake of Thun. Further, the Hotel Beatus sits in the middle of a beautiful park, has a private beach for a quarter of a mile, and its restaurant, terraces, verandas, and balconies all look across the lake to the white mountains of the Bernese Oberland.

The food is excellent. Some of the favorite main dishes include Fresh Ravioli with Sage Butter, Sole and Shrimps with Vegetable Strips on Rose Pepper, and Roasted Ribs of Lamb with Herbs. A tasty start to the meal is the fish soup with saffron.

Most of the diners will be hotel guests from all over Europe as well as the United States. Travelers in the area come to dine here as well. Paul O. Joss is still the general manager.

La Terrasse

Victoria-Jungfrau Grand Hotel
Hoheweg
CH-3800 Interlaken
Switzerland
Telephone: 036-21-21-71

All major credit cards
Breakfast, lunch, and dinner
Reservations requested
Jacket required
Liquor served
Dinner: $16 to $28
    full 3 courses, without wine
Lunch: the same
Chef: Erwin Leo Stocker
Maitre d': Dino Sotqiu and
    Raffael Esposito

About a hundred and seventy-five years ago a man named Stähli built the first Hotel Jungfrau. It had 15 rooms and two big verandas. But because he neglected it, the building fell into disrepair. Old Stähli decided to desert it all and he departed for America. No one ever heard of him again.

It was Friedrich Ruchti who built the Victoria in 1880 and named it in honor of Queen Victoria. The architects were Studer and Davinet, who had designed the Swiss Parliament and the Hotel Bernerhof in Berne.

In 1865, a modern Hotel Jungfrau was built right next to the Victoria. Soon afterward Ruchti bought it and put the two hotels together, thus creating the biggest hotel in Switzerland (then and now). The two big buildings burned down in 1905 and were rebuilt.

The top restaurant at this resort is La Terrasse, which features French cuisine and breathtaking views of the mighty Jungfrau, 11,500 feet above sea level. This grand view has been shared by many of the world's greats, among them Mark Twain, Lord Byron, Thomas Edison, and an impressive amount of presidents, vice-presidents, kings, ex-kings, and royalty. The Victoria Bar is another indoor viewing spot which converts to an outdoor one in the summer by opening a sliding glass wall.

La Terrasse features *nouvelle cuisine,* and the Jungfrau grill offers grilled meats and Swiss specialties.

LAUSANNE

Le Relais

Lausanne Palace
7–9 Grand-Chene
1002 Lausanne
Switzerland
Telephone: 021–20–37–11

All major credit cards
Lunch and dinner
Reservations necessary
Jacket not required
Liquor served
Dinner: $20 to $60
  full 3 courses, without wine
Lunch: $15 to $45
Chef: Franco Taufer
Maitre d': Vincenzo d'Amizia

In the very heart of the city, commanding a magnificent view of Lake Geneva and the Alps, the Lausanne Palace is one of the most elegant hotels in Switzerland.

Le Relais is the spacious dining room, with a rich decor featuring high ceilings and large windows facing the lake. You should reserve a window table in advance.

The cuisine is excellent, bringing into the dining room not only guests of the hotel but also travelers from the area. Among the highlights on a typical menu are Slice of Grilled Salmon in Lime and Mustard Sauce, Angler Flambé in Metaxa Brandy, Fillet of Dory in a Sabayon of Red Wine, Wild Salmon with Capers, and a Cutlet of Turbot in Saffron and Ginger. You can order a U.S. "T"-Bone Steak with Herbs and Shallots, for two; the Roast Fillet of Beef *Perigourdine* and the Roast Rack of Lamb with Herbs, Tomatoes and Aubergines also serve two. Fillet of Veal in Leek Cream and Fillet of Lamb with Rosemary are also available. Among the desserts are Chocolate, Lemon, or Grand Manier Soufflé, Apple Tart with Cinnamon, and Crêpes Suzette. Each of these desserts serves two.

The Lausanne Palace was opened in 1915 and has been the location of many historic events, such as the signing of a Treaty of Eternal Friendship between Poland and Turkey and various war reparations agreements in 1932.

La Terrasse-Rotonde

Le Beau Rivage Palace
CH-1000 Lausanne 6
Switzerland
Telephone: 021–26–38–31

All major credit cards
Breakfast, lunch, and dinner
Reservations suggested
Jacket required
Liquor served
Dinner: $30
  full 3 courses, without wine
Chef: Hans Martin Fopp

This traditional grand European hotel opened its doors in 1861 and is one of the classic palatial hotels surrounding Lake Geneva. Most of its neighbors were built in the 1900s in a final flourish of *belle epoque* luxury. The collection of hotels are a pageant of the period, the ultimate expression of the stately and dignified life-style of that time. Today the Beau Rivage Palace still wraps its guests in turn of the century comforts.

The ten-acre estate is located in the lakeside village of Ouchy, which used to be a poor neighbor of Lausanne. The two cities merged and now form a split-level city with hills and valleys joined by a modern free-form sculpture of bridges and slanting roads.

The view from the restaurant is magnificent, overlooking the old trees of the park, the lake with its pretty sailboats and ever-changing colors, the snow-capped mountains of the Haute Savoie in the rear, and the Alpine glow on the Dent d'Oche when the sun sets behind the Jura. When the lights go on in Evian and Thonon the shore becomes a brilliant necklace of shining-blue diamonds. It is easy to feel that this is some sort of paradise.

Hans Martin Fopp, 41 years old, is the hotel's executive chef. He's worked in the Schweizerhof in Berne, the Dorchester in London, the Eden-au-Lac in Montreux, and other hotels in Portugal and Greece. His cuisine is French, in the tradition of Auguste Escoffier and Fernand Point; it is a cuisine which does not overwhelm but instead uses subtlety to delight the guest.

There are many local specialties featured on the menu, from the fish of Lac Léman (Lake Geneva) to the delightful *Crepes de Gruyére,* which are popular with the gourmets of Lausanne. Other favorites are *Escalope* of Fresh Goose Liver with Orange, Calf's Sweetbreads and Lobster in Cream, and the John Dory *Aiguillettes* on Spinach and Cream Sauce.

The location of the Beau Rivage Palace contributes not only to the view but to the ambience as well. Edmond Jalous wrote of Lausanne: "The city changes but it always keeps its youthful appearance. There is a delicious perfume of easygoingness and adolescence in its air." That goes of Ouchy, too. The little port, with its sidewalk cafes, music, wine, and the joyous laughter of the people, makes you think of a Mediterranean fishing village.

MURTEN/MEYRIEZ

Le Vieux Manoir

Hotel-Restaurant Le Vieux Manoir au Lac
CH-3280 Murten/Meyriez
Switzerland
Telephones: 037–71–12–83/4

All major credit cards
Breakfast, lunch, and dinner
Reservations recommended
Jacket not required
Liquor served
Dinner: $20 to $30
   full 3 courses, without wine
Lunch: $10 to $20
Chef: Ch. Gobat
Maitre d': R. Pontet

This lovely old Manor House is set in its own park on beautiful Lake Murten. It has its own little harbor and a sunny terrace looking down upon the pretty unspoiled lake and shores.

This fashionable French-style restaurant offers some of the better food in Switzerland. Among the favorites are Truffled Goose Liver Terrine, Rack of Lamb, and fish specialties, which change depending on availability.

The town of Murten is still surrounded by the old rampart walls which were built in 1238; in fact, it is one of the best preserved medieval towns in all of Europe. The houses in the inner town are fascinating, many of them dating from the 17th and 18th centuries.

NEUVECELLE

Restaurant de La Verniaz

Neuvecelle
s/Evian-Les-Bains F74500
Switzerland
Telephone: (50)75-04-90

All major credit cards
Breakfast, lunch, and dinner
Reservations required
Jacket not required
Liquor served
Dinner: $20 to $30
    full 3 courses, without wine
Lunch: the same
Chef: Christian Metreau
Maitre d': Henri Gauthier
Owners: The Verdier Family

High in the mountains above Lake Geneva and Evian (the famous source of the pure bottled water) is La Verniaz. It is a secluded Swiss country inn with cottages and pools, surrounded by beautiful, unspoiled country.

La Verniaz has earned one star from *Michelin,* but we've seen write-ups by critics saying that they felt it deserved more than that. The cuisine is delightfully fresh and served in the generous Swiss country style. Among our favorites are fish selections from Lac Leman, chickens cooked on huge outdoor spits (during the summer), and the bubbly regional wine. The desserts and the pastries are freshly prepared each day and are not the same every day—so they do not appear on the menu.

Dining in the garden on a summer's day, under the umbrellas covering the tables, is a pleasure you can share with guests from all over Europe: there are people here from Switzerland, Belgium, Germany, and England. About 80 percent of the guests are Europeans, and about 20 percent are Americans.

ZÜRICH

Le Pavillon

Hotel Baur au Lac
Talstrasse 1
Postfach
8022 Zürich
Switzerland
Telephone: 01–221–16–50

American Express
Breakfast, lunch, and dinner
Reservations required
Jacket required
Liquor served
Dinner: $25 to $27
full 3 courses, without wine
Lunch: $20 to $25
Chef: Bernard Gothuey
Director: Michel Rey

The Baur au Lac, founded in 1844 by an emigrant Austrian baker, has been owned by the same family since its beginning. For five generations the Baur-Kracht family has maintained the hotel's well-earned reputation for elegance, hospitality, and grand cuisine.

Although the townspeople ridiculed Johannes Baur for facing his new Hotel Baur au Lac away from the medieval town and toward the lake, today the hotel is considered to be in a choice location. On one side is a canal that was once a part of Zürich's medieval fortifications. Overlooking this canal is the very popular Le Pavillon dining room.

The Baur au Lac has three restaurants: the famous Grill Room and its American Bar, open year-round; Le Restaurant Francais, operated during the winter months and recently redecorated under the direction of the famous French interior decorator, Henri Samuel; and the most attractive and certainly the most popular, Le Pavillon, open May through October.

This large glass-enclosed restaurant is set in the beautiful private park of the hotel overlooking the picturesque Schanzengraben River. With so many colorful flowers and plants all around the room, you have the feeling of dining in the midst of a delightful garden.

At the same time, there is the unique view of Lake Zürich and the Alps. Le Pavillon itself provides a delightful view, with its elegant white curtains and table linens and Chinese-red lacquered chairs.

At first you may find the splendid French menu a bit overwhelming, but the friendly maitre d' or any of his staff will be glad to work with you on this important decision. Among our favorites—there are so many—are, to start, Smoked Salmon followed by Cream of Leek Soup. Main courses offer Zuricher Creamed Veal, Veal Steak, *Homard en Mousseline ou Melon et Caviar,* and *Truffe en feuilletée;* the most popular entrée is *Emince Züricher Rösti.* Recommended for dessert is the *Tartes aux Pommes Normande,* but there is a tempting variety of fresh fruits—blueberries and black raspberries—on the dessert cart, as well as torts, ice cream, and cream caramel.

Chef Gothuey is an honorary member of the *Société Culinaire Philanthropique* of New York. He has received more than ten gold medals at international culinary expositions and contests in Europe. He is an expert on the staff of the famous hotel school in Lausanne. You're in good hands at this beautiful place.

Thailand

BANGKOK

The Normandie
The Oriental
48 Oriental Avenue
Bangkok 10500
Thailand
Telephones: 234–8621–9

All major credit cards
Lunch and dinner
Reservations necessary
Jacket and tie required
Liquor served
Dinner: $75 to $100
full 3 courses, without wine
Chef: Pascal Peignaud
Maitre d': Pierre Michard

The pinnacle of dining at the Oriental, hailed as the best hotel in the world by many surveys and polls, is at the Normandie atop the hotel's Tower Wing. Dining in this restaurant is a feast for the eyes as well as for one's taste buds. The sweeping view over the Chao Phya River and much of low-lying Bangkok is quite a sight, particularly at night.

This is an expensive restaurant but worth the price. The objective of Kurt Wachtveitl, the general manager of the Oriental, and his staff is to keep the Normandie highly ranked. They have succeeded—hardly anyone disagrees that it is the finest restaurant in Thailand, the best French restaurant in Asia, and certainly one of the twenty best restaurants in the world. Among the menu favorites we enjoyed were *Les Aiguillettes de Canette Caramelisees au Miel d'Orangeret aux Epices Chinoises* (Sliced Breast of Duck Caramelized with Orange Honey and Chinese Spices) and *Le Garoupa au Riz Thai Enrage du Curry, aux Courgettes et Aux Poivrons Doux* (Steamed Grouper in a Light Curry, accompanied by Thai Rice Courgettes and Sweet Peppers). For dessert, try *Le Feuillete aux Pommes a la Canelle et Son Carmela a la Creme* (Fresh Apple with Cinnamon in Puff Pastry and Creamy Caramel Sauce).

Some unusual things have happened in the Normandie, particularly among its celebrity guests. Two years ago, Her Royal Highness Princess Somsawali, the Royal Consort of Crown Prince Vajiralongkorn, asked the bar supervisor whether her sister could work as a steward and clean the dishes at the hotel. There was a long pause before everyone realized the Princess was joking.

Sometimes it is difficult to enforce the rule that men should be properly attired in coat and tie and ladies in elegant dresses. One night a Thai man came without a jacket and tie and Mr. Bernard, then the restaurant manager, wouldn't let him in. In Thailand, an insult of a personal sort is taken seriously. Not understanding that it was a restaurant policy, the Thai gentleman thought this had been a personal affront. The next day, Mr. Bernard received a letter telling him to leave the country within 24 hours. Diplomacy at high levels resulted in the explanation of the strict dressing regulations and eventually all was understood and forgiven.

Then there was the time that Elton John ordered one Russian Vodka straight up. The restaurant personnel were surprised to find that the drink was not for him, but for his diamond ring—he used Vodka to clean it since the liquor did the job so well.

This is a quiet setting. There is no music because the managers feel that the fine food and the magnificent view are enough. And they are right.

Turkey

ISTANBUL

Roof Rotisserie

Hilton International Istanbul
Cumhuriyet Caddesi
Harbiye, Istanbul
Turkey
Telephone: 146–70–50

All major credit cards
Dinner only
Reservations required
Jacket appreciated
Liquor served
Dinner: $15 to $50
full 3 courses, without wine
Chef: A. DeVries
Maitre d': Ismail Özkilic

This thrilling view takes in both Europe and Asia! The view over the Bosphorus, just 300 feet below, to the Asian shore from your hilltop perch in Europe, is unparalleled and unobstructed, since the hotel is a free-standing structure in a tree-filled 13-acre park in the middle of town. On the Asian continent, you can see the old city of Istanbul with identifiable sights such as the famous Topkapi and St. Sophia. From the Kizkulesi Bar, at the entrance to the restaurant, you have a view of the Leander Tower in the middle of the Bosphorus and a breathtaking view of the Bosphorus Bridge.

The Roof Rotisserie is the most popular deluxe restaurant in Istanbul and is located on the ninth floor, which is the top floor of the hotel. It is frequented by local connoisseurs, who make up about 40 percent of the dinner guests, and the rest are a mixture of some twenty nationalities, with Americans averaging about ten to 15 percent.

The Roof Rotisserie is a medium-sized dining room seating 200 guests; there are also semiprivate niches decorated in the old Ottoman style for private parties of up to 12 people. The staff is a delight. They are well trained and on the average have been with the restaurant for about 15 years. There are international chefs and experienced local cooks under the direction of A. DeVries.

The daily catch, directly from the nearby fishing harbor, is brought to the table displayed on a bed of ice in a trolley so that you may select the fish you wish to eat. Istanbul's variety of fish is unique, brought about by natural circumstances which exist nowhere else in the world. The Bosphorus connects the Black Sea with the Sea of Marmara and the Mediterranean. The Black Sea has a considerably lower salt content than the others, so its water is lighter. This causes a unique current in the Bosphorus, in which there is a layer of water on top which has somewhat less salt, a middle section with mixed water and a layer of heavier water towards the bottom. The Bosphorus has an average depth of 60 feet. Because of this three-layer situation, the different species of fish seek their own salt content layer. Normally, in order to have such a broad selection of fish, one would have to travel to three different seas to catch them!

Among the favorite specialties of the Roof Rotisserie are *Döner* (lamb on a vertical spit) and, for dessert, Baklava (Turkish pastry with honey and pistachios). Accompanying the dining and the magnificent view is live music provided everyday by Aysun Ercan and company and their violins.

One treat in the Roof Rotisserie is the *Meze* display at the center of the restaurant, offering a wide selection of Turkish and oriental appetizers, freshly prepared each day. This is the popular way to start dinner. *Raki,* the popular Turkish anis-flavored hard liquor, is recommended as the best accompaniment.

Giving the restaurant its name is the copper grill, where masters of Turkish cuisine prepare typical local dishes.

The United States

ALABAMA
BIRMINGHAM

Hugo's Restaurant

Hyatt Birmingham
at Civic Center
901 21st Street North
Birmingham
Alabama 35203
Telephone: 205–322–1234

All major credit cards
Dinner
Reservations recommended
Jacket optional
Liquor served
Dinner: $13.50 to $14.95
full 3 courses, without wine
Chef: H. Andrew Hamilton
Maitre d': Tommy Brown

The view to dine by from Hugo's is particularly nice after the sun has set and the lights of the city go on. But this is not to say that the daytime view isn't also impressive; it features important buildings such as the Museum of Fine Arts, the Jefferson County Courthouse, and several high-rise office buildings, including the Bell South Building.

The restaurant is one of the town's favorites, and has been since it opened in 1973. One local newspaper recently voted Hugo's "the best restaurant for a celebration." One of the more unusual and surprising events to occur here was when a guest videotaped his marriage proposal. Luckily, the lady said yes.

Among the menu's specialties are Artichoke Hearts, Pasta Primavera, Filet Mignon with Cabernet Sauce, Veal Florentine, Lemon Sole with Lychee and Citrus Sauce, Roast Prime Rib of Beef with Fresh Grated Horseradish, and Spit-Roasted Young Duck. A popular dessert is Hugo's Key Lime Pie.

POINT CLEAR

The Grand Dining Room at Marriott's Grand Hotel

Point Clear
Alabama 36564
Telephone: 205–928–9201

All major credit cards
Breakfast, lunch, and dinner
Reservations requested
Jacket and tie required after 6 P.M.
Liquor served
Dinner: $25 to $50
full 3 courses, without wine
Lunch: $7 to $12
Chef: Gerard Pinault
Maitre d': David Wilson

This resort has a 150-year tradition of serving its guests well. The Grand Dining Room offers local and Continental specialties and entertainment every night.

The view is of the expanse of Mobile Bay and its sailing boats and ships. If you eat breakfast early enough, you can see the boats departing for deep-sea fishing.

ALASKA
ANCHORAGE

Josephine's

Sheraton Anchorage Hotel
401 East Sixth Avenue
Anchorage
Alaska 99501
Telephone: 907–276–8700

All major credit cards
Dinner
Reservations advised
Jacket requested
Liquor served
Dinner: $26 to $40
*   full 3 courses, without wine*
Executive Chef: Anil Roy
Chef: Mark Linden
Maitre d': Mike Meek

Perhaps the best way to start exploring Anchorage is to have dinner at Josephine's. Here the view looking north is of Knik Arm, the port, Mt. McKinley, the Cook Inlet, and the Chugach Mountain Range. Toward the south you see most of the city of Anchorage. All this is viewed from the vantage point of the 15th floor of the hotel where the elegantly decorated (in shades of apricot and green) Josephine's is located. (If you want to sample the cuisine and the view at a lower price than a full dinner you can sit in Josephine's comfortable lounge, on the south wall.)

Josephine's menu is primarily Continental, but it leans toward *nouvelle cuisine* and is served with style. Each plate is prepared with concern for the arrangement and design of the food.

Named for the Empress Josephine, wife of Napoleon Bonaparte, this European-style restaurant has magnificent carpets and fabrics patterned after those in Napoleon's last palace. The recurring motif of the Trumpeter Swan—the emblem of Empress Josephine—serves as a reminder that this bird migrates across the Arctic. Six French-style chandeliers created in Spain add luster to the Continental decor.

A suggestion: one of the more delightful specialties of Josephine's is the *Lobster LaPagerie,* tender, moist lobster tail stuffed with shrimp mousse and baked in phyllo dough, served with champagne and cilantro sauce. Alaska is *the* place for lobster tail!

ARIZONA
TUCSON

Ventana

Loews Ventana Canyon Resort
7000 North Resort Drive
Tucson
Arizona 85715
Telephone: 602–299–2020

All major credit cards
Dinner
Reservations recommended
Jacket suggested
Liquor served
Dinner: $30 to $40
    full 3 courses, without wine
Chef: Akram Azzam
Maitre d': Al Chija

The elegant Ventana dining room has two full walls of windows and a third wall of lustrous glass bricks lighted from behind. The view through the windows of this gourmet restaurant offers a full panorama of Tucson's skyline, the Canyon Waterfall, and the desert and mountains beyond.

Ventana is rich in its decor, with Woodmere, German Schottz Wiesel crystal, and plush seats. The colors are muted and the lighting soft. The tables, set with white linen, are illuminated by the flame of an oil lamp in the form of a clear glass disk. Each table has a crystal glass bud vase holding a single rose. Harp and violin music set a romantic ambience.

The cuisine is exceptional. A recent guest, just come from a visit to Vienna, said, "This restaurant poses a serious threat to the finest dining establishments in Europe." Chef Azzam, an American who began his cooking career in Belgium and has worked with Swiss and German chefs, says he thinks of cooking as an art. This is reflected in the appearance of his dishes, where vegetables, cut by Akram himself, are prepared and presented so beautifully that each plate is a picture of gastronomic perfection.

Akram uses reduction sauces, made by preparing the stock daily, then adding sherry, vermouth, white, burgundy, or sauvignon wines. Besides being more healthful for consumption than roux (flour) sauces, the flavor of reduction sauces is more appealing and the sauce is smoother.

The Southern Arizona Chefs Association awarded Akram a silver medal for the Ventana Medallions of Lamb in Whole-Grain Mustard Sauce. This and the Poached Sea Bass in Saffron are the favorite main dishes here. Other delights include the Mesquite-Broiled Salmon Steak with Grilled Red Onions and Chive Butter; Venison prepared in thin, tender Scallops, served with wild mushrooms and red wine sauce; Mesquite-Broiled Duckling; and Rack of Lamb with Jalapeño Jelly.

Among the desserts are Chocolate Velvet in Tulips (a fancy concoction of soft chocolate mousse under flaky pastry, with a pool of vanilla sauce laced with a raspberry swirl), and a Creme Brulée.

CALIFORNIA
BERKELEY

The Landing

Berkeley Marina Marriott
200 Marina Boulevard
Berkeley
California 94710
Telephone: 415–548–7920

All major credit cards
Breakfast, lunch, and dinner
Reservations required
Jacket recommended
Liquor served
Dinner: $10.50 to $25
    full 3 courses, without wine
Lunch: $7 to $15
Chef: Gerry Glass
Maitre d': Nancy Webb

The Berkeley Marina Marriott, in which The Landing is located, sits directly on the San Francisco Bay shoreline. The hotel seems like a resort because of the marina setting and the lack of high-rise development in the immediate area. Yet it is only twenty minutes from downtown San Francisco.

The Landing features tiered seating so that every guest has a view. In the foreground is the Berkeley Marina with all its colorful sails, masts, and never-ending activity. In the distance one can see the entire San Francisco skyline and Golden Gate Bridge. Sunset from the restaurant is a grand experience as the sun sinks directly behind the bridge's silhouette.

The menu offers American Cuisine with an accent on seafood. Sunday brunch is offered from 10 A.M. until 2:30 P.M. with a gigantic and highly appetizing spread that keeps the guests coming back for more.

BIG SUR

Nepenthe

Highway 1
Big Sur
California 93920
Telephone: 408–624–1032 or 667–2345

All major credit cards
Lunch and dinner
Reservations not required
Jacket not required
Liquor served
Lunch and dinner: $5 to $16
full 3 courses, without wine

Nepenthe is on a mountaintop overlooking the Pacific Ocean and the Santa Lucia mountains along the famed and scenic Highway Number One. It is 26 miles south of lovely Carmel, three miles south of Big Sur State Park, and about 165 miles south of San Francisco.

Nepenthe is a word derived from the Greek meaning "no sorrow." Many years ago, Nepenthe was used as the central setting for a motion picture, *The Sandpiper,* starring Elizabeth Taylor and the late Richard Burton; it was selected because its singular beauty and because its atmosphere were deemed a perfect setting for the story.

It's an attractive place to eat, and we like the desserts, especially the Chocolate Butter Creame Pie.

CARMEL

The Covey Restaurant at Quail Lodge

8205 Valley Greens Drive
Carmel
California 93923
Telephone: 408–624–1581

All major credit cards
Dinner
Reservations necessary
Jacket required
Liquor served
Dinner: $14 to $21
full 3 courses, without wine
Chef: Bob Williamson
General Manager: Mr. Lynn Farrar

Just a short drive from the Carmel area of Monterey Peninsula is the delightful and tranquil Carmel Valley. It is an area protected by those who live there and love the lush verdant surroundings. Beautiful estates and excellent country clubs are quietly, privately supported by the affluent residents of the area.

One of these sanctum sanctorums can be enjoyed by those not among the area's residents. This is the Carmel Valley Golf and Country Club, on the premises of which is Quail Lodge. Within Quail Lodge is the Covey Restaurant, a gourmet establishment with seating at various levels affording both privacy and unobstructed views of a small man-made lake, glistening in perfect contrast to the subtle tones of brown, beige, and ebony

within the restaurant. Swans float beneath a tiny bridge, adding to the setting of restful and luxuriant beauty.

The Covey Restaurant has won stars from restaurant critics for its fine cuisine. We enjoyed the Rack of Lamb and a generous selection of fresh California vegetables. We left the choice of wines to the wine steward, who selected from a variety of wines from the fine smaller vineyards with such limited production that only a few California restaurants serve their products.

LA JOLLA

The Marine Room

2000 Spindrift Drive
La Jolla
California 92037
Telephone: 619–459–7222

All major credit cards
Lunch and dinner
Reservations preferred
Jacket optional
Liquor served
Dinner: $13 to $22
*   full 3 courses, without wine*
Lunch: $5 to $10
Chef: Robert O'Kelly
Maitre d': Dennis Rush

One of the great views of the Pacific is to be had from the Marine Room, built right at the edge of the sea. Sometimes you think you are in the midst of the ocean and will be splashed by the breaking waves. And sometimes you find that the Pacific is not always so pacific. In fact, the Marine Room had to be rebuilt after it was destroyed by raging storms and sea in December 1982.

The cuisine here—featuring daily fresh sea bass, sole, halibut, salmon, Sea Scallops in Lobster Sauce, and other specials—has received the Taste of San Diego award. The meal is an elegant one. Appetizers range from Shrimp à la Scampi to Pacific Crab Cocktail Marina to Oysters Rockefeller. The dinner entrées are served with New England Seafood Chowder or Tossed Green Salad with Bay Shrimps and a Medley of Vegetables. Some of the Marine Room specialties include Steak Armagnac (New York steak with fresh crushed peppercorns, sautéed in French brandy), Deep Sea Scallops in Lobster Sauce, and "The Imperial Pair"—a petite filet mignon and choice lobster tail.

The Sky Room at La Valencia Hotel

1132 Prospect Street
La Jolla
California 92037
Telephone: 619–454–0771

All major credit cards
Lunch and breakfast
Reservations strongly recommended
Jacket required; tie optional
Liquor served
Dinner: prix fixe $25.50
Lunch: buffet $12
Chef: Christian Gaborit
Maitre d': Salvadore de la Torre

The Sky Room of La Valencia is situated on the 10th and top floor. From the windows of the restaurant it is easy to find yourself dreaming of sailing toward the sunset on the Pacific Ocean. The unobstructed vista of the California coastline and the La Jolla Cove and caves are all reminiscent of the French Riviera. These views can be seen from one of the ten tables in the Sky Room.

This view has been enjoyed by so many famous people that to try to list them would be an endless task. But Norma Shearer, Tennessee Williams, Audrey Hepburn, Jonas Salk, Gregory Peck, Aimee Semple McPherson, Ramon Navarro, Charles Laughton, Raymond Massey, Joseph Cotton, Herbert Marshall, Joan Crawford, Bob Hope, Groucho Marx, Greta Garbo, Mario Lanza, Zsa Zsa and Eva Gabor, June Lockhart, and Marie Wilson—shall we go on?—have been among La Valencia's guests. The luxurious La Valencia opened its beautiful wrought-iron doors in 1926 under the name of Los Apartamentos de Sevilla as an apartment hotel. It is so beautifully built and the grounds so beautifully planned and kept that the hotel and its setting must be considered part of the view.

This small dining room is in demand. Among the favorites you might consider are Salmon with Melon Sauce and Shrimp Salad served with Asparagus Tips and a special orange sauce.

LOS ANGELES

Angel's Flight Restaurant

Hyatt Regency Los Angeles
711 South Hope Street
at Broadway Plaza
Los Angeles
California 90017
Telephone: 213–683–1234

All major credit cards
Lunch and dinner
Reservations recommended
Jacket suggested
Liquor served
Dinner: $16 to $20
full 3 courses, without wine
Lunch: $9 to $17
Chef: Wolfgang Wildoer

Angel's Flight is the revolving restaurant on the rooftop of the Hyatt Regency in Los Angeles. It makes a full revolution once every hour and offers a 360-degree view of Los Angeles. From this height, Los Angeles seems to go on forever.

Angel's Flight

The menu is less varied than that of Pavan, the hotel's other restaurant. Here the specialties include a diversified salad menu and a fish of the day; there is also an exotic drink menu. The restaurant is open from 11 A.M. until midnight and is a favorite romantic spot as well as a popular place for cocktails at sunset.

The Dining Room and Outdoor Terrace of the Hotel Bel-Air

701 Stone Canyon Road
Los Angeles
California 90077
Telephone: 213–472–1211

All major credit cards
Breakfast, lunch, dinner, and
Sunday brunch
Reservations necessary
Jacket required
Liquor served
Dinner: $25 to $35
    full 3 courses, without wine
Lunch: $15 to $20
Chef: Joseph Venezia
Maitre d': Albert de Kerazan

The Hotel Bel-Air's restaurant, a popular setting for hotel guests and nearby residents, is at the end of one of the graceful arcades in the hotel's Mission-style main building. It was recently redecorated by designers Louis Cataffo and Betty Garber, with walls upholstered in peachy beige and enhanced with original art, carpeting in beige with moss green floral patterns, spacious booths covered with waffle-finish beige leather, and country-inspired Queen Anne armchairs.

Under the direction of Chef Venezia, the cuisine reflects the traditions of California, France, and even the Orient, and emphasizes fresh ingredients and artful preparation.

The dining room is neatly tucked into a corner of the plush grounds of the hotel and for the past forty years has been the most romantic setting for dining in Los Angeles. It is not unusual for celebrity neighbors living in Bel-Air to be seated next to a young visiting couple here to enjoy the surroundings and magnificent food.

For guests who like alfresco dining in warmer weather, tables on the bougainvillea-draped terrace next to the restaurant overlook the hotel gardens and Swan Lake, providing the best view to dine by in Los Angeles.

146   *California*

The cuisine features interesting combinations made with fresh local foods and pastas. For example, there is the appetizer of Sweetbreads sautéed with basil noodles, arugula, and shittake mushrooms. Among the favorite entrées are Mesquite-Grilled Spot Prawns on Tomato and Cucumber, Medallions of Veal with Onion Marmalade and Port Wine Sauce, Smoked Seafood with Rye Toast (tuna, salmon, sturgeon, sea bass, and mussels arranged with a display of capers, lemon, and a *trompe l'oeil* egg), Roast Sliced Canadian Duck, and Grilled Loin of Lamb with Poached Garlic and Spinach.

And the desserts! Have you ever heard of Poached Cheesecake (it's like a cream cheese mousse) with Raspberry Sauce? Other unique offerings are the herb-scented sorbets. But for chocolate lovers this is paradise. Our favorites are Chocolate Truffle Cake and Chocolate Mousse Cake! There is also Almond Kirsch Cake decorated with currants on the stem, blueberries, and blanched almonds. Decisions!

On Sunday, a delightful brunch is served from 11:30 A.M. until 2:30 P.M. that costs between $13 and $16.

The after-dinner stroll on some parts of the eleven-and-a-half acre enclave is a must. It is hard to believe that the hotel is so close to the bustle of Los Angeles. In the lower garden, the Mission-style bell tower overlooks a romantic lake whose swans add a touch of elegance. What is now the hotel was originally the offices in the early 1920s of Alphonzo E. Bell, the developer of the luxury residential community of Bel-Air. In the 1940s it was transformed into a luxury hotel that immediately became a favorite of the residents because of its refined tranquility. The residents have taken a proprietary interest in it ever since and nervously watched its recent renovation. Fortunately, in the hands of the Rosewood Hotels Organization, nothing was destroyed, only freshened and enhanced.

Dining Room and Outdoor Terrace, Hotel Bel-Air

Top of Five

Westin Bonaventure
404 S. Figueroa Street
Los Angeles
California 90071
Telephone: 213–624–1000

All major credit cards
Lunch and dinner
Reservations recommended
Jacket recommended
Liquor served
Dinner: $25 to $30
  full 3 courses, without wine
Lunch: $8 to $15
Chef: Werner Glur
Maitre d': Tom Berning

There are two viewing possibilities here, one from the restaurant and another from the cocktail lounge. On the 35th floor of the Westin Bonaventure is the Top of Five, a restaurant with a 360-degree view of Los Angeles and beyond. At night it is particularly beautiful because of the endless sea of glittering lights. Viewing is even more fun from the BonaVista, a revolving cocktail lounge located just one flight below the Top of Five's dining room. It is even fun getting to it, down a grand staircase from the restaurant.

The Top of Five has just been beautifully redecorated. Instead of the original beige and terra-cotta color scheme, there is an updated mauve and blush decor. The tabletops in the restaurant and the lounge are made of polished black Belgian marble. The bar top is polished black granite. The original continuous bench seating that lined the perimeter of the Top of Five has been replaced with intimate booth seating without obstructing any of the view.

Chef Werner Glur has been named Chef of the Year by the California Restaurant Writers Association. His current menu features such items as mesquite-grilled Swordfish Steak Louisiana with Jumbo Shrimp and Cajun Hot Sauce, Yellowtail with Cucumber and Ginger Shoots, and Crabmeat and Oyster Fettucine. Chef Glur has taken "the fire of Louisiana Cajun cooking and mixed in timeless Szechuan recipes, creating a new spirited cuisine with East meeting West."

Lunch is served Monday through Friday, brunch on Saturday and Sunday, and dinner and cocktails are served seven days a week. The Top of Five guarantees that your dinner there will take no more than 45 minutes from arrival until departure. If they miss, they pay the check!

MONTEREY

Conservatory Room at the Sardine Factory

701 Wave Street
Monterey
California 93940
Telephone: 408–373–3775

All major credit cards
Dinner
Reservations recommended
Jacket preferred
Liquor served
Dinner: $17 to $29.50
  full 3 courses, without wine
Chef: Doug Robertson
Manager: Jeffrey Lesker

The Sardine Factory is located on historic Cannery Row on the Monterey Peninsula and has won awards for its cuisine and decor. Started by Ted Balestreri and Bert Cutino in 1968, it has collected a long list of honors, including the *Travel/Holiday* Magazine Award since 1971, the *Restaurants and Institutions* Magazine Ivy Award, *Nation's Restaurant News* Hall of Fame Award, the *Mobil Travel Guide* Award, and others.

In addition to the original dining room, there are four other dining areas. Among them are the Victorian-styled Captain's Room, with fireplace and crystal chandeliers, the Wine Cellar, an elegant lower-level room with medieval decor featuring many collector's items as furnishings, and the Conservatory Room.

Conservatory Room

The distinctive Conservatory Room is entirely covered by a glass dome and offers a unique turn-of-the-century garden setting. The room, with its green and white decor and plants in Roman containers, is dominated by a white iron crystal chandelier from Czechoslovakia and a central fountain topped with a statue of the *Birth of Venus* adapted from the famous Botticelli painting. The view to dine by is of the enclosed garden patio.

Among the menu favorites are Abalone Cream Bisque, Monterey Bay Prawns, Abalone, and, for dessert, Pear Cardinal.

Be sure to see the Wine Cellar Room with its 25-foot long banquet table, cognac bar, and tobacco humidor built by Craig Clark, a wine captain, from a 1,000-year-old redwood tree.

Ferrante's Restaurant and Bar

Monterey Sheraton Hotel
350 Calle Principal
Monterey
California 93940
Telephone: 408–649–4234

All major credit cards
Lunch and dinner
Reservations suggested
Jacket not required
Liquor served
Dinner: $8.95 to $16.95
    full 3 courses, without wine
Lunch: $5.95 to $10.95
Chef: Paul Gelose
Maitre d': Doug McCall

When natural pressure forced the coastal mountain range of the Monterey Peninsula into the waters of the Pacific, it created what has been described as one of the world's most dramatic meetings of land and sea.

At Ferrante's, on the tenth and highest floor of the Monterey Sheraton, this spectacular panorama comes with the meal. From here you have 270 degrees of view, which is a great deal for the eyes to digest. In the daylight hours you may see the colorful spinnakers of sailboats in regatta, the spray of migrating gray whales, and the far-away Santa Cruz mountains, changing colors with the seasons and the setting sun.

As evening approaches, the fishing fleet comes through the dusk to anchor and a quiet

settles on the shore. Lights begin to twinkle at the Fisherman's Wharf, over the Presidio, and on the streets of Old Monterey far below. The view is all-inclusive—the Cannery Row and Tortilla Flat areas of Steinbeck fame, the mist-shrouded pines of the Peninsula hills, and the magnificent Monterey Bay.

Regular visitors to Ferrante's have stories to tell of the ever-changing views—of storms rolling in off the Pacific, or the night that meteors lit up the southern sky with a brightness almost like daylight. They also might talk of the familiar faces they saw, such as Clint Eastwood, Joan Fontaine, or John Travolta, or of the old Italian families that made Monterey the colorful fishing community immortalized by Steinbeck's writing.

The restaurant is appropriately named for Pietro Ferrante, a Monterey Bay fisherman. Even he might have difficulty in deciding what to select from the *antipasti, minestre, insalate tramezzini, frittate, pasta,* and *carnie e pesci* that Chef Paul Gelose includes on his menu.

Specialties include Seafood Fettucine with succulent scampi, scallops, and clams sautéed in a light cream sauce and served with spinach fettucine. Another favorite is Shrimp Pomodoro. This delightful restaurant specializes in Northern Italian cuisine, and so, not surprisingly, is popular with the area's Italians. Desserts feature freshly baked items and delightfully rich and creamy gelato.

MORRO BAY

The Inn at Morro Bay

Morro Bay
California 93442
Telephone: 805–722–5651

All major credit cards
Breakfast, lunch, dinner, and
Sunday brunch
Reservations necessary
Jacket not required
Liquor served
Dinner: $15 to $17
full 3 courses, without wine
Lunch: $6 to $13
Chef: James G. Magee II
Maitre d': Esteban DeLuque

Here you get some clues as to why the California coast is like it is. The volcanic rock of Morro Bay juts out into the Pacific; you can't completely walk around it, nor can you climb it. Some have tried and found themselves stranded for a while. It is an unusual formation and you find yourself studying it. Many, armed with camera or paintbrush, have tried to capture it artistically. Others run to the nearest library to consult a geology textbook.

When we first wrote about this view, it was from a small modest lodging called the Golden Tee. Now, completely new and replacing it is the Inn at Morro Bay, a delightful place to dine and stay.

You begin your viewing and dining experience with a stop in the cocktail lounge, where you have a great view of the ocean and the local fishing boats. Don't worry about losing the view once you go to the dining room—from there you can see the volcanic rock formations in the Pacific Ocean, framed beautifully by eucalyptus trees. Chef Magee offers California cuisine with French overtones. The dining is accompanied by soft classical music, in keeping with the tranquil setting of the inn. Among the favorite main dishes are *Canard Roti du Soire* (fresh Roasted Boneless Duckling served with a sauce of that evening), *Pasta El Encanto* (fresh Sautéed Shellfish on Spinach and Egg Fettucini in Lobster Bisque), and *Saumon Moutarde* (fresh Salmon poached in Cream, served in White Wine Dijon Mustard Sauce). The desserts are all tantalizing French pastries.

The dining room is open for breakfast at 7 A.M. Dinner is ready at 5 P.M. Sunday brunch is served from 10 A.M. until 2 P.M.

The view is getting even better. This year a marina at the inn will be completed, and then you will be able to see guests arrive for dinner, or a stay, by yacht. The Inn at Morro Bay is a favorite eating place for both residents and visitors, some of whom come for dinner and decide to stay a few days to enjoy the view.

PASADENA

Skylights

The Pasadena Hilton
150 South Los Robles Avenue
Pasadena
California 91101
Telephone: 818–577–1000

All major credit cards
Lunch and dinner
Reservations necessary
Jacket required
Liquor served
Dinner: $19.75 to $25
* full 3 courses, without wine*
Lunch: buffet $9.75
Chef: Hermann Thoni
Maitre d': Denis Regnier

Pasadena is that famous California city known for its annual Tournament of Roses Parade and for the Rose Bowl, the football classic. It is also an important cultural city, home to the California Institute of Technology and its NASA jet propulsion laboratory, the Huntington Library and Art Gallery, four museums, and several magnificent gardens.

The restaurant atop the Pasadena Hilton, Skylights, provides a magnificent view of Pasadena. The view at night is particularly delightful as the lights seem to extend forever. On a clear night the lights of Los Angeles, only eight miles away, as well as those of Glendale, ten miles away, are visible as well.

José Lopez, director of Food and Beverages at the hotel, is proud of the French cuisine served in this lovely penthouse restaurant. He points out that the best possible ingredients are obtained for each dish; if not available locally, he stressed, they are flown in from England, France, or from anywhere else necessary to get what is required. Among the awards received by Skylights are the Epicurean, three stars from the *Mobil* guide, and two stars from the California Restaurant Association.

Favorites from the kitchen include *Tournedos Arlequin, Filet de Fletan Biarritz,* and *Escalopes de Veau a l'Estragon.* Among the desserts we recommend are Chocolate Mousse and Creme Carmel. There are excellent French pastries as well. Sunday brunch is very popular here.

SAN DIEGO

Sheppard's
in the
Sheraton Harbor Island East
1590 Harbor Island Drive
San Diego
California 92101
Telephone: 619–692–2255

All major credit cards
Dinner
Reservations required
Jacket required
Liquor served
Dinner: $25 to $40
　　full 3 courses, without wine
Chef: Cindy Black

Sheppard's

This exceptional restaurant was the final project in the $30 million renovation and addition to the 750-room Sheraton Harbor Island East Hotel. It was opened in September 1984, and thanks to the remarkable Chef Black, Sheppard's is considered the best restaurant in San Diego and possibly in all of California.

The complex is located on Harbor Island, in the middle of scenic San Diego Bay. The small, elegant restaurant looks out across the Harbor Island Marina, with its colorful boats. Generally, Sheppard's diners have a view through treetops of the garden. If you want to enjoy the water view, when you make your reservation ask for a window table on the right side (as you enter) of the restaurant. Some say the view of the interior of the restaurant is even more spectacular than the outdoor view. The restaurant is decorated in soft shades of coral, accented by live green plants and matching pin cushion protea flowers which grace the centers of the tables. In the Vintage Room, a private dining room without a view that is very much like a dining room in a fine home, are six fabulous oil paintings by Nancy Bowen, a local artist, depicting Monet's summer gardens in France. This room is available for parties of four to nine people.

Cindy Black, the chef, has generated a lot of excitement. She's only 28 years old, but she knows food and good cooking as well as any older master. Her father is a diplomat and was her first cooking teacher. Her formal cooking education came from Madeleine Kamman, who runs her Modern Gourmet Cooking School in Newton Centre, Massachusetts. Cindy worked as a cook in the southwest of France after finishing school. Robert Brody, executive chef at the Sheraton, met her when she worked briefly at Apley's Restaurant in Boston. When the hotel in San Diego was looking for a chef that would fit in with the French "country" theme and decor of the Sheppard's Restaurant they were about to complete, Brody recommended Black for the job. Sheppard's opened under her direction on January 28, 1983; in 1984, Cindy Black and Bob Brody were married, and everybody there celebrated "the wedding of two cuisines."

There is ample reason for joy—the cuisine is terrific. It has been awarded the 1985 *Travel/Holiday* Fine Dining Award and has garnered praise from all California critics. Among the many delights are Duck Confit Salad, Grilled Marinated Swordfish with Coriander, Loin of Lamb with Glazed Green Beans, Fresh Salmon with Lemon-Thyme Sauce, Scallops with Sage Butter and Roe, and Snapper with Chervil. The desserts are outstanding, among them Raspberry and Chocolate Marjolaine, Apricot Tart with Marinated Dried Apricots in Puff Pastry Shell with Pistachios, and our favorite, Belgian Chocolate Ice Cream.

SAN FRANCISCO

Chic's Place

202 A—Pier 39
San Francisco
California 94133
Telephone: 415–421–2442

All major credit cards
Breakfast, lunch, dinner, and
Sunday brunch
Reservations not necessary
Dress: casual
Liquor served
Dinner: $11 to $15
  full 3 courses, without wine
Lunch: $7 to $9
Chef: Joel Theriault
Proprietors: Chic Watt and George Martinez

Here's a delightful restaurant on Pier 39, San Francisco's picturesque shopping and dining tourist mecca. Even though reservations are unnecessary, you might want to phone ahead for a window table if you'd like to dine with a view.

But even if you don't see the outside view, you'll still enjoy the grand interior of this place. It was designed at considerable expense to recreate the style of old San Francisco. A marble-topped bar with brass rail is backed by artist-commissioned mirrors which go all the way from the entrance area to about halfway around the dining room. The lighting is gentle and the heavy green carpeting with the white tablecloths, silk flowers, and shaded candleholders, all contribute to a turn-of-the-century decor.

The style here is Art Nouveau. One of the interior's highlights is a painting of one of Mucha's ladies set off by smoky persimmon walls; Mucha was also the inspiration for the designs on the hand-sanded mirrors and the glass partitions. Antique buffs will like the floral-design of the chandeliers and the hand-carved sideboard. Through the beveled, hand-carved windows guests may watch boats slowly crossing the bay or people meandering down Fisherman's Wharf.

The view inspires most patrons to order seafood. The Chef's Special Dinner is guaranteed to satisfy; it features Grilled Salmon, Sautéed Prawns, Fried Scallops, Petrale Sole, and Oysters Rockefeller, accompanied by Potatoes Anna and salad or soup. The Broiled Red Snapper is also great. If you're more of a landlubber, there are veal and steak entrées.

Compadres Mexican Bar and Grill

Ghirardelli Square
900 Northpoint
San Francisco
California 94109
Telephone: 415–885–2266

MasterCard, Visa
Lunch and dinner
Reservations recommended
Jacket preferred
Liquor served
Dinner: $15 to $25
    full 3 courses,
    without wine
Chef: Agustin Iniquez
Manager: Pat Dulin

Late in 1985, the third of four Compadres Mexican Bar and Grill restaurants opened in San Francisco, atop what had been an old chocolate factory building, in Ghirardelli Square.

The square is now a delightful, fun-filled shopping complex and restaurant center, but only some of the restaurants have grand views of San Francisco Bay—Compadres has one of the best because it is higher than all the others.

Compadres is an airy restaurant decorated with cushioned wicker furniture, plenty of green plants, and an outstanding array of Mexican artifacts. There is an outdoor patio with a freestanding adobe fireplace and tables set under gas lanterns. The antique wood furniture and festive umbrellas add to the setting.

Critics praise the cuisine here. Some of the more popular items feature Potato Nachos made from thick Maui potato chips and topped with cheese, salsa fresca, guacamole, sour cream, fresh bacon pieces, and chopped scallions.

Another specialty is Chili *Rellenos,* which are freshly roasted and peeled before being stuffed with Monterey Jack cheese, Mexican *chorizo* (sausage), Dungeness crab, and other delights. The Shrimp (*camarones*) *Fajitas* are especially popular, made with marinated Gulf shrimp sautéed with onions and green peppers and then wrapped by the diner into soft tortillas. Some people like the Compadres platter, a generous combination starting with a Caesar Salad tossed tableside and followed by *Flautas,* Baby Back Ribs (smoked), Chili *Rellenos, Pollo Borracho,* and *Fajitas.*

One of the most popular and creative desserts here is the Apple *Chimichanga,* which features brandied apples in a deep-fried flour tortilla topped with vanilla ice cream and/or cheese. Also on the menu is a wonderful Taco Split, a golden fried tortilla boat filled with fresh bananas, ice cream, fruit topping, macadamia nuts, and a cherry. The Caramel Flan and Kahlua Parfaits are also very popular.

The Crown Room

29th floor
Fairmont Tower
Fairmont Hotel
Atop Nob Hill
San Francisco
California 94106
Telephone: 415–772–5000

All major credit cards
Lunch, dinner, and Sunday brunch
Reservations recommended
Jacket advised
Liquor served
Dinner: $22.50 adults
* $16.50 children*
Lunch: $17.50 adults
* $12.50 children*
Sunday brunch: $17.50 adults
* $12.50 children*
Chef: Kurt Kratschmar

The Crown Room, perched atop the Fairmont Tower on the 29th floor, has a sweeping panorama of San Francisco Bay, the Golden Gate Bridge, the Marin County headlands, Alcatraz Island and its famed prison, the Bay Bridge, the Financial District skyscrapers, and the hills of South San Francisco. The Crown can be reached by inside tower elevators for the more squeamish, or by the glass enclosed Skylift, an outdoor elevator providing a magnificent view of the city all the way up.

Inside the Crown, guests can have their views from the tables in the revolving bar carousel in the center of the room, if they wish. It makes a complete revolution every 17 minutes.

The Crown Room features a magnificent buffet, offering over forty salads, entrées, and desserts. Cold buffet items for lunch and dinner include six prepared cold salads with such items as sliced tomatoes, sliced cold cuts, artichokes, mushrooms, pasta, coleslaw, tossed greens, Bay shrimp, poached salmon, assorted pâtés, sliced duck, sliced Cornish game hen, and roast beef. Typical hot luncheon and dinner items include London Broil with Sauce Bordelaise, Sautéed Fillet of Salmon, Baked Sea Bass Portuguese, Osso Bucco, and Fillet of Sole Amandine. Cheeses, raisins, and walnuts are there, along with fresh seasonal fruits. Dessert items include Lemon Chiffon Pie, Banana Cream Pie, assorted French pastries and more. Sunday brunch adds Pancakes Oscar, Eggs Benedict, and Cheese Blintzes.

The Crown is open daily for lunch from 11:30 A.M. to 2:30 P.M.; dinners are from 6 P.M. to 10 P.M.; cocktails are from 11 A.M. to 2 A.M. Holiday and Sunday brunches are usually offered at 10 A.M., noon, and 2:30 P.M.

Kurt Kratschmar, the Fairmont executive chef and chef of the Crown, was born and raised in Vienna and has been at the Fairmont for six years; previously he worked at various Las Vegas hotels.

People from all over the world and from all walks of life come to the Crown Room, including such celebrities and dignitaries as Claudette Colbert, Phyllis Diller, Sean Connery, the late Rock Hudson, Ella Fitzgerald, King Gustav of Sweden, John D. Rockefeller, and Alexander Haig.

Dante's Sea Catch

Pier 39
Box 213
San Francisco
California 94133

All major credit cards
Lunch and dinner
Reservations not required
Jacket not required
Liquor served
Dinner: $7.95 to $23.95
  full 3 courses, without wine
Lunch: $4.95 to $11.95
Chef: Daniel Comforti
Maitre d': Scott C. Bridges

The panoramic view through the wall of windows at Dante's Sea Catch encompasses both old and new, natural and manmade splendors. From the San Francisco skyline with its historical Coit Tower and the modern TransAmerica building (called by some the pyramid with ears) to the expansive bay where sailboats are forever gliding among the luxury liners, the vista is an ever-changing painting of mood and light, vibrant by day, alluring by night.

Dante's Sea Catch

In its seven-year history Dante's Sea Catch on Pier 39 has prided itself on serving the finest and freshest seafood, pastas, and other specialties that, by combining the traditional with the unique, reflect the nature of the view to dine by. Award-winning Chef Comforti won first prize for his Crab Cioppino dish during a national Crab Cooking Olympics, and his clam chowder was honored as the very best at the San Francisco Fair and Exposition.

Certainly among the menu favorites are his Crab *Nouvelle Cuisine,* the Silver Dollar Scallops, and Prawns *Fra Diablo.* The food has to be good here—the Sea Catch is one of the 23 original restaurants on Pier 39 which is still in business.

The setting at Dante's Sea Catch is casually elegant, with its long, curving Art Nouveau dining room looking out over the marina and its colorful boats. Stained glass and Victorian lamps add to the ambience. The same green and amber color scheme in the main room is found upstairs at the bar, where guests can relax with a drink and either admire the view or just stare into the flickering flames of the fireplace.

The Mandarin

Ghirardelli Square
900 North Point Street
San Francisco
California 94109
Telephone: 415–673–8812

All major credit cards
Lunch and dinner
Reservations recommended
Jacket optional
Liquor served
Dinner: $15 to $25
 full 3 courses, without wine
Lunch: $10 to $15
Chef: Teh Ko
Maitre d': Linsan Chien

Dining in this superb Chinese restaurant is a delight partly because of the delightful view of San Francisco Bay but even more so for the authentic and beautifully served Chinese cuisine.

The original Mandarin restaurant was opened in San Francisco years ago by Cecilia Chiang and achieved its renown as the first restaurant in the United States to serve the dramatic and now very popular dishes of Szechuan and Northern China. Born and bred in Peking, Ms. Chiang opened her first restaurant in Tokyo simply because she could not find the good food to which she was accustomed. Today she commutes twice weekly between Los Angeles and San Francisco to make certain that the quality of the cuisine in her restaurants meets her rigid standards.

The cuisine here has won many awards, including five stars from the *Mobil Travel Guide* and the *Travel/Holiday* Magazine Award. Among the favorites, and there are too many to list, are Minced Squab, Peking Duck, Beggar's Chicken, Smoked Tea Duck, Prawns Szechuan, and Sweet and Sour Fish. For dessert, try the bananas dipped first in molten sugar and then in ice water to form a brittle sugar crust. A scrumptious discovery!

The pleasure of dining here is enhanced both by the view of San Francisco Bay and the exquisite Chinese furnishings. The Mandarin's many rooms are divided by screens of openwork tile or intricately carved wood. The floors are laid with jade and blue tiles and covered with colorful Oriental rugs. On the walls are needleworks done in the "Forbidden Stitch" (so called because the threads are so fine that the artisans stitching these used to go blind!). One delight is an impressive lotus blossom sculpture, handcarved and assembled from seventeen pieces of a unique light-colored Oriental wood.

Neptune's Palace Seafood Restaurant

Pier 39
P.O. Box 3730
San Francisco
California 94119
Telephone: 415–434–2260

All major credit cards
Lunch, dinner, and brunch
Reservations advised
Dress: casual elegant
Liquor served
Dinner: $9.95 to $25
 full 3 courses, without wine
Lunch: $7.95 to $25
Chef: Kevin Sadlier

This restaurant, too, has a magnificent view of San Francisco Bay and all of its activities. General Manager Jeanne Cambra tells of a single day of viewing in October 1985:

Fleet Week began at that time in San Francisco with ten to 15 U.S. Navy ships and aircraft carriers sailing in under the Golden Gate Bridge at 10:30 A.M., with the Blue Angels performance on the water of the Bay following at 11:30. The Coast Guard was all over the Bay that day keeping sailboats out of the pathways of the Blue Angels. Later that afternoon, just 30 feet off the end of the Pier and directly in front of our windows, a sailboat capsized and sank completely within 15 minutes. Fortunately all on board were unharmed.

As you see, this is often an exciting view to dine by.

The cuisine here has won a variety of awards, among them the silver award in the Baltimore Crab Olympics and the Overall Grand Prize at the New York Landing Seafood Festival. Favorite entrées include Baked Salmon with Three Cheeses and Swordfish Kontiki, and, for dessert, Chocolate Torta with Fresh Raspberry Sauce.

Neptune's Palace's location is exciting, too. Situated near the end of the pier, it is surrounded by the bustling activity of the pier itself. Pier 39, which opened on October 4, 1978, is an exciting collection of shops, restaurants, marinas, docks, and much more—a full-fledged entertainment center for tourists and San Franciscans alike.

One-Up

Hyatt on Union Square
345 Stockton Street
San Francisco
California 94108
Telephone: 415–398–1234

All major credit cards
Lunch, dinner, and Sunday brunch
Reservations recommended
Jacket required at dinner
Liquor served
Dinner: $28
  full 3 courses, without wine
Lunch: $18
Chef: Jeff Moogk
Maitre d': Ramona Lashley

The Hyatt on Union Square has a restaurant on top of its penthouse, thus the restaurant's name: One-Up. It offers a thrilling view of the key landmarks of San Francisco, including Coit Tower, the Transamerica building, Alcatraz Island, and the Golden Gate Bridge.

One-Up was refurbished in 1983 by Denis Allemand and Associates Design, Inc., of Los Angeles. It was given an elegant decor with a pale blue and mauve interior, accents of brass, contemporary furnishings, and an Asian influence through the use of original artworks.

Under the direction of Executive Chef Moogk and One-Up Chef Ted Rowe, the One-Up menu features New American cuisine at its finest. It offers creative, light, and exquisitely prepared dishes using the freshest, most tender regional products in addition to lots of seafood from San Francisco Bay. Cooking time is short, sauces are light, and the food is artfully presented. There is a fine wine list, including the new Hyatt Cuvee Domain Chandon sparkling wine available by the glass or bottle.

An elaborate champagne brunch is served every Sunday featuring eggs, omelets, oven-warm breads, flaky pastries, breakfast meats cooked to perfection, imported pâtés and cheeses, and the freshest fruits of the season.

The One-Up Restaurant is open for lunch Monday through Friday from 11:30 A.M. until 2 P.M. Dinner is daily from 6 P.M. until 10:30 P.M. Sunday brunch is from 10:30 A.M. until 2 P.M.

Two suggested entrées are Warm Salad of Mixed Baby Lettuce with Sautéed Lobster, Sea Scallops, and Salmon with Mango-Walnut Vinaigrette and Sliced Loin of Lamb with Comfit of Eggplant, Red Pepper Relish, Sweet Garlic, and Rosemary Natural Jus.

Among the tempting desserts are Puff Pastry Filled with Fresh Berries in Caramel Sauce and Creme Brulée au Grand Marnier. Best of all are the soufflés, either raspberry or pistachio.

Top of the Mark

Mark Hopkins Intercontinental
Number One Nob Hill
San Francisco
California 94106
Telephone: 415-392-3434

All major credit cards
Sunday brunch; cocktail lounge
at other times
Reservations recommended
Jacket requested
Liquor served
Sunday brunch: adults $19.50
children under 12: $12.50
Chef: Tony Breeze
Manager: Steve Rice

Only on Sunday is this a view to dine by. On weekdays it is a view to drink by. The Top of the Mark is in this book simply because it is a great viewing spot, and because it is probably one of the best-known vantage points in San Francisco, and has been so for many years.

The Top of the Mark opened on May 11, 1939, and since then more than 25 million people from all parts of the world have come to view all of San Francisco from its lofty perch 257 feet on top of Nob Hill and 537 feet above sea level. Not only can one see the city of San Francisco, but in addition seven surrounding counties, mountains along the Pacific Coast, three giant bridges (including the Golden Gate), and the Pacific Ocean are all seemingly within your grasp. It is a 50-mile panorama that has few to equal it in all the world.

From the time it opened as a hotel in 1926 until 1936, the 19th floor (now the Top) was the private apartment of D.C. Jackling, a copper magnate. The floor was built to his specifications with unusually high ceilings to accommodate his prize collection of mammoth oil paintings. When Jackling moved to his country estate in 1936, George D. Smith, builder, owner, and general manager of the Mark Hopkins, decided to build a skyroom bar.

Timothy Pfleuger, San Francisco's leading architect of that era, created a room in which all four walls were actually huge glass panels—especially designed to withstand 120-mile gales (no winds have ever reached this velocity in San Francisco).

The Top of the Mark reopened during the year of the San Francisco World's Fair, in 1939, but it was World War II that gave the Top its worldwide reputation. Hundreds of thousands of Allied servicemen shipped through San Francisco, and the Top of the Mark became their figurative Port of Embarkation. It was the last place they remembered and the first they wanted to come back to; as servicemen met and passed each other on Pacific fronts, the watchword was "meet you at the Top of the Mark."

When the war ended, the United Nations Charter Conference came to San Francisco. The diplomats and other dignitaries were charmed by the Top of the Mark and its grand panorama. Anthony Eden used to have his morning tea there, all alone, gazing at the magnificent view, before departing for each day's work of attempting to build a charter for world peace.

The lavish buffet is different each Sunday, and features hot and cold entrées with a great selection of appetizers and desserts as well. It is a favorite spot for local residents to take their first-time San Francisco visitors to get a bird's eye view.

Vannelli's Seafood Restaurant

Pier 39
Box 210
San Francisco
California 94133
Telephone: 415–421–7261

All major credit cards
Lunch and dinner
Reservations not necessary
Jacket not required
Liquor served
Dinner: $8.75 to $22.50
full 3 courses, without wine
Lunch: $4.50 to $12.50
Chef: Claus B. Iversen
Maitre d': Tucker Short

Located at the end of Pier 39, overlooking the Golden Gate Bridge, the Bay Bridge, and all three of the Bay islands—Angel, Yerba Buena (Treasure Island), and Alcatraz—the V-shaped Vannelli's has a spectacular 180-degree panoramic view. The yacht marina just below the restaurant is always busy and interesting to watch, as are the incoming and outgoing cruise ships.

The cuisine here includes a vast selection of fresh and specially prepared seafood, meat, and poultry dishes. Among the popular entrées are Shrimp Louie, Combination Seafood Platter, Halibut Florentine, Veal Piccata (you can also have both the halibut and veal), and Baked Salmon Wellington. Another favorite is the Lobster-Fillet combination.

SANTA BARBARA

Harbor Restaurant

210 Stearns Wharf
Santa Barbara
California
Telephone: 805–963–3311

All major credit cards
Lunch and dinner
Reservations not necessary
Jacket required only in Santa Barbara Room
Liquor served
Dinner: $8.95 to $20
  full 3 courses, without wine
Lunch: $4.95 to $12
Chef: Kevin Sherry

Some feel that the view of old Stearns Wharf from the Harbor Restaurant is as delightful as the view from Stearn's Wharf itself. The wharf looks like a tiny New England fishing village mounted on a long pier, and, set against a background of palm trees and bright blue water, it is very picturesque.

Stearns Wharf has been around since 1872, when John P. Stearns, financed by a Santa Barbara millionaire, Colonel William Welles Hollister, got the city council to give its blessings for the construction of a town wharf. It has had many owners, including the Coast Guard (during World War II) and actor James Cagney, and it often suffered from physical neglect. Today the wharf is operated by the city of Santa Barbara and has, in addition to the luxurious Harbor Restaurant, an enclave of shops and other restaurants in rustic seaside-style buildings.

Like the wharf, the Harbor Restaurant has had a checkered history since its inception in 1941. It was first opened in what had been the Santa Barbara Yacht Club's old wharf-end clubhouse. In 1963, it was refurbished and became a successful showplace, only to be destroyed by a fire in 1973. Rebuilt, the new Harbor Restaurant manages to capture the decor and spirit of its three-decade history. It offers extensive lunch and dinner menus, featuring what it proclaims to be a "seafood menu unmatched on the Pacific coast, and is enhanced with pasta made fresh daily in the grand style of Northern Italy."

Popular with local residents, it is also a favorite of tourists in the area.

UNIVERSAL CITY

Oscars at the Premiere

Sheraton at Universal City
555 Universal Terrace
Universal City
California 91608
Telephone: 818–506–2500

All major credit cards
Lunch and dinner
Reservations necessary
Jacket required
Liquor served
Dinner: $17 to $26
  full 3 courses, without wine
Lunch: $12 to $27
Chef: Tim Knowlton
Maitre d': Bill Simmons

How would you like a view to dine by in Hollywood? Well, this is the most elegant one to be had.

Oscars at the Premiere, the signature dining room of the Sheraton Premiere Hotel, is a luxury dining room providing a formal yet intimate setting. Right next door to the Universal Studios, this 24-story glass hotel tower, designed by famed architect William Pereira, overlooks Hollywood and the San Fernando Valley. The tower contains 450 guest rooms and has 19 suites on its top five floors, including two 2,400 square foot presidential suites—bona fide Hollywood opulence. The restaurants of the hotel and meeting places are in three 40-floor high pavilions, also mostly glass enclosed, adjoining the residential tower.

The smallest full dining room in this hotel is the extravagant and elegant Oscars at the Premiere, named for the award many of its guests strive to earn. It seats 80 people.

Oscars at the Premiere

Chef Timothy A. Knowlton features fabulous foods of the newly rediscovered American cuisine, which is rapidly becoming a national favorite. The menu includes such items as New Orleans-style Blackened Tenderloin and Smoked Scallops with Raspberry Vinegar.

Opened in April, this extraordinary dining room is a delight for the eye. Its decor features antique mirrors, elaborate crystal chandeliers and flower arrangements, and a coffered ceiling. There is a central banquette as well as large individual tables with beautiful wood-framed, brocade-covered chairs. Sparkling Villeroy and Boch crystal, Mintin and Royal Doulton porcelain china, and richly designed Reed and Barton silver allows each table to be a study in elegance.

In keeping with the level of the decor and the settings, the ceremony of guest service is genteel as well. The menu is presented in a large white envelope, addressed with each guest's name.

It is a long and varied menu, so time is needed just to read it, let alone make a decision. To avert painful hunger pangs, guests are treated to complimentary chicken liver pâté served with toasted French bread. The pâté is very light and silky in texture because it has been blended with port and cream. Guests here are encouraged to forget restraint and order everything that looks good. Unfortunately, everything looks good!

Among the appetizer delights, for example, are a New Orleans-style skillet-fried Shrimp in Spicy Butter and Glazed Lobster with a sauce of puréed fresh chives and white wine.

Salad choices include red leaf lettuce pieces tossed with toasted pine nuts, wisps of carrots, red peppers, and smoked-on-the-premises duck in a honey-fresh lime dressing, or the endive salad with warmed goat's cheese tossed with walnut oil vinaigrette.

The main dishes are all special. It seems an effort is made to make the usual unusual. There is, for example, the usual prime rib, but it is roasted in a smoker. Other entrées include tender chunks of lobster smothered in a richly flavored reduction of crayfish stock, cream, brandy, and tarragon. Placed in the center of the lobster plate is a mound of fresh pasta made with Pinot Noir wine.

If you have room for dessert, you'll have a problem in deciding, of course. Oscars' fresh fruit soufflés are the favorites here. Blueberry and raspberry are featured.

This dining room is open Monday through Friday for lunch from 11:30 A.M. to 2 P.M., and for dinner Monday through Saturday from 6 P.M. until 10 P.M.

COLORADO
DENVER

Augusta
The Westin Hotel
Tabor Center Denver
1672 Lawrence Street
Denver
Colorado 80202
Telephone: 303–572–9100

All major credit cards
Lunch and dinner
Reservations recommended
Jacket and tie preferred
Liquor served
Dinner: $20 to $30
  full 3 courses, without wine
Lunch: $10 to $13
Chef: Serge Delage
Maitre d': James Twiford

The Augusta is a dining room featuring American cuisine, located directly off the lobby of the Westin Hotel, with which it shares a view of Denver's downtown skyline and Skyline Park. The dining room itself is very dramatic, with its background of padded gray satin walls showing off the polished brass and etched glass panels, ebony-lacquered furnishings, and peach-colored upholstery. The design is reminiscent of Art Deco.

The American cuisine features dishes either from the rotisserie or ones that are grilled, broiled, or steamed. The food is always light and sometimes consists of unique and exciting, or at least interesting, combinations. Among the favorites are duck and chicken prepared on the rotisserie. Local critics have rated Augusta among the best dining rooms in the city.

Desserts include a rich and sinful Chocolate Mousse, rich fancy cakes, and our favorite, Bread Pudding with Whiskey Sauce.

The hotel is situated in Tabor Center, which contains the 420-room Westin Hotel, a collection of 70 shops and eateries, and a 32-story office tower. It is named for Horace Tabor, an early pioneer developer in Colorado. The Augusta restaurant is named for the first wife of this legendary figure.

EL RANCHO

El Rancho Colorado

18 Miles West of Denver on I-70
El Ranch Exit #252
Denver/El Rancho
Colorado 80401
Telephone: 303–526–0661

All major credit cards
Lunch, dinner, and Sunday brunch
Reservations not required
Dress: casual
Liquor served
Dinner: $10 to $20
full 3 courses, without wine
Lunch: $5 to $11
Owner: Paul R. McEncroe

El Rancho Colorado, at 7,686 feet above sea level, is a great mountain dining lodge that offers what many writers claim is one of the most photographed views in Colorado and, some say, in America as well. It is indeed spectacular—the snowcapped Continental Divide of the Rocky Mountains rises dramatically in the distance.

The restaurant here has seven fireplaces, and has been expanded over the years. Back in 1954 72 guests could be seated. Today the seating capacity has increased to 225 in three mid-level areas, and in three lower-level dining rooms there's room for 125 more. All this additional seating has been provided without spoiling the elegant atmosphere.

Lunch is served from 11:30 A.M. until 2 P.M., dinner from 5 P.M. to 10 P.M., Sunday brunch from 9:30 A.M. until 1:30 P.M., and Sunday dinner from 2 P.M. until 8:30 P.M. Among the main dish specialties are Australia Rock Lobster Tail, Filet Mignon Rock Lobster Tail, Beef El Rancho, New York Strip Sirloin Steak, and Fresh Mountain Trout. A great favorite here (which you can also buy and take with you) are the delicious home-baked cinnamon rolls. The dessert selections are different and exciting every day.

Best time to dine with a view is just before sunset.

VAIL

Wildflower Inn at the Lodge at Vail

174 East Gore Creek Drive
Vail
Colorado 81657
Telephone: 303–476–5011

All major credit cards
Dinner
Reservations recommended
Jacket and tie required
Liquor served
Dinner: $25 to $35
    full 3 courses, without wine
Chef: Jim Cohen

At the magnificently refurbished Lodge at Vail, in the heart of Vail Village, there is a delightful new gourment restaurant called the Wildflower Inn. It is so beautiful that it won the first-place award for its interior design for 1985 from the restaurant industry publication, *Restaurant Hospitality.*

The prize-winning interior was created by Warren Platner of New Haven, Connecticut, known for having designed New York's Windows on the World Restaurant at the World Trade Center (also discussed in this book). The theme of the decor is that of a spring garden in bloom, giving the restaurant an overall atmosphere of warmth, elegance, and charm. Huge baskets of colorful silk flowers were personally arranged by Mr. Platner. The tables are richly set with Villeroy and Boch China, Reed and Barton silver, Zwiesel crystal, and Laura Ashley table linens.

The view from the Wildflower Inn is spectacular: the Rocky Mountains, covered with wildflowers during the spring and summer, snow-capped peaks glistening in the sun, or submerged under layers of crystalline snow in winter.

The superb cuisine served by Chef Cohen features a small but diverse menu whose specialties include Fresh Tuna Steak prepared in a peppery Tuscany oil, Rack of Lamb covered with Pine Nuts, Garlic, and Jalapeño Peppers, Breast of Pheasant, Lamb Loin, and Veal Chop Sauté.

CONNECTICUT
STAMFORD

The Swan Court

The Inn at Mill River
26 Mill River Road
Stamford
Connecticut 06902
Telephone: 203–325–1900

All major credit cards
Breakfast, lunch, and dinner
Reservations necessary
Jacket required at dinner
Liquor served
Dinner: $30 to $45
    full 3 courses, without wine
Lunch: $15 to $30
Chef: Maxime Ribera
Maitre d': John Zerega

One of the most elegant restaurants in Stamford, indeed in all of Connecticut, the Swan Court was awarded three stars by the food critic of the *New York Times.*

The Inn at Mill River is a favorite of the more affluent business people in Stamford, which is home to many national corporations' headquarters. The Swan Court Restaurant has windows overlooking a Japanese cherry tree promenade along the Mill River, which winds through the city limits and empties into Long Island Sound. While it is most delightful here at cherry blossom time in the spring, this restaurant affords a pleasant and tranquil view any time of the year.

The dining room is beautifully decorated, with latticed walls in peach and cream tones and Oriental touches such as blue and white vases and other decorative objects. The skirted tables are beautifully set with fine Wedgwood porcelain and handblown crystal. The authentic French cuisine is enhanced by the finest of local ingredients. The food is prepared on the premises with the expertise and original recipes of the Inn's well-known culinary advisers, including the French chefs Jean-Michel Gammariello and Jean-Pierre Vuillermet, and Clive Ranfay, an English pastry expert.

The menu is excellent. For starters you can have Tuna and Swordfish, a Three-Vegetable Mousse, or a savory Sauté of Artichoke Hearts in an orange-sparked Provencal sauce. All are presented as colorful and artistic masterpieces which look as grand as they taste.

Among the popular main dishes are Grilled Half Cornish Hen, Baked Monkfish, Breast of Long Island Duckling, and Sliced Medallions of Veal.

All of the desserts are fantastic. Among them are a tantalizing deep dark Chocolate Mousse in a toasted almond brioche crust, floating in vanilla sauce with toasted almonds; warm Almond Tart, composed of pear, almond cream, and caramelized pear sauce; Tart Nougatine with three homemade sorbets—black currant, raspberry, and passion fruit, neatly packaged in a crisp pecan-caramel box; homemade Pistachio Ice Cream in Sabayon; Mill River Mosaic of Three Ice Creams; and Chocolate Plaisir, a velvet-rich dark and white chocolate mousse, with a topping of pastry and chocolate sauce. Had enough?

Sunday brunch is available, too, from 11 A.M. until 2 P.M., for a reasonable $7 to $15 for entrées.

WESTON

Cobbs Mill Inn by the Waterfall

Old Mill Road
Route 57
Weston
Connecticut 06883
Telephone: 203–227–7221

All major credit cards
Dinner
Reservations preferred
Jacket recommended
Liquor served
Dinner: $14.75
full two courses, without wine and dessert
Proprietor: Julie P. Jones

In one of the oldest structures in the country, you can enjoy dinner with a view of a forty-feet-high waterfall formed as a small part of the Saugatuck River passes over a two hundred year old dam. Cobbs Mill Inn sits at the edge of a pond that is home to a number of ducks, adding to the quaint scene. The Inn itself was built between 1750 and 1775, predating the Revolutionary War, so you get to absorb some New England history as you dine. It sits within a Colonial style garden, attractively interrupted by outcroppings of rugged rock. The view can be enjoyed from the dining room at the top of the falls, or from the cocktail lounge, a floor below, at the foot of the falls.

The cuisine is American, featuring fresh foods of the season, all attractively prepared and pleasantly served.

FLORIDA
BAL HARBOUR

Coco's Sidewalk Café

9700 Collins Avenue
Bal Harbour
Florida 33154
Telephone: 305–864–2626

All major credit cards
Breakfast, lunch, and dinner
Reservations not required
Dress: casual
Liquor served
Dinner: $15.95
    full 3 courses, without wine
Lunch: $5.95
Owner: David Migicovsky
Maitre d': Lori Migicovsky

People-watching, particularly if these people are fashionable shoppers in a chic area, can be an entertaining experience. Coco's offers just such enjoyment, whether you're there for breakfast, twilight dinner, or the happy hour that takes place some time in between. And if that sort of entertainment isn't enough for you, some other type of diversion is always provided—a pianist, an accordionist, sometimes even a palmist.

Casual elegance is the catch phrase here. The waiters are all dressed as if they stepped out of the pages of a fashion magazine, and all are skilled in the art of food presentation, as part of a show put on by the proprietor, David Migicovsky.

When David came here from Montreal his objective was to achieve a Continental and cosmopolitan setting, and he decided that an outdoor café was the way to do it. He was the first to bring this style of dining to Florida.

Inasmuch as his customers were the stylish ladies who shop in the chic Bal Harbour stores, he elected to have a fashion theme for the restaurant's decor. Coco's was named for Coco Chanel, considered by David to be the first designer to "liberate women's fashions."

The style of the cuisine is called American, but it is a bit different because of the special Continental touches added by David. Salads, such as the famous Nicoise, are served in glass flowerpots. Specialties include homemade Lasagne, gourmet burgers, pita sandwiches, Asparagus Parmesan, and Cajun-style fish and steak.

Some of the favorite desserts include frozen Key Lime Pie, Oreo Biscuit Cheesecake, warm Apple Dumpling with Cinnamon Ice Cream and Caramel Sauce, Apple Pie with French Vanilla Ice Cream and Caramel Sauce, Pecan Pie, and Chocolate Kiss—a thick chocolate brownie topped with caramel ice cream and drizzled with coffee syrup.

In keeping with the chic location, this is one of the few spots in Miami where a guest can take her poodle to lunch and have him/her served out of a personalized water dish. Really.

BAY HARBOR ISLAND

Café Chauveron

9561 East Bay Harbor Drive
Bay Harbor Island
Florida
Telephone: 305–866–8779

All major credit cards
Dinner
Reservations necessary
Jacket required
Liquor served
Dinner: $45
    full 3 courses, without wine
Chef: Terry Left
Maitre d': Jean Claude Troadec

If you've wondered what happened to a wonderful New York restaurant called Chauveron, now you know: it's in Florida.

The late Roger Chauveron, restaurateur extraordinaire, opened the Chambord in New York City in 1935; it became one of the foremost restaurants in the nation. In 1957, he followed that achievement with another—Café Chauveron. It, too, was an immediate success, attracting the rich and the famous.

When Café Chauveron lost its least to Citicorp, Roger decided to move the restaurant to Miami, opening the Bay Harbor Island restaurant under the same name at the end of 1972. André Chauveron, who began learning the restaurant business in his dad's kitchen when he was only 17, became a partner in the enterprise and by October 1984 had taken over as the owner/host.

Apparently André has done a good job. The restaurant recently received the prestigious *Mobil Travel Guide* Five-Star Award for the 11th consecutive year. The *Miami Herald* restaurant critic awarded Café Chauveron top honors with four stars, the highest amount possible.

On a menu offering *"La Cuisine Francaise pour les Gourmets,"* these are the most popular items: Imported Dover Sole *Bonne Femme ou Sautée ou Grillee,* Red Snapper *Roti Beurre Blanc* and Fennel, *Les Belles Cailles Roties en Cocotte Flambees au Cognac* (when game is in season), and *Le Roi Faisan a la Mode du Maitre Perigourdin.*

The favorites among a lengthy list of tempting desserts are the *Mousse au Chocolate du Chef* with Sabayon Sauce and the three different soufflés—Chauveron, Grand Marnier, or Chocolate. These must be ordered at the beginning of the meal.

The restaurant itself is not as beautiful as the commanding view of the bay from its main dining room. The terraced dining room has a bar on a higher level; the dining tables here also have a nice view. André is spending time and money in beautifying the restaurant; in 1986 the color scheme will be changed to French blue with touches of apricot and the chairs will be replaced with ones in French Provincial style.

André is proud of the prestige his father achieved with his restaurants in New York and with Café Chauveron here in Florida. When his father died a few years ago, André was determined to keep up the standards that won this restaurant so many honors. Only Lutèce in New York, Ernie's in San Francisco, and La Maisonette in Cincinnati have received the *Mobil* guide's Five-Star Award more times than Café Chauveron.

One of André's fondest stories is about a couple who recently celebrated a wedding anniversary in his restaurant. They had first visited Café Chauveron in New York in 1962 and told André that nothing had changed, that everything was now as they recalled it had been in 1962. That, to André, is even more reassuring than a critic's stars.

FORT LAUDERDALE

Le Dome of The Four Seasons

333 Sunset Drive
Fort Lauderdale
Florida 33301
Telephone: 305–463–3303

All major credit cards
Dinner at 6 P.M. only
Reservations required
Jacket required
Liquor served
Dinner: $14 to $35
full 3 courses, without wine
Chef: Alain "Vincent" Barrere
Maitre d'/Proprietor: John Carlone

This penthouse restaurant, opened since January 1964, is one of the most elegant and distinguished in Florida. Situated atop the Four Seasons apartment building, which was purchased by Calvin Houghland in 1962, Le Dome is the product of one man's vision. Houghland, of Nashville, Tennessee and Fort Lauderdale, is a businessman, rancher, and international sportsman who likes the best. With an eye toward opening a restaurant of his own, he conducted a survey of the great restaurants of Europe; after a year and a half spent analyzing the results, planning, construction, and decoration, Le Dome was opened.

The view from the top of the condominium building is a panorama of Fort Lauderdale, the Intercoastal Waterway which flows by the building at its base, and the Atlantic Ocean. The food is also a highlight—Le Dome continues to receive honors and awards for what it calls "California Nouvelle Cuisine," among them the Golden Spoon Award and Four Stars from the *Mobil* guide.

The tasteful decor is by one of the country's leading designers, Wells M. Squier, of Fort Lauderdale. Most attractive is the enhancement of the interior by the display of original art. Five of the oil paintings are by Mrs. Houghland; others are contributions from the French artist Jean George Vibert from the Jay Gould collection; Gerard Ellis, who painted for the royal family of England; B. Delaroche, another French artist; Robert Curran Smith, of Orlando, Florida; and Jolie Gabor, mother of Zsa Zsa and Eva.

LAKE WALES

Chalet Suzanne Restaurant and Country Inn

P.O. Drawer AC
US Route 27 and 17A
Lake Wales
Florida 33859–9003
Telephone: 813–676–6011

All major credit cards
Breakfast, lunch, and dinner
Reservations preferred
Jacket preferred
Liquor served
Dinner: $33 to $43
6 courses, without wine
Lunch: $18 to $26
Chef: Carl Hinshaw
Hostess: Vita Hinshaw

This is a magnificent and imaginative hodgepodge of architecture housing an exuberant place to eat. You first realize you have a unique experience in store for you when you see the driveway to the inn, which meanders through orange groves leading to the restaurant on the edge of Lake Suzanne. You can't believe what you see! Turret-topped and rambling, this complex of buildings is painted in various pastels and features a mosaic-bordered pool, a French patio overlooking it, and much decorative wrought iron. There is also a 2,450-feet-long air strip nearby. Why so much variety? Simple—the Hinshaw family likes to feel that this inn reflects the diversity of the world at large.

The dining room is a delight, not only with its antiques, stained glass, and old lamps, but in its unique setting of quaint rooms on many levels. Just as no two rooms are alike, no two tables are set alike. Dinner is by candlelight, and fresh flowers are on every table.

The cuisine has been saluted with four stars from the *Mobil* guide and a Golden Spoon Award. Among the dishes featured are Broiled Grapefruit, Soup Romaine, Chicken Suzanne, Lobster Newburg, Shrimp Curry, Lump Crab, Shad Roe, Lamb Chop Grill, Filet Mignon, and, for dessert, *Gateau Christina*. This is down to earth, good, and substantial food.

MIAMI

The Cove

Miami Airport Hilton and Marina
5101 Blue Lagoon Drive
Miami
Florida 33126
Telephone: 305–262–1000 Ext. 67

All major credit cards
Lunch and dinner
Reservations required
Jacket not required
Liquor served
Dinner: $13.95 to $21.95
full 3 courses, without wine
Lunch: $4.95 to $8.95
Chef: Stephen Sappe
Maitre d': Bruce Ahart

The Cove

The Cove dining room at this airport/marina hotel has two views to delight its guests: interior and exterior. In fact, the view created within the dining room has received national recognition—the Cove was awarded the 1984 Designer Circle Award from *Lodging and Hospitality* magazine and the 1984 Table Top Award.

The decor of the dining room blends grays with real blues, accented by shades of shrimp. These colors form the muted backdrop for the Cove's featured item—a striking 1,000 gallon aquarium containing brightly colored tropical fish living in coral water. A large pastel painting in a single acrylic frame dramatically reinforces the ocean theme.

The exterior view complements the decor. Tiered levels within the dining room offer guests at every table breathtaking views of the Blue Lagoon: a delightful view to dine by.

The cuisine features some of Florida's most popular seafood, from Florida lobster and stone crabs to the more delicate flavors of pompano and swordfish. For the landlubber, Veal Princess and *Tournedos* Lichtenstein are on the menu. Other popular main dishes include Pompano *Francaise,* Minted Shrimp, and Scallops *Ticconese.*

Highlighting the spectacular dessert display are two favorites—Macadamia Pie and Chocolate Rum Cake. There is a new wine bar in the dining room.

MIAMI BEACH

Dominique's Restaurant

Alexander Hotel
5225 Collins Avenue
Miami Beach
Florida 33140
Telephone: 305–865–6500

All major credit cards
Lunch and dinner
Reservations suggested
Jacket requested
Liquor served
Dinner: $25 to $50
  full 3 courses, without wine
Owner: Dominique D'Ermo
Food and Beverage Director: Henry Sillman

Dominique's famous French restaurant at the Alexander Hotel on Miami Beach shares the name of its sister restaurant in Washington, D.C., long regarded as one of the capital city's best. The elegant main dining room in the Florida restaurant, filled with antiques and original artwork, overlooks the Atlantic Ocean and the lush gardens of the Alexander Hotel.

Dominique's

The restaurant is well appointed inside as well. From the sumptuous Renaissance Lounge on the mezzanine level, a glassed-in promenade walkway winds through tropical gardens, past a pair of antique brass gates and other treasures, ending at a striking marble foyer framed by intricate stained and beveled glass panels and a finely carved Victorian bench with ormolu embellishment.

To the left is Dominique's Lounge, an intimate spot for before- or after-dinner cocktails. To the right is the elegant main dining room, with bay windows overlooking a bubbling fountain and a meandering brook leading to cascades that tumble over coral grottoes into two lagoon swimming pools. Immediately beyond is a wide expanse of white sand beach and the Atlantic Ocean.

The decor blends soft tones of pink, deep burgundy, Hunter green, and beiges to complement the Alexander's lush tropical landscaping, creating a pleasant backdrop for Dominique's exquisite antique furnishings. Among the treasures in the dining room are an ornate clock, a lion sculpture, columns with a fruit motif carved in England (circa 1870), a turn-of-the-century piano with burled and inlaid wood detailing, and intricate

172   *Florida*

coffered paneling. Smoked mirrors create a *faux* balcony effect on three sides of the dining room, accentuated by provincial open chandeliers. Original oil paintings cover the walls; Oriental carpets are on the parquet floor.

The cuisine is also a major attraction. To ensure its reputation for freshness and quality, Dominique's flies in much of its produce and game directly from Dominique D'Ermo's estate on the eastern Shore of Maryland.

Dominique's fare often tends toward the exotic. Among the current unusual seasonal offerings are Buffalo Sausages, Diamondback Rattlesnake Salad, and Alligator Tail, all served as dinner appetizers. Those with less adventurous appetites shouldn't worry about finding enough on the menu to satisfy; Dominique's has exquisite conventional fare as well.

First course choices include *Quail Pâté en Brioche* with Raspberry Sauce, Shrimp with Ginger Sauce, and U.S. Senate Dining Room Bean Soup. Entrées include Grilled Salmon with Watercress and Dill Sauce (the house specialty), Marinated Rack of Lamb, prime New York Sirloin Steak stuffed with Escargots and Garlic Butter, and Veal Scallopini.

The desserts are a sight to behold. The Blackout Cake is at least six inches high, adorned with a thick, rich chocolate butter cream. Another tempting dessert, which combines chocolate-dribbled whipped cream with chocolate truffles, is named in honor of Farrah Fawcett and Elizabeth Taylor.

ORLANDO

Atlantis
Wyndham Hotel Sea World
6677 Sea Harbor Drive
Orlando
Florida 32821
Telephone: 305–351–5555

All major credit cards
Dinner
Reservations required
Jacket required
Liquor served
Dinner: $25 to $45
 full 3 courses, without wine
Chef: Michel Paton
Maitre d': Ralph Rendsland

The Atlantis Restaurant, the gourmet restaurant for Wyndham Hotel Sea World, is a pleasant surprise. Located just off the spectacular 65,000 square foot atrium/lobby—said to be the world's largest—of the new luxurious Wyndham Hotel Sea World in Orlando, the Atlantis offers the ultimate in elegance and has drawn rave reviews for its French nouvelle cuisine ever since the hotel and restaurant opened in December 1984.

At Atlantis the diners sit amid a lush decor of rich wood paneling, crystal chandeliers, fine European oil paintings, and warm-colored walls and furniture. A touch of Florida is provided by three large ceiling murals with tropical themes, painted by Dallas artist William A. Foley. Outside the restaurant is an astounding view—the hotel's spectacular atrium and lobby, which combined is longer and wider than a football field and features soaring palms, lush tropical foliage, a variety of shops, exotic Japanese Koi fish swimming in a large pond, and waterfall-filled pools.

The food is splendid and well-presented. Everything starts with a small portion of an *amusegueule,* which translated means "a bit of something to amuse the mouth." It might be, for example, Scallop Mousse with Oysters and Mussels in a suave sauce.

Other starters include Lobster and Truffle Bisque, Avocado Mousse with CrabMeat, and Assorted Leaf Lettuces adorned with goat cheese on tender toast points.

Some of the fine main dishes are Sliced Breast of Duck with Wine Sauce and Mango, Medallions of Spring Lamb, and Red Snapper Wrapped in Romaine Lettuce. Most expensive and delightful is the Lobster Mousse in Ravioli with Sliced Lobster Tail and Truffles.

The desserts are a threat to any diet and present a tough choice. Here are just a few of the favorites: Dacquoise Cake, Chocolate Mousse Cake, Bavarian Cream Cake topped with pears, and Raspberry Sauce over Strawberry and Almond Pastry—great!

Atlantis maitre d' Rendsland tells of the time that Bob Hope entered the gourmet dining room through the kitchen because of security reasons, much to the delight of the staff members, who gave him such a warm and enthusiastic greeting that Hope autographed everyone's chef's hat before going into the dining room.

Haifeng Restaurant

Wyndham Hotel Sea World
6677 Sea Harbor Drive
Orlando
Florida 32821
Telephone: 305–351–5555

All major credit cards
Dinner
Reservations necessary
Jacket requested
Liquor served
Chef: Danny Chu
Maitre d': Philip Yu

Like the Atlantis, this restaurant is located off the immense Wyndham Hotel Sea World lobby. Haifeng serves imaginatively prepared oriental food in a sophisticated setting.

The restaurant is uniquely decorated in neutral shades of gray and black to help set off the subtle yet powerful water color paintings on rice paper by the Chinese artist Li Shan, whose work also hangs in the Great Hall of the People in Peking.

A large glass window separating the restaurant from the kitchen provides an interesting view to dine by, that of the chefs at work.

A popular dining place, Haifeng's celebrity guests have included Bob Hope, Winnie Palmer (wife of the golfing great Arnold Palmer), actress Beverly Garland, a recent Miss Florida, and others.

PORT ST. LUCIE

The Brass Sandpiper Restaurant

The Sandpiper Bay Resort Hotel & Marina
Port St. Lucie
Florida 33452
Telephone: 305–335–4400

All major credit cards
Breakfast, lunch, dinner, and Sunday brunch
Reservations requested
Jacket requested
Liquor served
Dinner: $17 to $25
full 3 courses, without wine
Lunch: $8 to $12
Chef: Francois Peter
Maitre d': Allan Davis

The beautiful Brass Sandpiper Restaurant of the Sandpiper Bay Resort Hotel and Marina offers its guests luxurious dining in a room with massive wooden beams, a cathedral ceiling, a fine tapestry, and best of all, picture windows overlooking the waters of the mile-wide St. Lucie River.

This is the restaurant of a luxury resort, and as such it features an international cuisine, a daily change of menu, a choice of a dozen hot and cold appetizers, the freshest seafood, prime aged meats, crisp salads, vegetables—and, for dessert, scrumptuous soufflés.

Friday night a bountiful seafood buffet is featured, and on Sunday the brunch is generous and picturesque.

Among the favorites on the menu are the Mesquite-Grilled Fish as a main course, and, as desserts, Key Lime Pie and Mud Pie.

The cuisine won the 1985 Silver Spoon Award from the Gourmet Diners Club of America.

Port St. Lucie is an hour from the Palm Beach International Airport and two hours north of Miami. To reach Sandpiper Bay, take exit 54 at Port St. Lucie off the Florida Turnpike.

HAWAII
HONOLULU

La Mer

Halekulani Hotel
2199 Kalia Road
Honolulu
Hawaii 96815
Telephone: 808–923–2311

All major credit cards
Dinner and Sunday brunch
Reservations necessary
Jacket required
Liquor served
Dinner: $40 to $65
full 3 courses, without wine
Chef: Khamtan Tanhchaleun
Maitre d': Michael Flickinger

La Mer at the Halekulani Hotel ranks among Hawaii's finest restaurant; in fact, a recent review in the *Wall Street Journal* said that it is generally regarded by food experts as the best in Honolulu. That's saying a lot, for there are a number of very good restaurants in Honolulu and nearby Waikiki.

Creative French cuisine is offered nightly, along with spectacular views of the sea of Waikiki and the famous trademark of the area, Diamond Head rock.

The menus change weekly, with specialties including Fresh Duck Liver pâté, Island fish, and a spectacular strawberry dessert. Many of these dishes are the creations of consulting chef Philippe Chavent from Lyon, France, who visits La Mer at least three times a year. In exchange, Chef Tanhchaleun, in late 1985, went to Lyon for three weeks to work and observe in Philippe's La Tour Rose.

Meals are elegant here. A selection of items, from start to finish, will give you the picture: for appetizers, there are Prawn Bisque with Saffron and Scallions, Fresh Duck Liver Terrino, and Warm Spinach Salad with Sesame Prawns. Medallions of Lobster with Asparagus and Lobster Sauce, Sautéed Moana with Curry Sauce, Sautéed Makinnah Steak with Ginger and Lime Sauce, Beef Tenderloin with Sweet Bell Pepper Sauce, Breast of Duck with Green Peppercorn Sauce, and Medallions of Veal with Garlic Sauce and Snow Peas are just a few of the entrées. For dessert try a Strawberry Sunburst or Chocolate Mousse Cake—or pastries and fruits from the dessert cart.

The Willows

901 Hausten Street
Honolulu
Hawaii 96826
Telephone: 808–946–4808

All major credit cards
Lunch and dinner
Reservation suggested, particularly
    for the Kamaaina Suite
Dress: casual, but neat
Dinner: $15 to $35
    full 3 courses, without wine
Lunch: the same
Executive chef: Kusuma Cooray

The Willows is one of Hawaii's oldest and most popular restaurants; located in Moiiliili, a short ride from Waikiki, it has been in operation for more than forty years. The restaurant is made up of thatched cabanas which surround the main attraction—the koi-filled ponds where the *alii* (royalty) came to bathe. Tropical gardens add a wonderful touch.

The Willows offers award-winning cuisine, the preparation of which is supervised by Cordon Bleu-trained executive chef Cooray, a native of Sri Lanka. The cuisine blends the finest Eastern and Western ingredients.

Our favorite room to dine in is the Kamaaina Suite, a quiet, private dining room on the second floor of a building in the gardens overlooking the ponds. It has only a few tables and its special price-fixed menu is truly the *pièce de resistance* of the entire place.

Whether at dinner or brunch, the strolling musicians at the Willows are most entertaining. Lunchtime is very popular here, especially on Thursdays when an event called "Poi Thursday" is hosted by Auntie Irmgard Aluli and her Puama Trio. The show features dancers and singers and guests are invited to join in.

There are so many popular items on the menu that it is difficult to select just a few.

But some favorites include Sri Lankan Curry, using Chef Cooray's personal recipe, prepared with either fresh island chicken or shrimp; traditional Hawaiian Curry, rich with coconut cream and made with a choice of chicken, shrimp, or fresh vegetables; and Pacific Salmon, enhanced with a delicate seafood mousseline and an herb *beurre blanc*.

Among the appetizers, Chef Cooray's signature Spinach Timbale (a light spinach mousse topped with cheese sauce), *Lomi* Salmon and *Poi* (a Hawaiian favorite), and Angel Hair Pasta with prosciutto ham are fine choices.

The dessert menu at the Willows is a real challenge. One favorite is the coconut or lemon Sky High Pie with many inches of meringue. Another is Chef Cooray's chocolate *Gateau,* topped with chantilly cream—truly one of the world's best chocolate cakes! There are special desserts on holidays. At Thanksgiving, for example, you can order Pink Chiffon Pumpkin Pie with meringue!

Other desserts to ponder are Chocolate-*Haupia* Cake (dream cake with a layer of Hawaiian coconut pudding and a creamy mocha filling), Sinless Cheesecake, A Thing of Beauty (a deep chocolate confection in a macadamia-graham crust), Black Forest Crêpes (vanilla ice cream in homemade crepes topped with hot Bing cherries, whipped cream, and grated chocolate), and Sunny Lee's Guava Glue Sundae (a light fresh guava purée over macadamia nut ice cream). The *Nawiliwli* and *Keoki* coffees are very special, too.

The cuisine here has won the *Travel/Holiday* Magazine Award and the Golden Fork Award from the International Society of Food, Travel, and Wine Writers. *Gourmet* magazine has featured its Hawaiian food recipes. The *Poi* suppers and lunches offer local people and visitors a chance to sample native cuisine including *laulau,* sweet potato, chicken luau, *pipi kaula, lomi* salmon, fresh *poi, limu kohu,* Hawaiian rock salt, green onion, fresh pineapple, and *haupia.*

Windows of Hawaii

1441 Kapiolani Boulevard
Honolulu
Hawaii 96814
Telephone: 808-941-9138

All major credit cards
Breakfast, lunch, dinner,
 and late supper
Reservations recommended
Jacket not required
Liquor served
Dinner: $9 to $24
 full 3 courses, without wine
Lunch: $6 to $12
Chef: James Craig
Maitre d': Rory Horning

Twenty-five years ago, when this restaurant was opened under the name of La Ronde, it was the first revolving restaurant in America. It was a unique delight for visitors to Hawaii, for while dining they were able to see all of Honolulu and Waikiki.

Both the restaurant and the view have changed considerably. The restaurant is now called Windows of Hawaii and has just opened after being completely refurbished. Gone are the old, worn, cumbersome, space-consuming brown naugahyde dining booths that partially blocked the beautiful view, and the dull, drab, dark brown walls are now covered with a colorful Wyland mural called *Dolphin Heaven* which depicts dolphins and other beautiful sea creatures from the Hawaiian waters, some of which (not the dolphins!) are served at the restaurant.

The view is also better than ever because you can see more of it more easily. Located atop a building in one of the world's largest shopping centers, the restaurant offers a full view of the mountains, the Ala Wai boat harbor, the Ala Moana Beach Park, downtown Honolulu, and Waikiki, all dominated by Diamond Head. There are more skyscraper hotels and office buildings to see, but much to our surprise, these do not destroy the beauty of the view.

The food has improved, too. There's good reason: Windows of Hawaii's fish buyer has been buying fish for a long time and he personally knows the operators of all the major fishing boats working out of the island of Oahu. The restaurant has a perfect view of the sea and the harbors so the fish buyer can make sightings to determine when the fishing ships are coming in.

Lunch is popular at Windows on Hawaii because of a novel presentation called the "seawich" (which could just as easily be named the "crabwich," since it has a liberal offering of crab), which is served with the pleasant locally grown Manoa lettuce and slices of tasty wine-ripened tomato. The other sandwiches include roast beef, steak, sweet ham, chicken salad, tuna, and fresh fish. Lunch is served Monday through Friday from 11 A.M. until 2 P.M.

Dinner is our favorite time here. The spectacular sunsets turn the sky into a patchwork quilt of oranges, pinks, and magentas. And later you see the silvery glow of the moon on the tranquil ocean. Dinner offers a choice of appetizers such as shrimp and crableg cocktails, fettucine, sashimi, or escargots. The soups are special, including a zesty Portuguese bean soup, Queen's Seafood Chowder, or the favorite—Chef James' French Onion Soup. Among the classic entrée choices are Roast Prime Rib of Beef, Chateaubriand, Steak Kabobs, or Tarragon Veal Scaloppine. The fish is fresh and the meats are cut each day. There is also a choice of New England cuisine. Only fresh vegetables are served. Dinner is served from 5 P.M. until 10 P.M. On Saturdays and Sundays from 10 A.M. until 2 P.M. a continuous champagne and wine buffet is served. On Thursdays, Fridays, and Saturdays from 10 P.M. until midnight, moonlight suppers are served for the after-show people.

About half the patrons of Windows on Hawaii are tourists; the rest are local people. You can park just below the restaurant, or if it is easier, just take a number eight bus from any place in Waikiki and you'll be let off nearby.

Windows of Hawaii holds 350 people and is over 400 feet high, revolving 360 degrees each hour, at a rate of 3.5 feet per minute.

MAUI

Swan Court

Hyatt Regency Maui
200 Nohea Kai Drive
Lahaina, Maui
Hawaii 96761
Telephone: 808–667–7474

All major credit cards
Breakfast and dinner
Reservations necessary
Jacket not required
Liquor served
Dinner: $18 to $28
    full 3 courses, without wine
Chef: Harry Gabel
Maitre d': Ed Brea

Imagine selecting one of the most beautiful natural shoreline sites on the warm, dry side of Maui and planning every inch of 18.5 acres of beachfront land to create a resort complex of exceptional accommodations and services so fanciful and spectacular that everyone who sees it is awed and captivated by both the natural and the manmade beauty.

Christopher B. Hemmeter turned $80 million into the Hyatt Regency Maui resort on magnificent Kaanapali Beach. Part of the reason so much money was spent is that some astounding feats were required. For instance, in creating the grounds and the setting for a half-acre swimming pool and more than a mile of streams, lagoons, seven spectacular waterfalls, grottoes, and a genuine Swan Lake, Hemmeter brought to Maui 22,000 square feet of artificial lava rock made by a firm in Irvine, California, at a cost of $1 million, and combined it with 10,000 tons of the local lava rock. Some would say this is the classic instance of someone bringing coal to Newcastle. Why was this done? Because Hemmeter felt that the local stuff wasn't good enough; the edges were too sharp and the rock too coarse for his future guests to be able to climb and sit on comfortably.

There's more. A collection of art valued at over $2 million is scattered throughout the gardens, along with 38 different varieties of trees, 40 types of shrubs, and 23 different kinds of ground cover plants and vines. The art collection is also scattered through the atrium lobby, which is open to the sky, and in the corridors of the main floor as well.

The view to dine by in the Swan Court is superb. One entire side of this candlelighted restaurant is actually a 30 foot-high opening on the edge of manmade Swan Lake. The lake is fed by three waterfalls, and there is a graceful Japanese bridge at the far end. As you listen to soft piano music and dine on your selections from the Continental menu (which also features some delightful Hawaiian variations), you will most likely experience the ultimate in satisfaction.

Among the specialties are Fresh Island *Eichenholz* (fillet of fish baked on a plate of oak wood) and Veal Cutlet *aux Morilles.* For dessert, look at the cart and decide, or do as we did: order the large, luscious strawberries, glazed and then dipped in rich dark chocolate.

During the day, the Swan Court is open until 11 A.M. for breakfast. And what a breakfast! Even compared with the massive breakfast buffet spreads we saw in Scandinavia, the offerings here surpass anything we've seen both in quantity and richness. Not only are there many varieties of danish and other kinds of breakfast pastries and breads, but there is also a wide assortment of everything else—eggs, sausages, bacon, fruits, yogurt with all the toppings, cereals (including a Swiss cold cereal mixed with fresh fruits), and even miso soup.

We'll let a quote from the menu summarize our feelings for this view to dine by experience: "With regal bearing and white downy plumage, the swan is a creature of legend, a symbol of fragile, ethereal beauty. We think of swans on still lakes beside Rhine castles. . . . With the species Mute Swan and Australian Black Swan, the Hyatt Regency Maui celebrates these wonderous creatures at Swan Court."

ILLINOIS
CHICAGO

Ciel Bleu

Mayfair Regent
181 East Lake Shore Drive
Chicago
Illinois 60611
Telephones: 312–951–2864 or 787–8500

All major credit cards
Breakfast, lunch, and dinner
Reservations requested
Jacket required
Liquor served
Dinner: $40 to $50
    full 3 courses, without wine
Lunch: $17 to $22
Chef: Dominique Fortin
Maitre d': Pierre Robert

Ciel Bleu

This beautiful dining spot is on the 19th floor of the elegant Mayfair Regent Hotel, overlooking Lake Michigan, and only a few steps away from what is called "The Magnificent Mile" along the lake and the elegant Tower Place shopping and residential complex.

The restaurant's dominant feature is the view, which can be enjoyed from just about any seat. Try to sit next to the massive windows lining the eastern and northern walls. Somehow these give you the feeling of floating above the city. To the east, neighboring buildings stand out in sharp relief against the background of Lake Michigan. To the north is an urban landscape: Lake Shore Drive, Chicago's scenic highway, curving gently into the distance with luxury high rises marking the way as far as the eye can see. To the east lies parkland, beach, and shoreline, the huge expanse of the lake giving a sense of infinite distance. Stretching to the north, the clear, crisp lines of the city begin to blur, and the color blends into a soft blue haze.

The view at night—twinkling lights of the skyline, streaks of white and red from the lights of the automobiles on the drive, and street lights illuminating the park and the shoreline—is also very exciting.

Ciel Bleu offers Continental cuisine. It is open for breakfast from 7 A.M. until 10:30 A.M. (when some businesspeople meet to start the day), for lunch from 11:30 A.M. until 2 P.M., and for dinner beginning at 6 P.M., with the last sitting at 9:30 P.M.

The decor of Ciel Bleu, which means blue sky, enhances the view. It has soft rose floral-pattern table linens, fine lead crystal stemware, fine silver and china, and beautiful Palladian style mirrors along the wall reflecting everything inside and out.

Pat Bruno, food critic for the *Chicago Sun-Times,* has said, "the food is more than a match for the view," and awarded it a maximum four stars. Praise has come from other quarters as well—in 1981, the "Outstanding Dinner of the Year" award from *Chaine de Rotisseurs,* and, in 1984, the "Dinner of the Year" title from the International Wine and Food Society of Chicago. Among the esteemed entrées are Veal Medallion with Morel Mushroom Sauce and Albufira Rice, Ragout of Lobster and Sole with Vegetables covered with Tarragon-Lobster Sauce, and Sautéed Fresh Goose Liver with Mache Salad. Among the desserts are White Chocolate Mousse Cake with Raspberry *Coulis* and *Le Feuillette* of Fresh Berries in Caramel Cream Sauce.

The guests are as varied as the cuisine. Of course, the leading businesspeople come here, as do nearby residents of the elegant waterfront buildings. There are also out-of-towners, from all parts of the United States, and many parts of the world.

The Pinnacle

Holiday Inn Lake Shore
644 Lake Shore Drive
Chicago
Illinois 60611
Telephone: 312-943-0653

All major credit cards
Dinner
Reservations necessary
Jacket required
Liquor served
Dinner: $15 to $25
  full 3 courses, without wine
Chef: Glen Brittingham
Maitre d': Pedro Rodriguez

The Pinnacle atop the Holiday Inn Lake Shore on Chicago's famous Gold Coast is the city's only revolving rooftop restaurant.

While dining in the glass-enclosed restaurant at softly-lighted tables enhanced by richly appointed burgundy velvet decor and crystal chandeliers, it is possible to enjoy a gourmet meal and vintage wines while at the same time experiencing a breathtaking view of the Chicago skyline. The picture-postcard scene encompasses the twinkling lights and architectural brilliance of the Loop's corporate skyscrapers, thirty-five miles of Chicago's lakeside beach bordered by the elegant apartment buildings that dominate Chicago's legendary Lake Shore Drive, colorful yachts and sailboats anchored in Burnham and Delmont Harbors, and notable Chicago landmarks such as Grant Park and its majestic Buckingham Fountain, the Navy Pier, McCormick Place, and more.

This plushly carpeted dining room seats up to 180 people and makes a full rotation each hour. All diners, no matter where they are seated, have a panoramic view through the floor-to-ceiling windows that wrap this spacious room. There are even tables set on the perimeter of the revolving area, at windowside, for those who do not want to be on a moving platform. Piano music helps create a pleasant atmosphere during dinner. Among the main dishes served here are Shrimp *De Jonghe,* Steak Diane, *Filet Mignon Cordon Rouge,* Rack of Lamb (for two), and an assortment of fresh fish that changes daily.

The Pinnacle

LOUISIANA
NEW ORLEANS

Commander's Palace

1403 Washington Avenue
  at Coliseum Street
New Orleans
Louisiana 70130
Telephone: 504–899–8221

All major credit cards
Lunch and dinner every day,
  breakfast Saturday and Sunday
Reservations recommended
Jacket required
Liquor served
Dinner: $23 to $29
  full 3 courses, without wine
Lunch: $10 to $17
Chef: Emeril Lagasse
Maitre d': George Rico

What constitutes the best view here is in dispute. Some feel that this fine old 1880 restaurant and its building in the heart of the New Orleans Garden District is the primary thing of beauty. Others feel that the view of the interior dining court, by candlelight at night, is the more enchanting. We like both.

The structure of Commander's Palace is Victorian, with a turret, columns, and lots of gingerbread, painted bright turquoise with a crisp white trim. In 1880, Emile Commander established the only restaurant patronized by the distinguished families of the Garden District, the famed part of the city where George W. Cable entertained Mark Twain and where Jefferson Davis spent his last days. Mr. Commander chose the corner of Washington Avenue and Coliseum Street, a site that had once been a part of the J.F.E. Livaudais Plantation and later was the *faubourg* of Lafayette (which was subsequently engulfed by the westward expansion of the city of New Orleans in 1854). By 1900, Commander's Palace, fully a part of a bustling metropolis, was attracting gourmets from around the world.

It was during the twenties, under different management, that Commander's developed what might be called a spicier reputation. River-boat captains frequented the place, and sporting gentlemen brought their beautiful "ladies" for a rendezvous in the private dining rooms upstairs. Downstairs, however, the main dining room, with its separate entrance, was maintained as a place of impeccable respectability for family meals after church and for other special occasions.

The present owners, Ella, Dottie, Dick, and John Brennan, took over in 1974 and gave the splendid old landmark a new look. They decided to design rooms and settings indoors which complemented and enhanced the lovely outdoor setting—the deep green garden in back and the lovely patio with its fountain—creating an ambience that played up the sunlight and the garden atmosphere of the restaurant's setting. Walls were torn out and replaced with walls of glass, inviting the views to become part of the decor. Paintings were commissioned for each room to specially suit each one's particular color and design.

Commander's cuisine combines the best of the New Orleans Creole heritage with the creative concepts of modern cooking. Everything is as fresh as it can possibly be: seafood, meats, fruits, and vegetables. Among our favorites from a large and elaborate menu are, to start, Oyster Dome Soup, then Veal Chop Tchoupitoulas or Soft Shell Crabs Charone, and, for dessert, a Bread Pudding Soufflé.

Every Saturday and Sunday there's Commander's Jazz Brunch, with muted jazz played throughout the restaurant by Alvin Alcorn, an old-time jazz great, and his groups. It's a festive atmosphere, with balloons everywhere and a special Jazz Brunch menu. Generous portions of everything are featured.

Le Jardin

The Westin Canal Place
100 Rue Iberville
New Orleans
Louisiana 70130
Telephone: 504–566–7006

All major credit cards
Dinner
Reservations necessary
Jacket required
Liquor served
Dinner: $25 to $35
*   full 3 courses, without wine*
Chef: Edward Fitzpatrick
Maitre d': Manual Estrada

Here, in what had opened in 1984 as the Hotel Iberville but is now known as the Westin Canal Place, is a restaurant with one of the best views of New Orleans, situated on the 11th floor of the building which towers above New Orleans's shopping complex, Canal Place.

Called Le Jardin, this restaurant is an elegant room blending the styles of Victorian England and Frank Lloyd Wright, with spans of golden wood, sparkling marble, china-filled hutches, brocade-backed chairs, and palm-filled Chinese urns. Le Jardin is more like a European dining salon than a garden.

The most exciting part of the decor is the splendid view of the Mississippi River through the vast spread of glass that surrounds the dining room on two sides; the glass wall continues, unobstructed, through the full length of the lobby of the hotel. Adding to the dinner charm is soft piano music, the fashionably dressed guests, and the tuxedoed waiters.

Le Jardin's cuisine is a blend of modern and traditional French. Among the delightful entrées are Lobster Thermidor, Fillet of Dover Sole marinated in raspberry vinegar and hazelnut oil on a *coulis* of fresh papaya, and Fillet of Beef baked in pastry with Bearnaise and Bordelaise sauces lightly applied.

The desserts are grand! The three favorites, in order of popularity (according to Chef Fitzpatrick), are Pecan Cheesecake, Praline Soufflé, and *Creme Brulée au Chocolat.*

Afternoon tea, or a bit of caviar and champagne, are available at Chic Celebration, the lobby lounge. A violin and harp are played at tea time, and music from a grand piano can be heard in the evening.

Kabby's Seafood Restaurant and Bar

Riverside and Towers
The New Orleans Hilton
Poydras at the Mississippi River
New Orleans
Louisiana 70140
Telephone: 504–561–0500 Ext. 3660

All major credit cards
Lunch and dinner
Reservations not required
Jacket not required
Liquor served
Dinner: $10 to $15
    full 3 courses, without wine
Lunch: $5 to $8
Chef: Louis Jesowshek
Maitre d': Richard Frische

With a 200-foot window that runs the full length of Kabby's Seafood Restaurant, the view of the Mississippi from here is spectacular. Most views, including that of the Rain Forest in the same hotel, look down the river at the crescent bend. Kabby's view looks toward the bridge and upriver, offering great views of the various kinds of cargo and passenger boats that ply this famed waterway.

The restaurant got its name from Lester D. Kabacoff, who developed the riverfront from an old warehouse district into the bustling riverfront it is today. "Kabby" and a few other city leaders are primarily responsible for helping the people of New Orleans rediscover the beauty of the majestic Mississippi River.

Featured on the menu are clams from the Atlantic, Maine Lobster, shrimp, oysters, crabs, and crayfish from local bayous and lakes across the country. Traditional New Orleans-style dishes such as jambalaya, etoufée, and gumbo are also featured, as well as shark. One favorite is Blackened Redfish; for dessert we recommend the Mississippi Mud Cake.

The 190-foot *Creole Queen,* the newest paddlewheel boat on the river, is now docked alongside the Riverside building and is said to be the "people's favorite" part of the view.

The interior of Kabby's is worth seeing, too. It has the largest stained-glass bar canopy in the United States; designed by Gordon Bender, it measures 20 feet in diameter. The ceiling is New-Orleans style antique bronze, and the floor is of mosaic tile. The restaurant has other interesting features as well, including a bubbling fountain at its entrance, custom-designed lamp posts and wrought-iron accessories, and a floor made of 100-year-old pine.

The Rainforest

Rooftop of
The New Orleans Hilton
Poydras at the Mississippi River
New Orleans
Louisiana 70140
Telephone: 504–561–0500
          Ext. RAIN (7246)

All major credit cards
Lunch
Reservations not required
Jacket not required
Liquor served
Lunch: $5 to $8
Chef: Kathy Vogel
Maitre d': Dawn Marino

We find this view down the Mississippi River one of our favorites, taking in the crescent-shaped bend in the river and the old French Quarter of the city. Sometimes you find yourself so enchanted by the view you forget to eat.

The Rainforest used to be a place for evening dancing, but now it is also open for lunch, and the management has done something very interesting with that. Featured is something called the Prudent Diet, "a creation of the Hilton Chef under the guidelines of the American Heart Association. The Prudent Diet is a well-balanced buffet comprised of low-fat, reduced-sodium, low-cholesterol, low-calorie, and high-fiber selections." Among the items to be discovered are Indonesian Gado Gado, Ricotta Lasagna, Romaine and Radish Salad, Yogurt Mint Soup, Tabouli, Broiled Tofu with Mirin Sauce, and Tofutti.

This restaurant, located on the 29th floor, is a welcome respite from the excitement of New Orleans. But not for long—as darkness falls, it too becomes part of the city pulse, with cocktails, dancing, and the lights of the city and the river becoming positively electric.

MAINE
KENNEBUNKPORT

Olde Grist Mill

1 Mill Lane
Kennebunkport
Maine 04046
Telephone: 207–967–4781/5670

All major credit cards
Dinner
Reservations necessary
Jacket not required
Liquor served
Dinner: $11 to $25
          full 3 courses, without wine
Chef: Marco P. Ramirez
Owner and Maitre d':
          David F. Lombard

Although it hardly looks like a fortress, the Olde Grist Mill was used by natives of the "Port" as a temporary redoubt against hostile Indians some 200 years ago. Except for the addition of some replacement shingles, a cupola, and minor repairs, the Mill is the same as it was then.

The present owner, Dave Lombard, told us that his mother bought the mill from her father in 1940. Dave has been running the restaurant since 1965, so this is, to quote him, "probably the longest-running business in southern Maine that is owned and operated by the same family."

The building was placed on the Register of Historic Buildings in 1973 and is the *only* tide-water (operated on the change of height of the tidal waters) grist mill in the nation. Old mills and millstones are becoming a rarity. The Olde Grist Mill is on a little estuary about a half-mile above the Kennebunk River; it is picturesquely weatherbeaten and situated on the edge of a small stream where the inflowing waters of the river are imprisoned by a dam. This mill had ground corn unceasingly for more than two centuries and had been in full operation until recent years.

The interior has changed little, too. It has the old scales, the hopper, and the slender little elevator which carried the grist up in an endless chain of little carriers. On the wall is a lovely old map of the northeastern coast of North America as it was in 1821, with corrections and changes noted by the millers through the years. The floor of wide boards is brown and polished; the hand-hewn beams and crosspieces supported by ship's knees are browned with age; and the wooden blinds, true to the 1740's, swing upon the inside of the window instead of in the open.

The Olde Grist Mill is called "Maine's Most Unique Eating Place" because of its Colonial atmosphere and its delicious Johnny Cake, Baked Indian Pudding, and other old fashioned dishes in New England tradition.

David tells us that the favorites from a bountiful menu are Poached Salmon Doria, Baked Stuffed Shrimp Macadamia, and Steak *au Poivre*. The dessert menu is overwhelming; among the favorites are Baked Indian Pudding (the house specialty), Deep Dish Apple Pie à la Mode, and a selection of about a dozen different ice cream desserts, including all kinds of sundaes and parfaits.

MASSACHUSETTS
BOSTON

The Dining Room of The Ritz-Carlton

15 Arlington Street
Boston
Massachusetts 02117
Telephone: 617–536–5700

All major credit cards
Breakfast, lunch, dinner, and Sunday brunch
Reservations advised
Jacket required
Dinner: $22 to $30
    full 3 courses, without wine
Lunch: $16 to $20
Chef: John Vyhnanek
Maitre d': Joseph Lucherini

The Ritz-Carlton in Boston is one of a group of Ritz-Carlton hotels in the United States that prides itself on being deserved of the Ritz name. Colgate Holmes, president of the Ritz-Carlton Hotels of North America, believes sincerely that his hotels must earn their reputations each day. The lovely dining room of the Ritz-Carlton, Boston, can help boost the hotel's good name. The personal dining room of King Ludwig of Bavaria was used as a model for this room. The cobalt blue which beautifully enriches the restaurant's decor has come to be known as "Ritz-Carlton blue." The signature cobalt glasses were inspired by the cobalt blue in the original chandeliers installed when the hotel was built in 1927; these chandeliers still hang there today.

This is a sophisticated dining room in a hotel that has firmly stood by its dress code throughout the years. Some say it is more Bostonian than Boston itself. This has meant turning away movie stars and other celebrities who arrive in jeans or outlandish apparel. We're very prejudiced and think it's great that the elegance and tranquility that is so respected here is not allowed to be destroyed.

From the expansive windows in the Dining Room is a view that only the Ritz-Carlton can offer—a panorama of the Public Garden's flowers in the spring and ice skaters on the pond in winter. The Public Garden's fleet of swan boats, each one of which looks like a raft with a giant swan in back, is also visible, weather permitting.

The dining room offers superb Continental cuisine. On the menu cover is a reproduction of a beautiful painting of the Ritz-Carlton, the Garden, and its pond, by Kamil Kubik. Inside, the dinner menu features a wide range of fine items. We are told that the favorite main courses here are Lobster with Whiskey and Sautéed Dover Sole. Starred items on the menu are the chef's selections of light and nutritious dishes; some of them are, as appetizers, *Saumon Marine Norvegien, Sauce Moutarde* (marinated fresh salmon with mustard dill sauce), and Oysters or Little Neck clams in Season, and, for soup, Gazpacho *Andalous.* For your main course, Medallions of Venison with cracked peppercorns and currants, Broiled Boston Scrod, and Grilled Thin Veal Cutlet with chive butter are all starred.

A grand brunch, on Sundays from 11 A.M. until 1:30 P.M., is accompanied by chamber music from the Nuages Chamber Players. The pianist at dinner and at lunch plays a combination of popular melodies and classics from the stage and screen. At lunch, on Saturday, there is a fashion show—another attractive view to dine by.

CAMBRIDGE

The Empress

Hyatt Regency Cambridge
Overlooking Boston
575 Memorial Drive
Cambridge
Massachusetts 02139
Telephone: 617–492–1234

All major credit cards
Dinner and Sunday brunch
Reservations requested
Jacket required
Liquor served
Dinner: $18 to $25
Chef: Steve Jayson
Maitre d': Y.P. Lou

Conscious that Boston is a pretty city to look at, this restaurant takes advantage of it from the ground up. A glass elevator takes guests to the 14th floor and a grand restaurant, the Empress. At the top, there is a spectacular view of the city's skyline.

The Empress has exquisite Oriental decor and serves gourmet Oriental specialties from a long and varied list. According to a local critic, the Empress is the "most ambient" restaurant in the Boston area.

Most popular is the Sunday brunch, which features Oriental, Continental, and a bit of New American cuisine. Also on Sundays guests are invited to see another, most unusual, view . . . they are encouraged to enter the kitchen, which is actually an authentic recreation of a Chinese kitchen, where they can watch the chefs prepare the lavish specialties offered that day.

Dinner is served nightly, Monday through Thursday and Sunday from 6 P.M. until 10:30 P.M.; on Friday and Saturday dinner is from 6 P.M. until 11 P.M.; Sunday Brunch is served from 11 A.M. until 3 P.M.

DEERFIELD

The Main Dining Room of
The Deerfield Inn

The Street
Deerfield
Massachusetts 01342
Telephone: 413–774–5587

All major credit cards
Breakfast, lunch, and dinner
Reservations required
Jacket required
Liquor served
Dinner: $20 to $27
full 3 courses, without wine
Lunch: $9 to $12
Chef: Chris Opalenik
Maitre d': Georgiann Kopf

Dining at The Deerfield Inn gives one a glimpse of life as it was in Colonial America. Located in the center of historic Deerfield, a town with 12 beautifully restored museum houses, the inn is so well preserved that it looks much as it did when it was opened in 1884. The village of Old Deerfield has been designated a National Historic Site by the federal government, making it an authentic living monument to early New England life. This is only fitting, considering that the village was settled about 300 years ago and was once an outpost in the wilderness of Colonial America.

The inn has been modernized, with air-conditioning, 23 deluxe guest rooms, a cocktail lounge, two bars, a coffee shop, and a dining room. The decor features glistening mahogany and cherrywood tables, Queen Anne, Chippendale, and Federal-style chairs, oriental rugs, floral draperies, and brass chandeliers.

The luncheon menu includes traditional favorites such as Broiled Fresh Haddock, Scallops, Shish-Kebab, and daily specials featuring a *Crêpe du Jour* and fresh fish from New England waters. Dinner features more specialized gourmet dishes such as New England Baked Shrimp, Veal Orloff, *Tournedos au Poivre,* and Boneless Breast of Chicken Kiev. Among the desserts are Indian Pudding, Brandied Custard Bread Pudding, and a Queen Anne Torte.

MICHIGAN
DEARBORN

The Early American Room

The Dearborn Inn
20301 Oakwood Boulevard
Dearborn
Michigan 48124
Telephone: 313–271–2700

All major credit cards
Lunch: Monday through Friday;
dinner: Monday through Saturday
Reservations preferred
Jacket preferred
Liquor served
Dinner: $15 to $30
full 3 courses, without wine
Chef: Kevin Corcoran

Henry Ford (1863-1947) loved automobiles and the transportation industry. He also loved Georgian architecture. When he built the Dearborn Inn in 1931 he combined the two. Located across from what was then the Ford Airport, it is said to be the world's first airport hotel.

Mr. Ford took an active part in the design of the Inn, personally overseeing the development of many of its unique, charming features—such as the Alexandria Ballroom on the second floor. It's reported that Mr. Ford and his wife Clara led 250 guests around the ballroom in a grand march which ended with one of Mr. Ford's favorite pastimes: an evening of American dancing, followed by a buffet supper.

Because Mr. Ford admired the hospitality of New England and southern inns he made certain that the Dearborn Inn offered that same old-fashioned, warm, personal service. Making the guests feel at home has sustained the Inn for over 50 years.

The Inn and the adjacent Colonial homes, which can be seen from the Early American Room, reflect Henry Ford's fondness for (and, indeed, his involvement in) American history.

The Early American Dining Room, with its rose-print wallpaper and draperies, and its chandeliers, has an air of elegance and grace. Luncheon and dinner entrées served here include early American dishes, many of which come from Michigan and the Great Lakes region. A guest may start the meal with an appetizer such as Michigan Bean Soup. Main dishes include Roast Prime Rib of Western Beef and a large array of tasty seafood: Fillet of Fresh Scrod, Whitefish from the Great Lakes, Fresh Gulf Shrimp, Trout from Lake Superior, Golden Pickerel, and Great Lakes Perch. Popular at lunch are the wide selections of sandwiches including Prime Rib, Club, and Reuben.

A special children's menu with smaller and, for them, entertaining items, includes "Fife and Drum" drum sticks and the "Minute Man" hamburger, both served with French fries and milk.

On Friday night a Seafood Fantasy is served until 10 P.M. And on Saturday, traditional American cuisine is featured until 11 P.M.

DETROIT

The Summit
Hotel Westin
Renaissance Center
Detroit
Michigan 48243
Telephone: 313–567–2300

All major credit cards
Lunch, dinner,
*   and Sunday brunch*
Reservations required
Jacket not required
Liquor served
Dinner: $14.95 to $21.95
*   full 3 courses, without wine*
Lunch: $5.95 to $12.95
Chef: Beat Richei
Maitre d': Tom Dupar

The Summit is a trilevel restaurant and lounge located atop the Westin Hotel in the Renaissance Center of Detroit. Its position on the 71st through 73d floors of the tower provides a spectacular view; two of its levels revolve almost imperceptibly. Diners can see the buildings of downtown Detroit directly below, as well as the Detroit River, with its constant flow of varied shipping traffic, and, to the south across the river, the town of Windsor in the Ontario province of Canada.

The Summit is a fantastic spot to enjoy beautiful sunsets. And, as evening falls, the mood changes and the city lights become a lovely accompaniment to a fine meal. Especially pretty is the strand of lights which adorn the Ambassador Bridge to Canada.

The Summit menu includes a wide variety of fresh seafood, poultry, and meat dishes from different regions of North America. The Westin Hotels, in its system-wide competition, awarded the Summit the Silver Spoon Award for fine dining at lunch and brunch.

Among the specialties on the menu is the Great Combo, which features Lobster Tail and *Petit Mignon.* For dessert there is the Summit Orbiter, Harvey Wallbanger Ice Cream sprinkled with Chocolate Chips, topped with whipped cream, and served in a container with dry ice beneath it for a spectacular presentation. The favorite drink is the Summit Spinner—blended rum, two brandies, Triple Sec, and fruit juices, served in a souvenir glass which is a replica of the Westin, the world's tallest hotel.

The Westin Hotel is 710 feet above Jefferson Avenue. To reach the restaurant at the top, take the Sky Lobby elevator which takes off from the third floor of the hotel, the Ontario level. Since the hotel is very popular for conventions, make your reservation well in advance if you want to be sure to get one of the limited number of seats available in the Summit.

GRAND RAPIDS

Cygnus Restaurant
Grand Plaza Hotel
Pearl at Monroe
Grand Rapids
Michigan 49503
Telephone: 616–776–6145

All major credit cards
Dinner
Reservations necessary
Jacket required
Liquor served
Dinner: $30 to $50
  full 3 courses, without wine
Chef: Rudolf Van Nunen
Maitre d': Erich Ploetz

The Cygnus Restaurant opened in 1983 on the 28th floor of the 29-story glass-enclosed tower of the Grand Plaza Hotel, the tallest building between Chicago and Detroit.

Cygnus is named for the swan constellation seen through the glass roof of the restaurant. Diners have a spectacular view of the city of Grand Rapids, including the Grand River and the Gerald R. Ford Presidential Museum. To the far west, the outline of sand dunes along Lake Michigan is discernable.

When readers of *West Michigan Magazine 1985* were asked, "If you could have only one more meal in West Michigan, where would you go?", the overwhelming response was Cygnus. It was also selected by the readers as the best restaurant in Grand Rapids and as the restaurant having the best service and atmosphere.

No wonder. Cygnus is upscale and elegant, a place where caviar is served with double cream and veal with sweetbreads. It is also expensive; $100 per couple is not unusual. Luckily, you get what you pay for. The room is dramatic. The walls and most of the ceiling are made of glass. A pink marble dance floor is surrounded by tall and feathery papier-mâché palm trees. The tables are set with maroon and white linens, the napkins folded like swans. The wine glasses are sparkling Romanian crystal.

Chef Van Nunen takes pride in his achievements and works extensively with local farmers to get them to deliver the freshest products available. Fish is procured fresh from Michigan streams.

Cygnus is famous for its Gin Tomato Soup à la Ritz, prepared for two at your table ($9). This unique concoction is said to have originated at the Ritz in Berlin. The entrées are imaginative, too, ranging in price from $18 to $24. Among them are Partridge with Truffle, Cooked Apple filled with chestnut purée, topped with two cooked chestnuts, wild rice, and asparagus spears, Noisettes of Veal with Sweetbreads, a dish featuring woven strips of salmon and whitefish in a sauce made of pink champagne, butter, and soup stock, and Veal Medallions and Fresh Shrimp in Green Chervil Sauce.

The desserts are artistic as well. A plate of chocolate mousse flowers and a delicate chocolate butterfly is decorated with a pale and delicious green mint sauce. Butter Pecan Ice Cream is served on a thin pastry island floating in a sea of fresh raspberry sauce.

ST. CLAIR

St. Clair Inn
500 North Riverside
St. Clair
Michigan 48079
Telephone: 313-329-2222

All major credit cards
Breakfast, lunch, and dinner
Reservations recommended
Jacket not required
Liquor served
Dinner: $10 to $21
    full 3 courses, without wine
Lunch: $5 to $9.50
Chef: Warren Zimmer
Proprietor: Donald W. Reynolds

Diners at the St. Clair Inn are treated to a constant panorama of lake and ocean steamers on the St. Clair River, which connects Lake Huron with Lake St. Clair. The quiet majesty of these giant boats, which come from many lands, as they pass closely by the dining room windows, never fails to awe the guests at dinner. The American shipping channel for the Great Lakes is only 30 feet off the dock. Guests claim that the view from here is the best in the state of Michigan.

This is a cozy country inn whose manager, Michael J. Laporte, is proud of the food served here. Among the favorite main dishes are Walleye Pike and Bay Scallops. For dessert, try the strawberry pie.

MINNESOTA
MINNEAPOLIS

The Orion Room
5000 IDS Tower
Minneapolis
Minnesota 55402
Telephone: 612–349–6250

All major credit cards
Lunch and Sunday brunch
Reservations preferred
Jacket required
Liquor served
Dinner: $8.95 to $22.50
full 3 courses,
without wine
Brunch: $15.95
Chef: Charles A. Venables
General Manager:
Martin J. O'Dowd

Recipient of the *Twin Cities Reader* Best View Award, the Orion Room is located on the west side of the 50th floor of the IDS Center. It offers an excellent view of Minneapolis and its suburbs during the day and an unsurpassed view of the city at sunset. By night, twinkling lights far below extend to the horizon in all directions.

The room itself is a beautiful place to dine. It is contemporary and sophisticated, with a decor influenced by classical motifs. The unique angles of the faceted IDS Building are used as a recurring theme throughout the restaurant. The decor features gray and teal with a terra-cotta accent. A tiered seating arrangement uses mahogany chairs upholstered in pinstriped gray wool and teal banquettes to seat 165 diners. The panoramic view is available to diners through floor-to-ceiling windows and is reflected by etched mirrors so that all may see it.

The Orion Room features the best in the new trends of cooking while retaining many old favorites, including Roast Prime Ribs of Beef, a lobster and fillet combination, and its famous Wild Rice Soup. The new menu features regional American cuisine and a variety of fresh cookery that reveals a wealth of tradition and history behind each dish. Appetizers include Sliced Salmon with Mustard and Dill Sauce, and entrées include Roast Duckling with Orange and Blueberry Sauce, Roast Rack of Lamb, and Fresh Broiled Walleye Pike. The American Field Salad is a nice accompaniment to almost anything you order. Among the desserts are seasonal fresh fruit tarts and *Gateau Marjolaine*.

If you're in Minneapolis on a Sunday, the place for Sunday brunch with a view is certainly the Orion Room. The spread of things to eat is endless and very good, not only with standard brunch items such as eggs, breads, and salads, but also with a lot of special things that wealthy gourmand brunch-goers would enjoy, ranging from champagne, Mimosas, and Bloody Marys to smoked salmon, pâtés, sliced turkey breast, an assortment of cheeses, and all kinds of fresh fruits. The dessert spread is amazing—French pastries, cheesecake, and apple flambé! If you are too filled for a dessert or two, settle for a plump strawberry dipped in white chocolate!

MISSOURI
KANSAS CITY

The American Restaurant

Atop Hall's Crown Center
2450 Grand Avenue
Kansas City
Missouri 64108
Telephone: 816–471–8050

All major credit cards
Dinner
Reservations suggested
Jacket required
Liquor served
Dinner: $9.75 to $17.95
full 3 courses, without wine
Chef: Kenn Dunn
General Manager: Rolf Wetzel

Just minutes away from the heart of downtown Kansas City is Crown Center, a complex built largely through the inspiration of the late Joyce Hall, founder and president of Hallmark Cards. We are prejudicially fond of this place, because we had the unique pleasure of working with Mr. Hall on its design. Far more than just another shopping center, this complex sought to display a panorama of American enterprise through its shops and restaurants as well as through all of its public spaces and halls. It seems to have succeeded; after it was built, Crown Center became the model for many fine shopping complexes around the world.

The American Restaurant plays an integral part in following through with Hall's concept. It is an excellent reflection of America's finest cookery, offering impeccable service in elegant surroundings. The view looks over downtown Kansas City and the 10-acre Crown Center Square from approximately five stories up. During the warm summer months, the grass terraces, fountains, and flowers on the Square provide extra color. During the holiday season, the Square has a 70-foot Mayor's Christmas Tree which, when seen with the 20,000 twinkling lights on the trees surrounding it, provides a breathtaking spectacle.

The American is an award-winning restaurant, counting among its honors a *Mobil* Four Star rating, the Cartier Award, *Travel/Holiday* Fine Dining Award, the *Wine Spectator* Award of Excellence, and others.

Among the menu highlights are Barbecued Shrimp over Kansas Wheat (as featured by the American Restaurant at the 1984 presidential inaugural celebration) and Lobster in White Wine with Blue Corn Tortillas—a great salute to our American colors! The menu also features such American fare as fresh rainbow trout, creamy brie from Illinois, Kentucky ham, and of course, the celebrated Kansas City Strip.

The American's buffet is set on an immense brass, wood, and beveled glass fixture, laden daily with over 50 diverse and sumptuous offerings including vegetables tossed with farmer's cheese, Duck Salad with Orange Vinaigrette, Red Potato Salad in Hot Mustard Dressing, California Artichokes, Apple and Ham Pâté, Shellfish Salad in Garlic, Basil, and Pine Nuts, and on and on!

The dessert is the grand finale. Included are Chocolate Whiskey Cake, Sugarbush Mountain Maple Mousse, Frozen Hazelnut Soufflé, Candied Ginger Crepes, and the pastry chef's own homemade ice cream.

The American Restaurant is open for dinner from 6 P.M. to 10 P.M. Monday through Thursday, and until 11 P.M. on Friday and Saturday. It's very popular with the citizens of Kansas City and visitors from around the world.

The Crystal Pavilion

Crown Center
25th and Grand Avenue
Kansas City
Missouri 64108
Telephone: 816-471-2003

All major credit cards
Lunch and dinner
Reservations suggested
Dress: casual
Liquor served
Dinner: $18
    full 3 courses, without wine
Lunch: $8
Chef: Keith Fuemmeler
General Manager: Mark Wadsworth

The Crystal Pavilion is a glass-enclosed restaurant stretching out from the Crown Center shops, offering an appealing view of the Crown Center Square through picturesque arched windows in bright and casual surroundings.

Less costly than its neighbor, the American Restaurant, and with a different menu, the Crystal Pavilion has popular appeal for those working and shopping in the Crown Center. During the summer months, the guests enjoy a view of the 10-acre Square and can actually sit in the Square at tables under sun umbrellas, as the restaurant has outdoor seating. At holiday time, the scene is of the big Christmas tree and the colorful lights which reflect so excitingly through the restaurant's crystal canopy.

The menu's highlights include everything from steaks, broiled salmon, and Raspberry Duck to some of the city's best bar appetizers. Lunch is served Monday through Saturday from 11:30 A.M. until 2:30 P.M. Dinner is from 6 P.M. to 10 P.M., Monday through Thursday, and until 11 P.M., Friday and Saturday. The popular Happy Hour is from 4 P.M. to 6 P.M., Monday through Thursday, and until 7 P.M. on Friday.

Skies

Hyatt Regency Kansas City
at Crown Center
2345 McGee Street
Kansas City
Missouri 64108
Telephone: 816–421–1234

All major credit cards
Dinner
Reservations not necessary
Dress: semiformal
Liquor served
Dinner: $13.95 to $24.50
full 3 courses, without wine
Chef: Phil Guttendorf
Manager: Terri Stielow

It is said that on a clear day diners in the Skies revolving restaurant, on the 45th story of the Hyatt Regency Kansas City Hotel, can see as far as twenty miles away. But in case it is cloudy and the exterior view is not at its best, this dining room has a unique substitute—a view of the state's prairie past. Wrapped around the center core of this restaurant-in-the-round is a 360-degree photomural capturing the essence of the Kansas prairie.

In these days when the concept of a revolving restaurant is grand but not unusual, what better improvement could there be but a revolving interior mural? This 186-foot panorama is a horizon-to-horizon vista of the Konza Prairie, the largest untouched area of native prairie tallgrass in the nation, located 100 miles west of Kansas City. So when diners tire of straining to see the new Kansas City airport 20 miles away, they can relax and look back over their shoulders to see "how it used to be."

Dinner at the Skies is a delight. The cuisine features such main dishes as Certified Black Angus Beef, T-Bone, Strip, and Fillet steaks, Blackened Redfish, and *Pollo* Pesto Florentine. A favorite dessert here is Sky High Ice Cream Pie.

NEVADA
INCLINE VILLAGE

Hugo's Rotisserie

Hyatt Lake Tahoe
Country Club Drive and Lakeshore Boulevard
Incline Village
Nevada 89450
Telephone: 702–831–1111

All major credit cards
Dinner
Reservations suggested
Dress: casual
Dinner: $12 to $20
Chef: Yasu Suzuki
Director: Robert Simeone

As Mark Twain wrote upon looking at Lake Tahoe: " . . . The view was always fascinating, bewitching, entrancing. The eye was never tired of gazing, night or day, in calm or storm; it suffered but one grief, and that was that it could not look always, but must close sometime in sleep."

Hugo's picturesque waterfront location, across the street from the Hyatt Lake Tahoe, offers diners an unobstructed view of Lake Tahoe and the surrounding Sierra Mountain Range. The mountains reach to the clouds and remain capped with snow year-round. The lake, which is 1,645 feet deep, 22 miles long, and almost 13 miles wide, can be glassy and clear like a pond or rough with waves crashing on the beach like the ocean.

In *The Saga of Lake Tahoe* writer Edward B. Scott also weighed in with his thoughts on this famous lake: "Brilliant blues, vivid greens, intense ultra marines, magnificent deep indigo with delicate shadings of purple, violet, and cobalt. These and other combinations of chromatic colors and tints may be seen in the crystal purity of Tahoe's snow waters."

The cuisine is a delight, too, having been awarded three stars in the *Mobil* guide. The house specialty is the spit-roasted fresh duckling.

NEW HAMPSHIRE
NORTH WOODSTOCK

Clement Room of
The Woodstock Inn

Route 3, Main Street
P.O. Box 118
North Woodstock
New Hampshire 03262
Telephone: 603–745–3951

All major credit cards
Breakfast, lunch, and dinner
Reservations necessary on
    Friday and Saturday
Jacket not required
Liquor served
Dinner: $9.50 to $18.50
    full 3 courses, without wine
Lunch: the same
Chefs: Scott Rice and Erik Nelson
Maitre d': Eileen Rice

The Clement Room at the Woodstock Inn is a glass-enclosed petticoat porch open year-round for breakfast, lunch, and dinner. It is named for the gentleman who lived in the home for sixty years and who was the town's postmaster.

The Inn contains an interesting hodgepodge of New Hampshire history. For example, just recently Scott and Eileen Rice, the owners, bought Lincoln's original railroad station and moved it from its previous location and attached it to the Inn. Then they added a few other pieces and parts, such as the 100-year-old four-station barber shop behind the bar, old sewing machines (now used as tables), and seats from the old Lakeport Opera House. All this plus a new outdoor patio for dining on warm summer days contributes to a most unusual view to dine by.

Called the "Woodstock Station," the menu here is an entertaining bill of fare. The categories in it are in keeping with the railroad theme: "All Aboard for Appetizers" features Arti Choo Choo, artichokes marinated in pesto and baked with melted cheese. Other appetizers include Railroad Ties, which are fried cheese sticks with a Dijon mustard sauce; Box Car of Shrimp—"peelum and eatum," with cocktail sauce; Split Rails, a half pound of spicy barbecued pork ribs; and Frog that got Caught on the Tracks, frog legs sautéed in butter and garlic.

Under "Station Soups," there are the Hobo Soup of the Day, the Montrealer (baked French onion soup), and Maine Central (seafood chowder "that's loaded!").

The Station Salads include the Acapulco Express, a salad in a flour tortilla with chili and avocado slices; and the Train Just Pasta, orzo pasta salad with shrimps and artichokes.

"Sandwiched Between the Tracks" includes the Crabby Conductor, the Fall River Connection, the Smoke-Stacked Sandwich, the Cattle Crossing, and the Rushin' Reuben.

"The Main Line" items include Coastal Express, with scallops, shrimp, and fish fried in a Newburg sauce with a crumb crust, Twenty Tiny Twisted Tunnels, which is mushrooms and Gruyere tortellinis topped with pesto and marinara, and a Station Steak, charbroiled and lots more.

In the dessert area, the names are truly crazy. Waffles offered include Before the Tornado, Somewhere Over the Rainbow, There's No Place Like Home, If I Only Had a Brain, and the Wicked Witch's Waffle.

This, as you gather, makes your meal enjoyable, but we must point out that the food is seriously good. Among the favorites are Roast Duckling, Clement's Classic (beef tenderloin layered with crabmeat and asparagus with Hollandaise Sauce), and the hand-cut veal, the most popular of which is Veal Oscar, which is crabmeat, asparagus, and Bearnaise Sauce.

NEW JERSEY
HIGHLANDS

Bahrs Landing

Two Bay Avenue
Highlands
New Jersey 07732
Telephone: 201–872–1245

All major credit cards
Lunch and dinner
Reservations not required
Jacket not required
Liquor served
Dinner: Moderate
Chef: Gordon Dingman
Proprietor: Ray Cosgrove

It is said that this is the approximate spot where the first white man—Henry Hudson—set foot on the soil of New Jersey. He landed his ship, the *Half Moon,* here on September 5, 1609, as part his historic journey in the New World.

The Landing has been a comfortable, down-to-earth restaurant ever since it was started by the Bahrs in 1918. It features a sweeping view. Behind it are the Highlands of Navesink, "world-famous portals at the gateway to the United States." Atop these hills, which are the highest elevation on the East Coast, are the famous Twin Lights lighthouses, the last lingering bit of America visible as ships sail east, and the first to be sighted by ships arriving from Europe. To the north is desolate Sandy Hook, separating the waters of the Atlantic Ocean from the broad stretches of Lower New York Bay. Beyond that is the sketchy outline of Coney Island. At night it appears to be a distant fairyland floating in the sky. As you dine you may see great passenger liners, warships, barges, sailing ships, and many other kinds of vessels moving in and out of view. Directly in front of the restaurant is the Shrewsbury River, noted for fishing and crabbing.

There is more history attached to this spot. It was here that what was called the American Riviera began—in the late 17th century the wealthy patrons of New Amsterdam had their summer cottages on the slopes of the Highlands of Navesink. Many of the scenes in James Fenimore Cooper's *The Pilot* took place here. And Gertrude Ederle, the first woman to swim the English Channel, was taught to swim at a point less than a hundred feet from the restaurant.

The building that contains the restaurant was originally a boat house built in 1890. It was eventually beached, put on pilings, and a second floor was added. From 1903, it was a hangout for fishermen.

A typical seafood restaurant, the menu features clam chowder, lobsters, coleslaw, and hot biscuits. For dessert, a picturesque Mile High Pie (lemon chiffon) is a good choice.

PRINCETON

Greenhouse Restaurant
Nassau Inn

Palmer Square
Princeton
New Jersey 08542
Telephone: 609–921–7500

All major credit cards
Breakfast, lunch, and dinner
Reservations suggested
Jacket not required
Liquor served
Dinner: $5 to $15
    full 3 courses, without wine
Lunch: $5 to $10
Chef: Tony Sindaco
Food and Beverage Director: Kevin M. Howard

The broad windows of the Nassau Inn's airy Greenhouse Restaurant overlook picturesque Palmer Square in the college town of Princeton. The square's diversity of Colonial architecture tells the story, in part, of Princeton's place in American history.

The Nassau Inn, which is now an Omni Hotel, was built in 1937 by Edgar Palmer, who had a vision of a town square containing apartment, office, and retail buildings, with the Nassau Inn as its hub and the beautiful Gothic spires of Princeton University as the backdrop.

The cuisine is excellent and reasonably priced. It won two silver medals at the 1984 Culinary Olympics in Frankfurt, West Germany. Among the favorite main dishes are Steamed Turbot with Basil Cream Sauce and fresh Tomatoes and Sautéed Veal Medallions with Sun-Dried Tomatoes, fresh Basil, and Dijon Cream Sauce.

SEA BRIGHT

The RiverHouse on the Quay

280 Ocean Avenue
Sea Bright
New Jersey 07760
Telephone: 201-842-1994

All major credit cards
Lunch and dinner
Reservations required
Jacket required
Liquor served
Dinner: $25
full 3 courses, without wine
Chef: Avrum Wiseman
Owners: Raymond and Dorothy Cosgrove

The RiverHouse on the Quay has a view of the magnificent Navesink River and its environs. Viewed from across the river are the verdant Highland hills, the highest point on the East Coast, and the historic Twin Lights lighthouses (atop the Highlands), beacons that once guided sailors into the harbor of New York City. In the summer it is pleasant to watch the never-ending parade of pleasurecraft that ply the waters outside the restaurant.

The recently built RiverHouse is situated on a strip of land between the Atlantic Ocean and the Navesink River. Decorated in muted shades of peach and blue, the restaurant seats 156. Because of the generous use of glass in the architecture of the building, there is a striking river view from every table. The comfortable lounge, with rustic tiling throughout, has a welcoming fireplace to warm visitors during the chilly winter months.

The menu features lobster and veal specialties, and other fine examples of American cuisine. The wine list is excellent. RiverHouse is on the Top 100 Restaurant Wine List compiled by *Wine Spectator* magazine.

NEW YORK
ALEXANDRIA BAY

Voyageur Room
Pine Tree Point Resort
P.O. Box 68
Alexandria Bay
New York 13607
Telephone: 315–482–9911

All major credit cards
Breakfast, lunch, and dinner
Reservations recommended
Jacket not required
Liquor served
Dinner: $9 to $23
  full 3 courses, without wine
Lunch: $3.75 to $7.50
Chef: Ray Bartholomew
Proprietors: Therése T. Thompson,
  Richard S. Thompson, and
  Roland Graham Thompson

The view of the Thousand Islands seen from the dining rooms, called the Voyageur Room and the Captain's Table, remind one of the Oslo Fjord; the dining room is similar to the one at the Highlands Inn near Carmel, California; and the view of Boldt's Castle is something like a Rhine view, near Bingen and Oppenheim.

This lodge is situated on its own private peninsula, surrounded on three sides by the tideless St. Lawrence River in a spot of scenic grandeur. The Indians named the area *Monatoana,* which means "Garden of the Great Spirit."

As you sit at your table, looking at the islands of the St. Lawrence, you are particularly impressed by the view of Heart Island, so named for its shape, and the beautiful Boldt's Castle you see on it. The castle's story is bittersweet. George C. Boldt spent $2.5 million building this castle, which he never finished, as a monument to (and summer home for) a great love, his wife. He started construction in 1895 but when his wife died in 1903 all work was stopped. The only parts of the structure that had been completed were the castle's shell, a power house, an Arch entrance, and the Alster Tower, which the Boldts used as a summer home while work was progressing.

Boldt's fascination with castles started as a poor boy in Prussia. He often saw castles along the Rhine and dreamed that he would someday have a castle of his own. Both the large castle, which we see from the Voyageur Room, and the smaller "playhouse," or Alster Tower, were modeled after Rhine castles. Boldt came to America and became the greatest hotel mogul of his day, owning the Waldorf-Astoria in New York and the Bellevue Stratford of Philadelphia. He died a multimillionaire.

There's more history to contemplate while dining—that of the St. Lawrence, which has been the scene of many important developments in U.S.-Canadian relations. For instance, the waters you look upon were the center of activity of Bill Johnston, who burned the British steamer *Sir Robert Peel* in an attempt to free Canada from British rule. Both British and Americans tried to capture this "pirate," as they called him, but he knew the Thousand Islands so well that he was able to avoid being caught.

Capt. C.S. Thompson bought the original site of the resort in 1911, sold it a while later, and bought it again in 1953, developing it as a resort. He further enlarged it in 1960, after a fire. He and his son, Andrew Graham Thompson, made it into a popular and successful resort. "Cap" passed away in 1967; Andrew died in 1969. The hotel is currently owned by Andrew's widow, Thérése; her sons Richard and Ronald help her run the operation. The dining room has been expanded to seat 235, while a newer dining room, the Captain's Table, seats 85. New, too, is a Sunday brunch featuring a six-course meal. There is also a Terrace Luncheon Sandwich Buffet, started last year; the terrace is the only place in the area where you can dine directly on the water with a view of Boldt's Castle.

The menu has been enlarged, offering appetizers ranging from Fresh Fruit Cup to Breaded Mushrooms. Entrées offer six selections of beef, four of veal, and various assortments of pork chops, chicken, and duck. There are eleven seafoods, ranging from Crabmeat Dewey (Alaskan King Crab in a cream-mushroom sauce laced with brandy and topped with Swiss cheese), to Maine Rock Lobster Tails.

A large salad bar, all of whose salad dressings are made in the Pine Tree Point kitchen, features, of course, Thousand Islands salad dressing.

BOLTON LANDING

Trillium

The Sagamore Hotel
  on Lake George
Bolton Landing
New York 12814
Telephone: 800–648–4901

All major credit cards
Reservations required
Jacket and tie required
Lunch: Monday through Friday; dinner: daily
Liquor served
Dinner: $26 to $35
    full 3 courses, without wine
Lunch: $12 to $15

The view to dine by here includes the rolling mountains of the Adirondacks and the sparkling freshwater Lake George. The Sagamore is a private island resort set on this lovely upstate New York lake.

This magnificently restored historic main hotel is surrounded by clusters of private cottages. The resort's top restaurant is called Trillium, named after a glorious light rose-colored lily which stands out as a solitary flower among a whirl of three leaves.

Dining here is supposed to bring the diner back in time to the resort's turn-of-the-century heyday, enabling guests to savor seasonal fare and chef specialties along with elaborate dishes offered more than 100 years ago. Dr. Lorna J. Sass, in her role as culinary historian, was commissioned to research and prepare a menu to include recipes of the late 19th century. The results are delightful.

Luncheon guests are offered *Pâté Maison* with Pear Cumberland Sauce, Jellied Borscht, Mallard Duck Salad with Warm Raspberry Vinaigrette, and Sole Sagamore, a poached sole with Lobster Ragout and White Wine Butter Sauce.

Among the dinner offerings are Partridge Camelia in Armagnac, Raisins, Port Wine, and Cream, Atlantic Salmon baked in Parchment with Mushrooms, Zucchini, and Fine Herbs, Maine Lobster with Cucumbers and Fresh Mint, and Gulf Snapper poached with Scallops and Shrimp. The appetizers, soups, and salads are just as varied: Lobster and Truffle Ravioli, Snails Trillium wrapped in Spinach, Phyllo Dough, and Fresh Tomato, Adirondack Fish Chowder, Asparagus and Truffle Salad, and a special Trillium Salad—a beautiful combination of Sea Scallops, Green Beans, and Caviar sprinkled with Basil Vinaigrette.

The Trillium flower appears in more than 20 shades of rose and pink and is resplendent on delicate linens, crystal, and fine Lilien Bellevue Austrian china designed for the Sagamore.

With such food to choose from one would think the view might play second fiddle. Well, it's hard to say which is more spectacular. The Trillium is a peninsula of windows surrounded by exterior verandas overlooking scenic Lake George. The center of the dining room is raised so that nearly every guest is able to enjoy the view of the lake and the towering Adirondacks.

BROOKLYN

The River Café

1 Water Street
Brooklyn
New York 11201
Telephone: 718–522–5200

American Express, Diners Club
Lunch and dinner
Reservations necessary
Jacket required
Liquor served
Dinner: $45
full 3 courses, without wine
Lunch: $12 to $19
Chef: Charles Palmer
Maitre d': N. Azzolini and J. Collison

The view from the River Café is simply stunning. You see the Brooklyn Bridge, the Wall Street area, the Statue of Liberty, the World Trade Center, the Woolworth building, and that's not all.

The view at night inside the restaurant is impressive, too. A pinstripe of light illuminates a beautiful floral arrangement on each table. The soft lighting creates a subtle ambience that permits celebrities to dine almost unnoticed. It is not unusual for Robert Redford, Frank Sinatra, John Huston, Mary Tyler Moore, or Elizabeth Taylor to be seated in this restaurant, sometimes at the same time. Heads of state, including the late Princess Grace of Monaco, Princess Margaret, the King and Queen of Sweden, and Queen Juliana of the Netherlands, have dined here.

The River Café is actually a coffee and spice barge dating from the 1940's. In 1977, it was positioned on an underwater pier in the East River and refitted with six-foot high windows spanning the length of the 90-foot barge. The owner, Michael O'Keefe, traveled extensively to provide many unusual decorating touches. The rattan chairs were made in Paris; the cobblestones on the driveway are from England; the oak floor is Australian; and

the extruded steel porch doors are from Belgium. Mr. O'Keefe tells us that this is the most photographed restaurant in America because of its intrinsic excitement. He says that guests of any age often stand in awe when they see the panorama of New York City on a crisp, clear night. He claims that it is probably for this reason that more people are proposed to at the River Café than at any other restaurant. While not provable, this is certainly believable.

The cuisine is exceptional and, in some instances, extraordinary. The chef specializes in unique domestic products, such as fresh buffalo, Muscovy and Mallard ducks, and seasonal game. The cuisine might be called refined American cooking.

Easy to find, the River Café is located on the East River, under the Brooklyn Bridge, on the Brooklyn side.

NEW YORK

Devereux's

The Essex House
160 Central Park South
New York
New York 10019
Telephone: 212–247–0300 Ext. 136

All major credit cards
Breakfast, lunch, dinner, and Sunday brunch
Reservations suggested
Jacket required
Liquor served
Dinner: $23 to $40
full 3 courses, without wine
Lunch: $15 to $25
Chef: Uwe Toedter

Seated at a window table in Devereux's Restaurant at the Essex House, you can gaze out on Central Park South and be fascinated by the contrasting metropolitan sights: the changing seasonal beauty of Central Park; horse-drawn carriages making their way through honking taxis and a stream of limousines; a steady flow of joggers and walkers in an amazing range of clothing. It's a scene that is uniquely New York City, and at the same time, it's a kaleidoscopic view of the peoples of the world. This is the ultimate people-watching vantage point.

Devereux's, at New York City's landmark Essex House, is characterized by roomy comfort, understated elegance, and a full-length view of Central Park and 59th Street. With a decor featuring shades of dusty pink, Devereux's has pastel fabric-covered walls, embroidered seat covers, burgundy patterned carpet, a pink marble floor, and mirrored walls. The color scheme is enhanced by crystal chandeliers and sconces, Oriental-style ceramic and brass urns filled with leafy plants, baskets of straw flowers, and a collection of Victorian-style paintings that includes one of Robert Devereux, the Earl of Essex.

The restaurant is divided into three sections so as to foster privacy. The elevated middle section is enclosed within banquettes mounted with etched-glass dividers in brass settings. The sunken area is distinguished by its fine wood paneling.

Prior to his arrival at Essex House, Executive Chef Toedter earned a reputation as one of the East Coast's most creative chefs while serving at the Vista International in Washington, D.C. He also conducted classes for students interested in the field of gastronomy. Toedter, a native of Hamburg, West Germany, has also been associated with a number of prestigious hotels and restaurants in Europe.

The cuisine features seafood and beef. Sunday brunch is served.

During the evening the view is a blur of lights, but one of fascinating movement; it is accompanied by a pianist playing softly to enhance the gracious dining.

Devereux's

Edwardian Room

in the Plaza
Fifth Avenue at Fifty-Ninth Street
New York
New York 10019
Telephone: 212-759-3000

All major credit cards
Breakfast, lunch, and dinner
Reservations necessary
Jacket required
Liquor served
Dinner: $40 to $55
   full 3 courses, without wine
Lunch: $20 to $35
Chef: Reiner Greubal
Maitre d': Paul Nicaj

   The view to dine by from the Edwardian Room is a privileged one. There are only a few tables situated by the high windows overlooking either Central Park or the plaza in front of the hotel's entrance, but the good news is that by asking for them well in advance you can usually get one with a view to dine by.

   The view to the north, of Central Park, is nice but not the best. We prefer the view looking east, toward the General Motors skyscraper and Fifth Avenue. The bustling scene of horse-drawn carriages and well-dressed passersby is an animated and interesting one, and the little park between the hotel and Fifth Avenue is especially stimulating.

   Its centerpiece is a large pedestal holding the equestrian statue of General Sherman done by Augustus Saint Gaudens. The piece won a gold medal at the Paris Salon in 1899. A statue of Pomona, goddess of Abundance, created by Karl Bitter, is also on the pedestal. Both statues rise above a fountain, around which is a favorite lunchtime spot for workers in the nearby buildings. This view was created as the result of a $50,000 bequest by Joseph Pulitzer to create a fountain in this mini plaza/park, which had had only General Sherman and some trees there since 1903. What you see was created in 1913. In 1923 the space was officially named Grand Army Plaza, in honor of the Union army of the Civil War.

   Competing with the view is the decor and design of the Edwardian Room itself. When New York's Plaza Hotel opened its doors on October 1, 1907, advertised as "The World's Most Luxurious Hotel," it did not have the Edwardian Room. Nor did the space have a name; its patrons called it the Fifth Avenue Café. In 1955 it was formally named the Edwardian Room. For a brief time in the early 1970's it was changed to try to capture the mood of other trendy places in town; fortunately, good sense prevailed and its days as the "Green Tulip" will soon be forgotten, if they haven't been already. In 1974 the Edwardian Room was restored as the grand and elegant place it was and probably always will be.

   The Edwardian Room was originally intended to provide the atmosphere of a private club for men only, a place where gentlemen could relax and enjoy masculine company, free from feminine "distractions." In the early days, certain unwritten rules were observed, as in private clubs. One of them prohibited the discussion of business; if one wanted to do that, he had to go to the famous bar in the back of the hotel (which came to be called the Oak Bar when it was reopened after prohibition and after E.F. Hutton and Company, which had occupied the space during prohibition, moved upstairs).

The view to dine by has changed over the years. In 1928, what had been the Vanderbilt mansion on the south side of "the plaza" was torn down to make way for the Bergdorf Goodman store, which is still there. Across Fifth Avenue, to the east, was the Hotel Savoy, which was also torn down in 1928, to be replaced by a more magnificent Savoy-Plaza Hotel. That too is gone, replaced in 1968 by the General Motors building designed by Edward Durrell Stone. In our opinion, Mr. Stone must never have dined in the Edwardian Room or he would not have designed such a bland, massive wall of a building.

Dining in the Edwardian Room, for any meal, is a special treat. When Westin Hotels bought the hotel in 1975, they resolved to keep the Plaza the fine hotel that it had been through the years. The Plaza is still one of New York's most beautiful sights, a designated landmark both by the city of New York and the National Register of Historic Places. So the superb cuisine of the Edwardian Room remains.

Among the dining room's specialties are Glazed Salmon Mornay with Mustard Seed, omelets made table-side, and Veal Paillard in Basil Sauce. All the desserts, including the gorgeous pastries, are made in the Plaza's bakery. All are wonderful.

Lutèce

249 East 50th Street
New York
New York 10022
212-752-2225/6

American Express, Diners Club, Carte Blanche
Lunch and dinner
Reservations recommended
Jacket and tie required
Liquor served
Dinner: $55
    full 3 courses, without wine
Lunch: $29 fixed price
Chef/owner: André Soltner

Frankly, although very pretty and enjoyable, the view to dine by at Lutèce is a modest one. It is to be had in the lovely skylighted garden room at the rear of this grandest of grand restaurants, where the sound of birds chirping (actually a recording) lends a nice touch to the proceedings.

The view may be modest, but the cuisine is not. Lutèce is said by many to be the finest restaurant in New York City. Since 1980, *Playboy* magazine, in its annual survey of the 25 best restaurants in the United States, has put Lutèce in first place three times. It is the efforts of the famed André Soltner and his wife, Simone, that make this restaurant so delightful and earn it so many awards. A full page of this book would be needed to list all of the culinary awards Soltner has received since he was an apprentice in Mulhouse in 1951. The 120-seat Lutèce, whose name comes from the old Roman name for the city of Paris, *Lutetia,* has been open since 1961.

Soltner's 20,000-bottle wine cellar is one of the restaurant's high points, but what contributes most to the charm and greatness of the Soltner dining room is that it embraces you with warmth rather than overwhelming you with too much service, too much decor, or too much food.

Quality is the obvious and understated concern, ranging from pâtés to pastries, from the zinc bar to the garden room, from the elegant linen to the tasteful silver place settings. You can scan the menu yourself, but many diners seem to prefer a careful consultation with the chef/owner himself. Among the specialties he might recommend are a simple roast chicken, *Medaillons de Veau,* and *Saumon en Croute.* The desserts, too, are tantalizing; we suggest you try the *Soufflé Glace.*

The more affluent of New York's big business and high society world congregate at Lutèce. Located in a small townhouse in the center of Manhattan, it has a staff of 16 in the kitchen. André spends about three-quarters of his time in the kitchen while his wife, Simone, takes care of the front of the house.

Is the cuisine French, international, or American? André says that he runs this restaurant as if it were in Paris, but he is reluctant to give a nationalistic label to his food. "French cuisine is good because France is blessed with wonderful food, with wonderful ingredients with which to start. America is the same. I've been here about 25 years. Italian, Chinese, Spanish, French, this is all American food here. I believe in only one cuisine— good cuisine."

Riveranda and Empress of New York

Pier 62
West 23rd Street and
    the Hudson River
New York
New York 10011
Telephone: 212–929–7090

All major credit cards
Dinner and Sunday brunch
Reservations required
Jacket requested
Liquor served
Dinner: $40 to $45
    full 3 courses,
    without wine
Lunch: $22 to $25
Chef: Bruce Sacino

At last, New York can compete with the Paris *Bateaux Mouches* on the Seine and other dinner ships around the world. In fact, according to articles that have appeared in *Gourmet, Travel & Leisure,* and other publications, New York's dinner cuisine is the best of them all.

New York's first and only (at the moment) restaurant yachts are the Riveranda and the Empress of New York. You may stroll on the promenade decks, relax with a cocktail, and then dine on freshly prepared and beautifully served selections from the on-board galleys. And all the while you will have a view to dine by of the incomparable Manhattan skyline and its dramatic, continuously changing vistas, as the restaurant yacht sails through New York's harbors and waterways. In addition to an international cuisine offering a wide choice of salads, appetizers, hot and cold entrées, fresh vegetables, and fine desserts, music, dancing, and entertainment are offered. Fully enclosed, the dining room offers the meals and views year-round.

The Empress seats 375 at dinner and the Riveranda seats 275; both took their first dinner voyage on July 30, 1984. The Empress is a luxuriously converted U.S. Navy ship that crossed the Atlantic during World War II; the Riveranda is a vessel designed and built to be a cruising restaurant.

The ships normally leave at 7 P.M., but guests often arrive early, mainly to get window tables; don't worry, though, if you can't arrive early—all seats have views.

Operated by a company called World Yacht Enterprises, the Empress and the Riveranda travel some thirty miles of waterways around the island of Manhattan. It is a refreshing journey, particularly on a nice day or on a sunset cruise. On Thursdays to Saturdays there is a pre-theater cruise from 4:30 P.M. until 6:30 P.M. and there is a starlight cruise from 9 P.M. until midnight. Most popular is the 7 P.M. cruise. The weekday lunch cruises are from 11:30 A.M. until 1:30 P.M., and the Sunday brunch cruises start at 12:30 P.M. and return at 2:30 P.M. There are midnight cruises at which only hors d'oeuvres and drinks are served.

The Sea Grill

Rockefeller Plaza
19 West 49th Street
New York
New York 10020
Telephone: 212–246–9201

All major credit cards
Lunch and dinner
Reservations necessary
Jacket required
Liquor served
Dinner: $35
    full 3 courses, without wine
Lunch: $16 to $24
Chef: Konstantin Schonbachler
Maitre d': Peter Wyss

The Sea Grill is a new restaurant (opened in 1984) in the heart of Rockefeller Plaza. In the summer and spring, its side is opened and the restaurant is expanded to provide outdoor dining in a flower-filled garden setting. This "garden" is set up every spring in the area which in winter becomes an ice-skating rink, and thus a different view to dine by. At Christmastime, the view also encompasses the famous gigantic Rockefeller Center Christmas tree. The golden Prometheus Fountain by Paul Manship can be seen year-round (though the fountains do not run in winter).

The Sea Grill itself has a delightful decor designed to conjure up the sea. The North Light bounces in the windows on Rockefeller Plaza, moonlight flows down through the glass-bottomed pools set in the ceiling, and light filters through the bottles of garnet and amber wines, making them look like stained glass windows. Soft wools in the colors of the seashore carpet the floor.

The deep armchairs are modeled after those welcoming first-class passengers on transatlantic liners. A ruddy cherrywood is used on the ceiling, in the columns and arches, and on the walls. Below the pools in the ceiling, a second pair of pools add the sparkle and murmur of cascading water to the room.

The kitchen is visible, set behind chilled marble counters where the day's catch, herbs and vegetables, and pastries are all displayed.

Regional dishes featuring native finfish and shellfish are prominent on the menu, served grilled over hardwood coals and grapevines in the light and exquisite West Coast-style and in simple raw-bar style. Maine Lobsters weighing from two-and-a-half to three pounds are served steamed, poached, or grilled. Breast of Pheasant, Calf's Liver, veal, and steak are grilled, too. All of the desserts, including ice creams and fruit ices, are made in the Sea Grill pastry shop.

The Sun Garden and
The Crystal Fountain

of the Grand Hyatt New York
Park Avenue at Grand Central Station
New York
New York 10017
Telephone: 212–883–1234

All major credit cards
Breakfast, lunch, and dinner
Reservations not necessary
Dress: casual but neat
Liquor served
Dinner: $16 to $35
    full 3 courses, without wine
Lunch: $8 to $16
Chef: Helmut Leuck

The Grand Hyatt opened in 1980 as a modern showpiece in the heart of New York City. Its architecture is a delightful interplay of space, marble, water, and glass.

The hotel is a 34-story glass edifice which reflects the historic architecture of its neighbors, including the famous art deco skyscraper, the Chrysler building. The Grand Hyatt has a dramatic waterfall cascading over a marble wall in its three-level entryway. The lobby has fashionable boutiques and attractive restaurants with views.

The Crystal Fountain is the name given to the 365-seat restaurant on the lobby level. Here tables surround the fountain from which the restaurant takes its name. The huge floor-to-ceiling windows that flood the restaurant with natural light provide diners with a dramatic view of the landmark Chrysler building across the street. The Crystal Fountain features an open bakery and serves food far superior to that of the average hotel.

Overlooking the rush and hubbub of midtown Manhattan's 42nd Street is the Sun Garden cocktail lounge, a lush, plant-filled greenhouse actually cantilevered over the sidewalk. The Sun Garden is an ideal place to have lunch or cocktails while watching the endless march of people below, many of whom are going into or coming from Grand Central Station, located next door. This is one of the few spots where rain or snow enhances the dining atmosphere. There's also a view of the waterfall in the atrium. In the evening, guests enjoy refreshments under the stars while listening to a string trio perform.

Tavern on the Green

in Central Park
at Central Park West and 67th Street
New York
New York 10023
Telephone: 212–873–3200

All major credit cards
Lunch and dinner
Reservations recommended
Liquor served
Dinner $9.50 to $21.50
full 3 courses, without wine
Lunch: $8.50 to $19.50
Chef: Reto Demarmels
Pastry Chef: Dieter Schoener

The Tavern on the Green is situated in New York City's Central Park, on city-owned space rented to Warner LeRoy, the restaurateur who also created Maxwell's Plum.

The view of the park is unquestionably beautiful, encompassing trees and lawns, horse-drawn carriages, equestrians, joggers, and other staples of New York City life. The view inside is equally impressive: huge reflective chandeliers and twinkling lights wherever you look. The atmosphere is so festive that this is certainly one of the city's most popular places for celebrations and parties of all sorts, although couples, too, find it a romantic and even private spot to be.

Among the recommended main dishes are Red Snapper with Julienned Sweet Vegetables, Rib Roast, Green Pasta Dressed with Chicken, Mushrooms, and Cream, and Tagliorini (fine egg pasta) with Scallops, Sole, Basil, Tomato, and Cooked Vegetables. The desserts are colorful and, if you're watching your weight, downright sinful.

Top of the Park

One Gulf & Western Plaza
60th and Central Park West
New York
New York 10023
Telephone: 212-333-3800

All major credit cards
Dinner
Reservations recommended
Jacket required
Liquor served
Dinner: $19.50 to $27.50
  full 3 courses, without wine
Chef: Alain de Coster
Maitre d': Andre Fevrier

In 1970, when Gulf & Western built this skyscraper overlooking Central Park, Stuart Levin, the owner of a famous New York French restaurant, Le Pavillon, was asked to create a dining room on the roof of the building. Both a private dining room for executive luncheons and a stylish rooftop dinner spot for a sophisticated clientele were requested.

Levin agreed, but with the understanding that he could set it up not as a tourist attraction, but rather as an elegant dining room serving, for the most part, the residents living in the luxury condominium and cooperative apartments nearby, all having magnificent views of their own of the broad expanse of beautiful Central Park.

Levin knew that the restful view was really nothing new to most of his guests, so he designed a dining room with beauty and charm. Levin has just completed a full remodeling, changing the decor after 15 years. A rich brown, red, and black carpet has replaced the royal blue and red one of old. The table lights have been changed from red to crystallized glass, and all the walls are mirrored, adding light and providing a fuller panoramic view of the city. The dining room seats 120 and is 43 floors above Central Park.

As you enter the reception area you can see the sparkling New Jersey skyline. In the center of this panorama is the brightly lighted Meadowlands sports complex. And the Hudson River seems dramatically dark and close, even though it isn't.

Walking to the dining room on the opposite side of the bar in the reception area, you look right down into Central Park and over to Fifth Avenue, on the other side of the park. This spectacular view is visible from any table and gets better as it gets darker.

The food competes with the view. Alain de Coster has earned recognition in all the guidebooks for his international cuisine. One favorite is Rack of Lamb; others include the Tournedo of Beef and Roast Duckling with Peaches. Among the tantalizing desserts, we suggest the Frozen Sand Pie, which is made with coffee ice cream, crushed Italian cookies (called amaretti), and crushed coffee beans which are placed in a graham cracker mold, frozen, and then served with hot chocolate sauce and whipped cream. Because the meal portions are so generous you might be tempted to skip dessert. Don't skip this one.

The View
New York
Marriott
Marquis

1535 Broadway
New York
New York 10036
Telephone: 212–398–190

All major credit cards
Lunch and dinner
Reservations necessary
Jacket required
Liquor served
Chef: Willy Ribbe

Photo courtesy of John Woodward

In October 1985, the 1,877-room New York Marriott Marquis hotel opened its doors in Times Square, the heart of New York City. This is a hotel of superlatives: it has the largest hotel atrium in the world, it is the largest—at 50 stories—of the Marriott hotels, and it is the first building to go up as part of a major effort to restore Times Square's badly tarnished luster. The hotel's arrival has begun to inspire others to contribute to the upgrading and beautification of the world-renowned center of America's largest international city.

Most exciting to us is the area of the hotel on its 46th through 48th floor, where there is a three-level revolving restaurant complex. Although there are revolving restaurants all around the world, this is the first of its kind in Manhattan. On clear days one can see three states (New York, New Jersey, and Connecticut) and four bodies of water—the Atlantic Ocean, Long Island Sound, and the Hudson and East Rivers.

You enter from a special elevator from the ninth level of the hotel, which carries the restaurant guests up through the immense atrium, past skylights and ivy-covered internal terraces to the 46th floor. The View seats 196 and offers an international menu. Opened in December 1985, it is furnished in dark, rich fabrics, accented by sparkling brass.

Above the restaurant is the View Lounge, which seats 505 guests comfortably. It has the same spectacular revolving view and is destined to become the spot for New York's sophisticated set to enjoy cocktails while watching the sun set.

The New York Marriott Marquis is the newest luxury hotel in New York City. Its history started in 1972 when Mayor John Lindsay approached the Atlanta-based architect and developer John Portman with an idea. The Mayor envisioned a larger-than-life hotel on an 85,000 square-foot Times Square site that could accommodate the growing influx of visitors and conventioneers to New York City. Portman, an innovator whose efforts led to the building of the first floor-to-ceiling atrium hotel, the Atlanta Hyatt Regency, in the 1960s, said he was ready to accept the challenge.

A challenge it was. There were problems with financing and conservationists, as well as debates over air rights. Eventually, Mayor Ed Koch and his administrative associates gave Portman the collaboration he needed. A partnership was eventually formed involving Marriott and Portman, and the project, originally planned to cost $170 million, was started.

Now, more than a decade after it was conceived, the New York Marriott Marquis (which ended up costing some $450 million) is a major Times Square attraction. The hotel has its own 1,500-seat Broadway theater, 141 exquisite and luxurious suites, glass elevators gliding through a 46-story atrium, the largest grand ballroom in New York City, which can accommodate up to 3,500 guests, four lounges and four world-class restaurants under the direction of executive chef Willy Ribbe, who has been an executive chef for 18 years in six different countries.

Windows on the World

107th floor
One World Trade Center
New York
New York 10048-0605
Telephone: 212-938-1111

All major credit cards
Breakfast, lunch, dinner,
*   and Sunday brunch*
Reservations recommended
Restaurant: jacket and tie required
Hors d'Oeuvrerie: jacket required
Liquor served
Restaurant:
*   Dinner: $29.95 prix fixe,*
*   without wine*
*   À la carte: entrées $17.50 to $23*
*   Hors d'Oeuvrerie:*
*   Breakfast: $3.95 to $12;*
*   other meals, hot/cold*
* $4.95 to $9.50*
Chef: Hermann Reiner
Maître d': Lee Harty

Unless you are eating in an airplane, or in heaven, the highest view to dine by in the world is the aptly named Windows on the World, on the 107th floor of the World Trade Center in the financial district of New York City. The view is truly startling; in fact, some people have trouble getting used to it. It is not as high as the view from an airplane, but it sure seems that way. It is actually better than an airplane view because you see it, leisurely, from an elegantly set table through large windows, rather than stretching to catch a fleeting glimpse of a swiftly passing panorama.

Even when the weather is not clear enough to secure the 55-mile visibility you get on a clear day, the view is enough to make poets of ordinary people. One patron seated next to us said, when lightning flashed, "It's so beautiful that God took a flash picture." Another saw the Queen Elizabeth II float ethereally from the Hudson River into a fog-covered Atlantic Ocean and called it a movie dream sequence. Another sour-faced guest was silent as he took in all of the views of Manhattan and beyond and said, "It goes to show you that even the ugly is beautiful if you just step back and take a long look."

Philosophers, dreamers, and ordinary sightseers, too, find the view a grand experience whether it is a first or fiftieth visit. You can see Manhattan, Brooklyn, Long Island, and much of Northern New Jersey. The Statue of Liberty, the Empire State Building, the green expanse of Central Park, and the 747s rising from and landing at John F. Kennedy International Airport—these are the elements of your view to dine by.

Not only do many New Yorkers bring their out-of-town and foreign visitors here to see New York City from its most beautiful vantage point, but they bring their families, too, particularly for Sunday brunch. Windows on the World is truly an international dining spot, for whenever we have been here, the languages spoken by the diners made it seem as if the United Nations general assembly had adjourned to dine here.

Upon contemplating this scene, you are also moved to ask a somewhat intriguing question: did the founders of New York City—the Dutch, the English, and then the Americans—ever imagine that their small city would reach such huge dimensions in so many ways? The men that built the nearby historic landmarks, such as the stock exchanges, Trinity Church, the Wall Street office buildings, Federal Hall (where George Washington was inaugurated as president), the original South Street Seaport, and City Hall, would probably never believe that their work would be looked down upon from a dining room some 1,350 feet (412 meters) above!

Windows on the World is actually a collection of dining rooms. The largest is simply

Windows on the World

called The Restaurant and has the best views from all of its 350 seats. Despite its size, it is cozy and intimate because it is sectioned off and terraced so everyone can see everything. It offers a truly international cuisine, representative of the makeup of its guests. It is open for dinner Monday through Saturday from 5 P.M. until 10 P.M., on Saturday from noon until 2:30 P.M. for brunch, and on Sunday from noon until 7:30 P.M. Lunch is served Monday through Friday from noon until 2:15 P.M., when The Restaurant is a private club mostly for occupants of the World Trade Center buildings. Nonmembers are charged a $7.50 cover charge at lunch only, but for an annual fee anyone can join. In the center of The Restaurant is the Grand Buffet Table, where pastries are temptingly displayed at dinner-time, and where the Grand Buffet is displayed for Saturday luncheon and all day Sunday.

The menu of The Restaurant features charcoal-grilled meats, the special Rack of Lamb James Beard, and what the menu describes as "always the freshest oysters around." The desserts offer such treats as Chocolate Sabayon Cake, luscious White Chocolate Mousse, and Warm Apple Tart. The staff in this room speaks 11 languages.

The Hors d'Oeuvrerie is smaller, but not small, with 240 seats, and bills itself as "America's first international hors d'oeuvre restaurant." It is designed to look like a dinner theater, with tiered seating to provide a view of the open kitchen—the International Cooks' Table—as the stage. Cooks in colorful national dress prepare and serve their countries' regional specialties. From a selection of over 20 hot and cold hors d'oeuvres such as sushi, sashimi, Moroccan kefta, Indonesian sates, Kyoto beef roll, coconut fried shrimp, and Szechuan hacked chicken, you can put together an entire meal. The Hors d'Oeuvrerie also contains the City Lights Bar.

It is open at 7:30 A.M. on weekdays for breakfast and the rising sun. At 3 P.M. the bar opens and samples of the hors d'oeuvres are served. The piano begins at 4:30 P.M. and a trio takes over at 7:30 P.M. and plays until 1 A.M. Tuesday through Saturday (12:30 A.M. on Mondays). On Sunday tea dancing begins at 4 P.M. There is a $2.75 cover charge whenever there is dance music. Sunday brunch is served from noon until 3 P.M. Jackets are required and denims are not permitted. The Hors D'Oeuvrerie also offers views of Manhattan and beyond.

There is a restaurant here which has no view because it is in the heart of the Windows on the World complex; called the Cellar in the Sky, it is a small romantic dining room which seats only 36. This really isn't a restaurant; rather, it is the working wine cellar for the complex, so the guests are surrounded by thousands of bottles of wine. Dappled lights reflect the wine's ambers and reds on the cool marble floor, so there is a view of sorts. This room has a special gourmet menu for its limited guests with a prix fixe of $70 a person. Reservations are necessary.

Windows on the World is an operation of Inhilco, Inc., a wholly owned subsidiary of Hilton International. Anton Aigner is the president of Inhilco, which is responsible for serving 25,000 to 30,000 guests every day at Windows on the World. The vice-president, director, and host is Alan Lewis, who calls Windows "the biggest neighborhood restaurant in the world."

NORTH CAROLINA
MAGGIE VALLEY
The Cataloochee Ranch

Route 1
Maggie Valley
North Carolina 28751
Telephone: 704–926–1401

All major credit cards
Breakfast, lunch, and dinner
Reservations required for non-guests
Dress: informal
Dinner: $11 to $15
    full 3 courses, without wine
Lunch: $4 to $7
Managing Partner: Alice A. Aumen

The views from the mile-high surroundings here are spectacular. Most people consider the Balsam Mountain Range of the Great Smokies to be the primary view (to the east and south), but the northern view, of the Great Smoky Mountain National Park and the grazing meadows for the cattle and ranch horses, is magnificent, too. Included in this view is the trout pond where guests of the ranch may catch their own breakfast or lunch; later they can look out over the pond from the dining room while enjoying their trout.

The dining room is in the ranch house itself, which is a recently (1982) remodeled stone and log barn. During 1986-87 the dining, public, and kitchen areas will be completely redone. The new dining room, like its predecessor, will be filled with antiques and hand-crafted furniture. The dining tables are solid cherry wood. Centerpieces with freshly arranged wildflowers from the surrounding woods and meadows are used. Several times a week, lunch or dinner may be served on the terrace just outside the dining room, making the diner feel more a part of the majestic view.

The new dining room will reflect the same refined, rustic informality that the old one did. Because of the cool climate, the fireplaces will be lighted most of the time.

At dinnertime usually one or two meat dishes are offered. Occasionally outdoor meals like trout fries or steak cookouts are organized. But dinner is generally served in the dining room. Salads and vegetables in large quantities, such as Zucchini Creole and Fresh Steamed and Buttered Snow Peas, as well as homemade breads and great desserts like Chocolate Upside Down Cake and fruit cobblers are featured.

Because appetites are stimulated by the fresh mountain air, generous portions are always served. And although until recently only guests of the ranch could be served in the dining room, now visitors and residents in the area are welcome so long as they make reservations, particularly for breakfast and dinner.

PENNSYLVANIA
BOILING SPRINGS
The Carriage Room

at Allenberry "on the Yellow Breeches"
Resort Inn
Route 174
Box 7
Boiling Springs
Pennsylvania 17007
Telephone: 717–258–3211

All major credit cards
Dinner
Reservations recommended
Jacket not required
Liquor served
Dinner: $11 to $18
    full 3 courses, without wine
Chef: Danial Raudabaugh

This fine dining room is located on the same resort property as Fairfield Hall (see next entry), but its dining room serves à la carte regional cuisine and it is known for its excellent food and fine self-service wine cellar, featuring a broad selection of Pennsylvania wines made in nearby wineries. The Carriage Room is in an addition built on the 1812 Stone Lodge.

It has a different view than Fairfield Hall, with large windows looking out on the shady maples and abundant rhododendrons planted around a charming brick patio and fern-encrusted limestone walls. Birds, chipmunks, squirrels, and ducks parade by for the entertainment of the diners. And here you hope for at least a chill wind, since that becomes an excuse to have a fire in the beautiful large stone fireplace at the end of the room.

The Carriage Room's menu is unique in the area. It offers such entrées as Broiled Rainbow Trout, Barbequed Baby Back Ribs, Cajun Redfish, Sautéed Veal with Mushrooms, Broiled Oysters with Lump Crab and Garlic, and Grilled Breast of Duck. They are served with soup, such as Danny's Seafood Chowder, salads including Marinated Artichoke Hearts, and hot garlic bread with brie and stilton cheeses. There are chilled summer soups and seasonal vegetables. Desserts include a hot fudge sundae served in a "Paul Bunyon"-sized champagne glass, chocolate/fresh fruit fondue, and homemade carrot cake.

Fairfield Hall

at Allenberry "on the Yellow Breeches"
Resort Inn
Route 174
Box 7
Boiling Springs
Pennsylvania 17007
Telephone: 717–258–3211

All major credit cards
Breakfast, lunch, and dinner
Reservations recommended
Jacket not required
Liquor served
Dinner buffet: $12.95
Lunch buffet: $8.25
Proprietor: The Heinze Family
 President: John J. Heinze
 Manager: Jere S. Heinze

Fairfield Hall was constructed around 1785 as a limestone dairy barn but has been made into a delightful place to dine. It is one of the largest remaining bank barns in central Pennsylvania, and is set in the hillside above the Yellow Breeches Creek. The creek was so named during the Revolutionary period when soldiers who waded or washed their white breeches in the waters found they turned yellow from the churning silt.

Looking south from the Hall, guests can see the creek, now one of the best trout fishing streams in America. Next to the creek is the small Still House; a guest house now, it was once the home of a distiller who made the grains of the large productive farm into a popular "cash" product. Also in the view is Mansion House, the private residence of Mrs. Mary Lu Heinze. Among its past owners was a relative of the folk hero, Davy Crockett. Mansion House became a farm in 1685, when the land was granted.

Fairfield Hall is open every day for breakfast and lunch. Buffet dinners are served Wednesday through Saturday. The buffet dinner consists of Country Ham, Roast Steamship of Beef, Roasted Chicken, Seafood Newburg, fresh vegetables and salads, fruits, cheeses, famous Pennsylvania Dutch Lebanon bologna, and their own delightful sticky buns and homemade ice cream. Fairfield Hall is located on Route 174, 20 miles southwest of Harrisburg.

RHODE ISLAND
NEWPORT

Le Bistro
Bowen's Wharf
Newport
Rhode Island 02840
Telephone: 401–849–7778

All major credit cards
Lunch and dinner
Reservations necessary
Jacket not required
Liquor served
Dinner: $18 to $38
 full 3 courses, without wine
Lunch: $9 to $22
Chef: John Philcox
Proprietors: John and Mary Philcox

Le Bistro is a delightful restaurant on the second and third floors of a semimodern building on Bowen's Wharf, at West Pelham Street in Newport. It is in an area busy with tourists and the sailors who frequent the wharf, but, located as it is above the activity, it is free of the hubbub.

From both floors one has beautiful views of the harbor, particularly delightful when the sun sets. The two dining rooms are on the second floor and each seats 50, while the bar on the floor above seats 20.

John and Mary Philcox are glad that visitors enjoy the view but they themselves concentrate on preparing fine cuisine. Dinner is served from 6 P.M. until 10 P.M., with about a dozen main courses and appetizers, plus the daily offerings of seafood. Everything is very fresh, purchased that day. In addition to a dinner menu, there is a simpler menu available in the bar all day and at lunch that includes sandwiches, salads, and some country-style entrées such as *Saucisson Chaud* and *Bouillabaisse*. The dining room has become known for its unusual specialties, such as sweetbreads and veal kidneys, and its own *pâtés* and *terrines*.

Special wines come from a neighbor, the Sakonnet Vineyards in Little Compton.

This dining room has received many complimentary reviews, has been called one of the best restaurants in New England by a number of critics, and has had its recipes featured in several magazines.

Newport is really two different towns. In summer, it is a very busy tourist city, with a regular summer colony and sightseers who come to see the mansion "cottages" built during the turn of the century by some of America's most wealthy families. During the rest of the year it is a small New England town with more restaurants than it really needs. Le Bistro is one of the few restaurants that requires guests to make reservations year-round.

TENNESSEE
KNOXVILLE

The Volador Room

Hyatt Regency Knoxville
500 Hill Avenue S.E.
Knoxville
Tennessee 37901
Telephone: 615–637–1234

All major credit cards
Dinner
Reservations recommended
Jacket required
Liquor served
Dinner: $15 to $20
    full 3 courses, without wine
Chef: Jim Higgins
Maitre d': John Shanks

Looking to the southeast from the Volador Room, toward the rolling East Tennessee Hills, overlooking the Tennessee River, one sees a breathtaking view of the main chain of the Great Smoky Mountains, climaxing with the peaks of Clingman's Dome and Mount LeConte.

It is so lovely here that the local people call the Volador Room of the Hyatt Regency Knoxville "the restaurant where the stars come out at night." This actually has two meanings. It refers, of course, to the great view, but it also means that the room is a favorite of local as well as national celebrities.

This is also a fun place. People are still talking about the time the waiters served a pig's head, with an ample cigar in its mouth, to the astonished mayor of Knoxville, who is, luckily, famous for his sense of humor. But the mayor's presence here was no surprise, since the Volador Room is the showplace of Knoxville. Opened in March 1972, this restaurant brought many new dining practices to town, including table-side service highlighted with flaming dishes and cordial and dessert carts, as well as an extensive presentation of soups, appetizers, exotic wines, and liqueurs.

The decor, featuring dark colors and soft lighting, produces a romantic atmosphere. The hotel itself is striking, with its atrium lobby and glass elevators which rise through the lobby and emerge on the exterior of the building, as they continue up to the top floor (the eleventh), where guests arrive at the Volador Room. So while riding in the elevator, you get a preview of the view to dine by.

TEXAS
DALLAS

Antares
Atop the Reunion Tower
Hyatt Regency Dallas
300 Reunion Boulevard
Dallas
Texas 75207
Telephone: 214–651–1234

All major credit cards
Lunch, dinner, and Sunday brunch
Reservations suggested
Jacket not required
Liquor served
Dinner: $20 to $28
  full 3 courses, without wine
Lunch: $5.50 to $7.50
Chef: Eddie Peyer
Manager: Norman Shiman

Antares

There's a lot of Dallas to see, and the best place to start is atop the 50-story Reunion Tower, where, in a revolving restaurant, you can get a 360-degree view of the city and its outskirts.

This is the best view of the area you can get, and it includes the popular amusement park, Six Flags Over Texas in nearby Arlington, the Arlington Stadium, home of the Texas Rangers, and the Fort Worth skyline to the south. You also see the Trinity River and the beautiful Green Belt, as well as the massive Dallas/Fort Worth Airport, which is larger than Manhattan Island. To the west, the Texas Stadium, home of the Dallas Cowboys, is visible, as well as the famous Dallas Market Center which includes the World Trade Center, the Apparel Mart, the Market Hall, the Home Furnishing Mart, the Decorative Center, and the Trade Mart. Also in view are Love Field, Southern Methodist University, and the 1891 Romanesque Old Red Courthouse (you can even see the gargoyles with a pair of binoculars). To the north is the John Neely Bryan Cabin, home of the Dallas settler who founded the city in 1841, the John Fitzgerald Kennedy Memorial designed by architect Philip Johnson, and the Dallas County Courthouse. In addition, toward the east you see the beautiful Dallas City Hall designed by architect I.M. Pei, the State Fair Park, with its Cotton Bowl Stadium, State Fair Music Hall, and the world's largest fair, the State Fair of Texas. Also to the east is the Old City Park, the Reunion Arena, and the Dallas Convention Center with an adjoining Memorial Auditorium.

The 50-story Reunion Tower has a unique geodesic dome, and it is the architectural landmark of Dallas. The three-level dome is studded with 240 light bulbs, creating a spectacular nighttime display. The dome weighs 50 tons, contains 114,000 separate parts, and uses over two miles of aluminum pipe. At 560 feet, its highest level is "At Top of the Dome," a revolving cocktail lounge that makes a complete turn every 55 minutes.

Antares, named for the brightest star in the Scorpio constellation, is the Continental restaurant at the dome's middle level. Guests are brought up to the restaurant in glass-enclosed elevators located in the tower's three outer concrete shafts.

The guests include out-of-town visitors, guests of the hotel, and local residents. One diner proposed to the young lady with whom he was dining by having an airplane fly by the window during dinner, trailing a sign that said "Will you marry me?"

Chicken in the Stars, half a young chicken with teriyaki marinade and fresh sautéed vegetables, is the recommended specialty at lunch. At dinner, a Texas favorite is, of course, Prime Ribs of Blue Ribbon Beef, a most tender serving of prize-winning beef along with fresh country vegetables. Other favorites include (at lunch) Tower Taco (the dining room's version of taco salad) and Reuben Pizza. At dinner, another popular dish is Seafood Teriyaki. The desserts include Double Chocolate Mousse and Profiteroles Zabaglione, tiny puffs filled with creamy custard set in cold zabaglione sauce, ribboned with hot bitterfudge sauce. At dinner you are served a *palette pacifier,* a cone of tart sherbet to refresh your taste buds between courses. Another dinner treat is a basket of grilled French herb bread.

Adjoining the modern Reunion Tower is the futuristic, 947-room Hyatt Regency Hotel, with its 18-story lobby, itself offering a view to dine by at Fausto's Sea Catch.

Laurel's

Sheraton Park Central Hotel
12720 Merit Drive
Dallas
Texas 75251
Telephone: 214–385–3000

All major credit cards
Dinner
Reservations recommended
Jacket and tie required
Liquor served
Dinner: $35 to $50
    full 3 courses, without wine
Chef: Tim Rodgers
Maitre d': Sal LaCayo

Laurel's is the only rooftop restaurant in North Dallas. The entire exterior wall of the restaurant is glass, providing diners with a full view of downtown Dallas and beyond. Local publications rave about the view, with the *Dallas Times Herald* calling it "magnificent" and *D* magazine labeling it "fabulous." The view has been credited as providing Laurel's with an ambience that makes it one of the most romantic restaurants in Dallas.

Laurel's

Both the hotel and the restaurant are new, having opened in 1983. Designed by Dallas architects Hellmuth, Obata, and Kassabaum, Inc., with interiors by Jutras and Nobill Associates of Bedford, Massachusetts, the Sheraton Park Central is a place of elegance and grace.

Its food is as fine as its view. The chef and chef artist have won awards for the beautiful presentation of the dishes served here. Among the more popular selections are Corn Velvet with Louisiana Lump Crab Meat, Steamed Salmon Fillet with Scallop Mousse and Seabean, Roast Loin of Lamb with Roasted Peppers and Southwest Salad, Symphony of Seafood on a Trio of Sauces, and Grilled *Poussin* with Fresh Pasta. The house-specialty accompaniment to most meals is the delicious molasses-nut bread. There's an after-dinner cordial cart offering diners a selection of exquisite liqueurs. For dessert, we recommend the fresh blueberries (in season) and whipped cream and the ricotta cheese/sponge cake.

FORT WORTH

The Old Swiss House

1541 Merrimac Circle
Fort Worth
Texas 76107
Telephone: 817–877–1531

All major credit cards
Dinner
Reservations advisable
Jacket encouraged
Liquor served
Dinner: $13 to $25
   full 3 courses, without wine
Chef/Owner: Walter F. Kaufmann
Maitre d': Pat Ragsdale (Ms.)

Fort Worth's first European-style restaurant also has the best view to dine by in the city. Diners seated at or near the high wall of windows overlook the scenic Trinity River. You can sometimes see the moon rising over the treetops and reflected in the tranquil river waters. Commenting on the view, the owner and chief chef, Walter F. Kaufmann, says that "all that's missing are the mountains; on a clear day, you can even see those."

When we first dined here, Chef Kaufmann, wearing his white outfit and chef's high hat, came to chat with us while we were enjoying our meal. "How wonderful," we thought, "he came out just to see us." Not so, we found out. Kaufmann talked to many other guests before returning to the kitchen. That's the kind of place this is. It is as if we are the chef's friends and are eating in his personal dining room.

For more than a decade, *Travel/Holiday* has listed this establishment in its *Guide to Fine Dining.* For more than two decades, Kaufmann and his wife Nancy have brought Continental cuisine at its best to Fort Worth. Kaufmann is responsible for introducing local restaurantgoers to such delicacies as *Escalopes de Veau "Oscar"* (veal sautéed in butter and topped with crabmeat and Hollandaise), *Filet Mignon Sauté King Henri IV, Carre d'Agneau Persillade* (rack of lamb with parsley, bread crumbs, and mustard), and others.

Asked what dishes his guests like, Walter told us that a favorite appetizer is cold cucumber soup, and the favorite main course is Poached Norwegian Salmon with Cucumber Sauce. Favorite desserts include Strawberries Walter and Cherries Jubilee.

Walter Kaufmann's cooking is special. When he uses herbs, sauces, and dressings, they are only employed to bring out the flavor of the meat, not to smother it. He feels that good meat and good seafood should be helped to preserve their natural flavor and not be so drowned in seasonings that they become unidentifiable.

HOUSTON

La Tour d'Argent

2011 Ella Boulevard
and T.C. Jester
Houston
Texas 77008
Telephone: 713–864–9864

All major credit cards
Lunch and dinner
Reservations necessary
Jacket required
Liquor served
Dinner: $28 to $32
  full 3 courses, without wine
Lunch: $13
Chef: Maurice Couturier
Maitre d's: Tony Vasquez and Mike Lahham

Quite a contrast from the original Tour d'Argent in Paris, this restaurant is called "The French Log Cabin," and it is indeed a log cabin, a beautiful one at that! The cuisine by Chef Couturier is very French, and earned the restaurant the coveted *Mobil* United States and Canada 1984 and 1985 Four Star Award for Outstanding Food Presentation, atmosphere, service, and extensive wine list.

This log cabin was built in the early 20th century by Alex Curpin, a French Canadian carpenter. It took him three years to build, using only a few simple tools—an ax, a hammer, an adz, and a saw. Logs of pine, oak, and cypress were used from the San Jacinto River bottom, along with a carload of Walker County stone for the fireplaces. In 1980, a fire destroyed *La Tour d'Argent,* but the owner, Sonny Lahham, in love with the cabin, had it rebuilt as close to the original as possible, and he did a very good job.

Because of its romantic atmosphere and its fine French cuisine, this restaurant attracts guests from major hotels in Houston. It is only eight minutes from the Galleria and ten minutes from the center of the city.

The exterior view is of the beautiful and well kept forest-like gardens. This is a very special view to dine by in Houston.

Windows on the Galleria

The Westin Galleria
5060 West Alabama
Houston
Texas 77056
Telephone: 713–960–8100

All major credit cards
Sunday brunch
Reservations recommended
Jacket required
Liquor served
Sunday brunch: $18 adults
children 12 and under: $11
Chef: Markus Bosiger
Maitre d': Tom Wise

Only on Sunday can you have the view to dine by at Windows on the Galleria on the 24th floor of the Westin Galleria Hotel. Located in one of America's most exciting shopping malls, the famous Galleria, "Windows" offers one of the best views of the Houston skyline.

From Monday through Saturday it operates as one of Houston's top nightclubs. On Sundays it is transformed into a relaxing restaurant offering brunch at reasonable prices from 10:30 A.M. until 3 P.M.

Chef Bosiger features international selections which vary weekly, ranging from Norwegian Salmon Salad to Stuffed Onions to chicken and oyster dishes. Specials such as Snapper with Grapefruit and Fish Mousse are occasionally among the delights offered. Prime Rib and a variety of hot dishes are served as well.

Desserts and special breads, including Chocolate Mousse, Carrot Cake, Black Forest Cake, and French pastry and eclairs, are beautifully prepared here. Apple Turnover lovers will be astounded at the variety that is available.

SAN ANTONIO

The Stetson Steakhouse

Hilton Palacio del Rio
200 South Alamo Street
San Antonio
Texas 78205
Telephone: 512–222–1400

All major credit cards
Dinner
Reservations recommended
Dress: casual
Liquor served
Dinner: $12.95 to $33.95
full 3 courses, without wine
Chef: Louis Spost
Maitre d': Chuck Heath

San Antonio was known to the Spanish missionaries as early as 1718, and the Spanish influence has never left. It is most apparent in its architecture, especially the many missions and the Spanish Governor's Palace. But the city's most delightful attraction, in our opinion, is the Paseo del River, the picturesque riverwalk in the downtown area. Because of the canal-type waterway, San Antonio is called the "Venice of the Southwest." The view of the riverwalk is delightful from the Stetson Steakhouse, the dining room of the Hilton Palacio del Rio.

The hotel was built in 1968—in a hurry. It was decided to have it ready in time for the Hemisfair, the Texas World Exposition of 1968. Using modules of pre-cast lightweight structural concrete, the hotel was designed and built in only 202 working days.

It wasn't until 1981 that the Stetson Steakhouse was opened in the hotel, exploiting the delightful riverwalk view. It is an excellent steak house and has received the Table Top Award. Pat O'Brien, the director of food and beverage, assures us that the beef served here is the best in all of Texas. Entrées include tender Filet Mignon, Sirloin Steak, Texas T-Bone Steak, fresh Norwegian Salmon, and New Braunfels Wiener Schnitzel—all served with Texas generosity.

UTAH
SALT LAKE CITY

The Roof
Westin Hotel Utah
Main at S. Temple
Salt Lake City
Utah 84111
Telephone: 801–531–1000

All major credit cards
Lunch and dinner
Reservations suggested
Jacket required
Liquor not served
Dinner: $14 to $22
*   full 3 courses, without wine*
Lunch: $5 to $9
Chef: Chuck Wiley
Maitre d': Carl Stubner

A favorite of local citizens and visitors is the rooftop restaurant on the tenth floor of the Hotel Utah. Not as high as other hotel rooftop restaurants around the country, it is nonetheless perfectly located for dramatic straight-on views of the Gothic-styled spires of the famous Mormon Temple.

The hotel is in the heart of Mormon history: a home of Brigham Young is almost next door, and in the square just across from the hotel is the Mormon Tabernacle, where on

The Roof

Thursday nights crowds of visitors go to hear the choir rehearsals and marvel at the acoustics.

There is entertainment in the Roof as well—a pianist plays familiar oldies while you dine. If you wish to drink with your meal, you must bring your own liquor. Out of respect to its neighbor, the Roof does not serve alcoholic beverages. But you may order delightful food from the menu prepared by Chef Chuck Wiley. In recent years, he has tended toward *nouvelle cuisine,* so that the food is lighter and less complex than it used to be. Among the menu favorites are the Utah Rack of Lamb. The fish is good, too—fresh and flown in from Boston the day you enjoy it. Another of the favorite dishes is Veal Oscar, a combination of veal, crab legs, and Béarnaise sauce. For something simple, try the Veal Piccata, prepared French style. *Travel/Holiday* has given the Roof awards from 1978 through 1985, and *Mobil* gave the dining room four stars. It is deserved.

VERMONT
CHITTENDEN

Mountain Top Inn

Mountain Top Road
Chittenden
Vermont 05737
Telephones: 800–445–2100 or, in Canada,
    802–483–2311

All major credit cards
Breakfast, lunch, and dinner
Reservations recommended
Jacket required for dinner
Liquor served
Dinner: $14 to $20
    full 3 courses, without wine
Lunch: $2.25 to $6.95
Chef: David Pierson
Proprietors: Jan and William Wolfe and Barbara
    and Bud McLaughlin

Mountain Top Inn, a charming country inn nestled in the Green Mountains on a 1,000 acre estate, has a spectacular panoramic view of the lake and the surrounding mountains. Each season offers a different scene—lush, verdant mountainsides in summer, an incredible mélange of foliage color in autumn, and the fantasyland of snow-covered mountains and trees in winter.

That view is enjoyed from the inn's dining room. The restaurant's interior provides an enjoyable view, too, with its post and beam construction, large exposed Douglas fir beams, an enchanting fireplace, and lovely antiques.

The inn was originally a barn but is now a full-service resort. In the 1870s the barn was part of the Long family's turnip farm. In 1940, it was purchased by William Barstow, an engineer from New York, who converted it into a wayside tavern as a hobby for his wife, Francoise. In 1945, William Wolfe and his wife Margery bought it after seeing a "for sale" advertisement in the *New York Times*. In 1955, one of its guests was President Eisenhower, who stayed here with his entourage during a fishing trip. In 1966, a ski resort was developed and, in 1979, it was completely rebuilt after a fire. This time, large windows and a glass silo staircase were added to take advantage of the views. Bill Wolfe died in 1983 but his family continues to manage the place.

The dining room's cuisine is wonderful. Among the favorites are Sautéed Bay Scallops in Dijon and Chutney as an appetizer, and, as an entrée, Stuffed Breast of Chicken with Veal Sausage in Cheddar Cheese, with McIntosh Apple Stuffing. For dessert, try the Chocolate Frangelico Cream Pie.

Not hard to find, the Mountain Top Inn is ten miles northeast of Rutland, Vermont, via Route 7 North to Chittenden Road, or via Route 4 East to Meadow Lake Drive. Follow the road to Chittenden and watch for signs directing you to the top of the mountain.

STOWE

Topnotch at Stowe

Mount Mansfield Road
P.O. Box 1260
Stowe
Vermont 05672
Telephone: 802–253–8585

All major credit cards
Breakfast and dinner, lunch in "Le Bistro"
Reservations necessary
Jacket preferred
Liquor served
Dinner: $14 to $20
     full 3 courses, without wine
Lunch: $6 to $12
Chef: Anton Flory
Maitre d': Bodo Liewehr

The view from the main dining room of Topnotch at Stowe is of the resort's sculpture garden on the terrace lawn with the highest peak in Vermont, Mount Mansfield, in the background. This peak is known for offering some of the best skiing on the East Coast of the United States. What is unique about the view is that the lodge is very close to the summit and thus the view is an unobstructed one. The peak is noted for its resemblance to a giant slumbering person; the highest portion of the rock that is visible is called the "Nose"—noted for its death-defying Alpine skiing. On either side of the "Nose" are a distinct "Forehead" and "Chin."

The different seasons clearly have an impact on the nature of the mountain view as seen from the dining room. During the spring, when crocuses bloom on the terrace, the mountaintop is still covered with snow. In the fall, the brilliant colors of maples and birches intermixed with the deep greens of the coniferous forest make for an unsurpassed show of color. During the winter, the snow cover stays on the ground from late December to early April, creating a fairyland atmosphere of light, captured and accentuated in the evenings by strings of bright white lights woven through and around the barren trees surrounding the dining room. And in Vermont the light of the moon on the snow is so special that it has inspired at least one song, *Moonlight in Vermont*.

At Topnotch there are two restaurants, the main Dining Room and a small cafe called Le Bistro. The original Dining Room was a part of Topnotch when it was a small country inn, from 1950 until 1973. In 1975, the Dining Room was enlarged from about 40 to about 100 seats. In 1983, the upper tier of the Dining Room was partitioned off into the charming cafe, Le Bistro.

The Dining Room is known for its award-winning cuisine. In September 1985, at the Taste of Vermont Culinary Competition and Tasting, it won several awards. (Not surprising, given that Chef Anton Flory is one of the fifteen Master Chefs in the United States.)

Topnotch

Continental foods and original specialties of the chef are served. Among the featured items are Pheasant under Glass and venison. Selected menu items are also prepared according to the guidelines of the American Heart Association's Creative Cuisine Program (low sodium and low cholesterol). Le Bistro features a lighter menu. Both menus change seasonally.

The Trapp Family Lodge

Stowe
Vermont 05672
Telephone: 802–253–8511

All major credit cards
Breakfast, lunch, and dinner
Reservations necessary
Jacket preferred
Liquor served
Dinner: $22 prix fixe
    full 3 courses, without wine
Lunch: $10 prix fixe
Chef: Michel Martinet
Maitre d': Anthony Czaja
Owner: The Von Trapp family,
    General Manager: Johannes Von Trapp

Situated on 1,700 acres overlooking the Green Mountains of Vermont, the dining room of the Trapp Family Lodge has one of America's more delightful views.

In 1941 the famous Von Trapp family, immortalized in the movie *The Sound of Music,* made their American home on Luce Hill in Stowe, Vermont, in great part because the land and the breathtaking scenery reminded them of their native Austria.

In 1980, the lodge was destroyed by fire. But in December, 1983, a new world-class lodge was opened, replacing the original. From the dining room of the new lodge the view is of the broad expanse of meadows which give way to woods and, beyond, a sweeping vista of the Worcester range of the Green Mountains.

A modern 73-room hotel replaced its 27-room predecessor, still retaining the intimate charm of the original Austrian-style chalet through the use of gables, steep sloping roofs, traditionally carved balconies, and the Trapp bell tower.

The lobby is not like a hotel lobby but more like the entry hall to a private home, which, by the way, it really is: the Baroness Maria Von Trapp has her apartment here, just as she did in the original lodge.

Mostly German and Austrian food are featured here; some of the specialties are *Wienerschnitzel mit Preiselberen* (Breaded Veal Steak with Lingonberries), *Gespickter Rehschlegel* in *Rahmsauce* (Roast Leg of Venison served with a Chestnut Purée), and *Rindgulasch mit Spätzle* (Beef Goulash served with Homemade Noodles). Favorite desserts include Black Forest Cake, Apple Strudel, and Linzertorte.

The lodge dining room seats 128 people. Windsor-style chairs and tables set with white linen, candles, fresh flowers, fine china with a Blue Danube pattern, lovely silverware, and crystal glassware contribute to the beautiful interior view. The waitresses wear dirndls, and during dinner classical music is played by a harpist or guitarist.

VIRGINIA
ARLINGTON

The View Restaurant

Key Bridge Marriott Hotel
P.O. Box 9191
1401 Lee Highway
Arlington
Virginia 22209
Telephone: 703–524–6400

All major credit cards
Dinner and Sunday brunch
Reservations suggested
Jacket required
Liquor served
Dinner: $18 to $35
    full 3 courses, without wine
Chefs: Donald Stern and Tony Harrington
Manager: Hamid Ghassemi

The View Restaurant is on the fourteenth floor of the Key Bridge Marriott, overlooking the Potomac River and the skylines of Georgetown and Washington, D.C. In unobstructed view are the Washington Monument, the Lincoln Memorial, the Washington Cathedral, and Georgetown University. Breathtaking!

The View Restaurant, opened in 1980, was designed by Barbara Lockhart, a well-known West Coast interior designer who has decorated many homes for the rich and famous, among them Carol Burnett and William Randolph Hearst. This was the first upscale restaurant to be built in a Marriott Hotel and has served as a model for the rest of the chain. It is decorated in pink and mauve, and all of the dining chairs are individually hand carved and hand painted. Mirrored backdrops are used in the upper tier of the restaurant to provide a view for those guests seated with their backs to the view.

This restaurant was the site of Aaron Copland's 80th birthday party, with guests including Leonard Bernstein and Mstislav Rostropovich.

Among the favorites on the menu are Lobster Bisque, Zucchini-Curry Soup, Veal Medallions with Fresh Mango and Pink Peppercorns, and Fresh Poached Salmon with Vermouth Sauce. Dessert includes a daily soufflé selection served with Vanilla Haagen-Daz ice cream.

WILLIAMSBURG

For an overview of eighteenth century life in America, there is no better place than Colonial Williamsburg. From 1699 to 1780, Williamsburg was the capital of Virginia and a proving ground for both ideas and leaders. A remarkable body of men reached political maturity in Williamsburg in this era: George Washington, George Wythe, Peyton Randolph, Edmund Pendleton, Patrick Henry, George Mason, Thomas Jefferson, and a score of other Virginians. The capital proved to be an ideal setting for and a stimulus to their growth as leaders.

Inspired by Dr. W.A.R. Goodwin, Mr. John D. Rockefeller began the restoration of Williamsburg in 1926, making sure that all work was done with an eye toward recalling the fundamental principles upon which the Williamsburg of two hundred years ago made its enduring contribution to contemporary America.

Today, for all to see, Colonial Williamsburg has several major appeals to the eye and mind. They lie in its history and heritage, gardens, architecture, furniture, handcrafts, and the preservation of research in all forms, including archaeology. There is an obvious, patient concern with being authentic in every aspect, from the flowers grown and the clothing worn to the meals served.

Here, history is also a view to dine by. We've selected six of the ten delightful dining spots in Williamsburg so that you may select from among them for your view to dine by of Colonial America.

The Cascades

Visitor Center Drive
Williamsburg
Virginia 23185
Telephone: 804–229–1000

All major credit cards
Breakfast, lunch, and dinner
Reservations required
Jacket preferred
Liquor served
Dinner: $16 to $26
    full 3 courses, without wine
Lunch: $7 to $15
Chef: Charles Madison
Manager: Charles F. Trader

The area surrounding the Cascades Restaurant—beautiful woods on the grounds of the Colonial Williamsburg Visitor Center—is the place most visitors to Colonial Williamsburg go to see an orientation film, explore the shops, and study the models and exhibits so as to better understand what they will be seeing.

This is an unexpected view to dine by. A stream of water cascades into three different ponds along the side of a hill next to the restaurant. Most tables in the dining room have a view of the water.

Among the delights on the menu are a Hunt Breakfast Buffet and, at dinnertime, Scalloped Oysters, Cheese Grit Soufflé, Cheddar Cheese Soup, Seafood Brochette, and a Seafood Feast. For dessert, try the Peppermint Ice Cream.

Christiana Campbell's Tavern

Waller Street
Williamsburg
Virginia 23185
Telephone: 804–229–1000

All major credit cards
Dinner and Sunday brunch
Reservations required
Jacket preferred
Liquor served
Dinner: $16 to $26
    full 3 courses, without wine
Brunch: $8 to $11
Chef: Edward Swann

Christiana Campbell's Tavern is located on Waller Street in the historic area of Williamsburg, with a view of the grand Colonial capitol building across the street. George Washington and other leading gentlemen of the colony periodically met with local residents at this tavern. Christiana Campbell was described by a traveler in 1783 as "a little old woman, about four feet high; equally thick, a little turned up pug nose, a mouth screw'd up to one side." She was, however, an experienced tavern keeper, having learned the skill from her father.

The restaurant is delightful, with such tasty dishes as Captain Rasmussen's Clam Chowder and shrimp, lobster, and Seafood Jambalaya served with Sweet Potato Muffins. For dessert, freshly made, Rum Raisin Ice Cream is an excellent choice.

Josiah Chowning's Tavern

Duke of Gloucester Street
Williamsburg
Virginia 23185
Telephone: 804–229–1000

All major credit cards
Lunch and dinner
Reservations required
Jacket preferred
Liquor served
Dinner: $13 to $26
    full 3 courses, without wine
Lunch: $7 to $11
Chef: Manfred Roehr
Manager: Tom Kojcsich

Josiah Chowning's Tavern, in the historic area next to the Market Square, is an 18th century alehouse with informal dining. "Gambols," featuring Colonial games, entertainment, and various "diversions," occur nightly. The tavern is a typical hearty food and drink spot, just as it was two centuries ago. Among the featured items are Barbecued Pork Backribs, Barbecued Ribs of Beef, Roast Prime Rib of Beef, and Chowning's Good Bread. For dessert—apple pie, of course, unless you prefer Black Walnut Ice Cream.

The King's Arms Tavern

Duke of Gloucester Street
Williamsburg
Virginia 23185
Telephone: 804–229–1000

All major credit cards
Lunch and dinner
Reservations required
Jacket preferred
Liquor served
Dinner: $16 to $24
full 3 courses, without wine
Lunch: $9 to $12
Chef: John Foster
Manager: Herb Harris

The King's Arms Tavern, originally owned by Mrs. Jane Vobe, was one of Williamsburg's most genteel taverns in the eighteenth century. The King's Arms, like other local taverns, served as the gathering place for discussions of politics, business, and the latest gossip. During the Revolutionary War, Mrs. Vobe and other tavern keepers supplied food, drink, and lodgings to American troops.

The cuisine specializes in traditional southern delicacies such as Virginia Peanut Soup, Sally Lunn Bread, Corn Muffins, Game Pie, and Leg of Lamb. Desserts include Pecan Pie and Fig Ice Cream.

Lodge Bay Room

South England Street
Williamsburg
Virginia 23185
Telephone: 804–229–1000

All major credit cards
Breakfast, lunch, dinner, and Sunday brunch
Reservations required
Dress: casual
Liquor served
Dinner: $15 to $25
full 3 courses, without wine
Lunch: $3 to $9
Chef: Ted Kristengen
Maitre d': Henry Verlander

The Lodge Bay Dining Room is a spacious and sunny room furnished with green captains' chairs, butcher block tables, and luxurious carpeting. The tables are arranged near neatly paned windows and French doors to give diners a view of the immaculately manicured gardens complete with fountain, wisteria, and rocking chair-lined courtyard.

Robert Burrell's seascapes of the Chesapeake Bay area adorn the walls throughout and help create a setting for the popular seafood feast offered every Friday and Saturday night. The Sunday brunch is popular, too, with made-to-order omelets, homemade breads, and a variety of fresh fruits. Dinner, served Sunday through Thursday, features both land and sea specialties. Favorites include the Bay Overture and Crabmeat Au Gratin. The favorite dessert is Chocolate Mousse Cake.

The Regency Dining Room
at the Williamsburg Inn

Francis Street
Williamsburg
Virginia 23185
Telephone: 804–229–1000
            Ext. 2450

All major credit cards
Breakfast, lunch, and dinner
Reservations required
Jacket required
Liquor served
Dinner: $22 to $35
    full 3 courses,
    without wine
Lunch: $8 to $12
Chef: Hans J. Schadler
Maitre d': Everaud Green

The Regency Dining Room of the grand Williamsburg Inn is a rare and satisfying aesthetic and culinary experience. Tasteful surroundings of ivory and green blend with the glitter of fine silver. The view overlooks beautiful Colonial gardens and the picturesque, contemporary Golden Horseshoe Golf Course. Breakfast and lunch are served in this delightful setting.

Opened in 1937, the Williamsburg Inn is one of America's distinctly luxurious hotels. It has received numerous awards, including the *Mobil Travel Guide*'s five stars, and has played host to many VIP guests, including the monarchs of Belgium, Saudi Arabia, and Sweden, as well as prime ministers and presidents of many nations. It was the site of the 1983 Economic Summit of Industrialized Nations, hosted by President Ronald Reagan.

The cuisine here is elegant American. Among the specialties are Veal Oscar and Crabmeat Randolph.

WASHINGTON
SEATTLE

The Emerald Suite and
**The Space Needle
Restaurant** of
The Space Needle
115 Warren Avenue North
Seattle
Washington 98109
Telephone: 206–447–3175

All major credit cards
Breakfast, lunch, dinner,
*   and Sunday brunch*
Reservations recommended
Jacket required in Emerald Suite
Liquor served
Dinner:
Space Needle: $13.50 to $19.25
Emerald Suite: $13.50 to $20.95
*   full 3 courses, without wine*
Lunch: Space Needle: $6.50 to $13.95
*   Emerald Suite: $7.50 to $13.95*
Chef: Steve Hartigan
Director of Food and Beverage:
*   K. Russ Goodman*

More than a million people, from all over the United States, Japan, Europe, Australia, India, and elsewhere come every year to see the view from Seattle's Space Needle.

Opened on April 21, 1962, as the dominant central structure for the 1962 Seattle World's Fair, the idea for the Space Needle was that of Edward E. Carlson, who, while relaxing in a coffee house in Stuttgart, Germany, in 1959, was inspired by the revolving restaurant in the Stuttgart Tower and began sketching his idea for a similar structure that he proposed to build in Seattle.

When completed, the Space Needle was the engineering feat of the day. Its underground foundation weighed as much as the Needle itself and established the center of gravity at just above ground level. The steel erection used massive and unusually shaped members to form slender legs and the tophouse. The five-level dome was completed with special attention to the revolving restaurants and an observation deck.

Storms have forced the closing of the Space Needle only twice, once on Columbus Day of 1962, when winds from a storm gusted as high as 83 miles per hour, and again in 1973 during 75-mile-an-hour winds. However, the Needle was built to withstand high wind velocity, and it has withstood several earthquake tremors, including one in 1965 that measured a healthy 6.5 on the Richter scale.

The view from over 500 feet is a 360-degree panorama of striking Pacific Northwest scenery—the Olympic and Cascade Mountain ranges, Mount Rainier, the downtown Seattle waterfront, the Port of Seattle, Puget Sound, and Lake Union.

Eighteen feet below the observation deck is the revolving restaurant level. There the Space Needle Restaurant serves fine food in an informal setting and the Emerald Suite offers elegant dining. Both feature Pacific Northwest cuisine, emphasizing fresh seafood and produce (from the fabulous Pike Place Market of Seattle), with Continental flourishes. The cuisine has been judged "exceptional" by *Pacific Northwest* magazine and has received several "Best in the West" awards from *PSA* magazine. Among the notable items on the menu are Seattle Stew, Space Needle Seafood Chowder, and Space Needle Apple Pie. Our favorite is the Dungeness Crab.

Through the years the restaurants here had many honored guests, including John Glenn, Prince Philip of Great Britain, Russian cosmonaut Gherman Titov, King Hussein of Jordan, the Shah and Empress of Iran, and many governors, vice-presidents, presidents, and movie and theatrical stars.

The King of Tonga was probably the Needle's heaviest visitor. He weighed 400 pounds and had to have a special chair carried up the service elevator.

WASHINGTON, D.C.

The Mayfair Restaurant

The Grand Hotel
2350 M Street, N.W.
Washington
District of Columbia 20037
Telephone: 202–429–0100 Ext. 4488

All major credit cards
Lunch and dinner
Reservations necessary
Jacket required
Liquor served
Dinner: $30 to $40
        full 3 courses, without wine
Lunch: $12 to $18
Chef: Richard J. Hill
Maitre d': Christian Mattei

A very distinguished new hotel with a European flavor, the Grand Hotel is reminiscent of some of Europe's superb small hotels. Although scaled to the baroque grandeur of the nation's capital, the Grand Hotel of Washington has the intimacy, charm, and elegance of a private mansion.

Located in Washington's West End, formerly the industrial area of the city, the building's Skidmore, Owings, and Merrill design gives it an air of timelessness. The Grand Hotel projects the monumental character of Washington with its copper-topped dome wedged between the corners of the building. The gray brick, granite, and concrete blocks of the building's exterior fit within the monumental scale yet are proportioned to impart a neighborhood residential feeling.

The lobby has double columns ringing its rotunda, resulting in a circular lounge area crowned by a 16-foot stepped dome. The graceful marble staircase leads to the Promenade and to the European-style interior courtyard.

This beautifully landscaped courtyard is the view to dine by from the Mayfair restaurant. A special sight is the wall-mounted fountain from which water cascades down a series of basins to the collecting pool below. There is also a stillwater pond stocked with eye-catching tropical fish.

Located off the lobby, the restaurant seats 110 people and is a pleasant setting for lunch or dinner.

The restaurant's dominant colors are warm tones of peach, deep coral, and camel. Peach silk covers the ceiling with a delicate shimmer of color, and the carpeting is patterned in deep coral and camel. The deep coral tone is repeated in the upholstery of the comfortable banquettes. Gold leaf covers the frames and the seating of traditional side chairs, accenting the Fortuny covering of white shot with pure gold. White linen tablecloths are a crisp setting for elegant china, silver, and crystal, as well as colorful floral arrangements.

The focal point of the room is the ceiling's dome. Beveled mirrors line the walls, reflecting the individual table lamps, the indirect light of the dome, and the courtyard. During the day, ambient light enters through the curved bank of French windows that open to the view of the courtyard and its gardens.

The Mayfair features French Continental cuisine exquisitely presented. While the menu for lunch and dinner is the same, the lunch menu is enhanced with daily special selections. The most popular and innovative specialties on the menu include Navarin of Lobster with Baby Vegetables, Lamb Noisettes with Truffle and Parsley, Salmon Quenelles with Morels and Herbs, and Veal Medallions with Shittakes and Roasted Shallots. Many writers are moved to say two things about the Mayfair: "it is the most beautiful restaurant room in the United States" and "its cooking rates with that of the finest restaurants in Washington."

WISCONSIN
MILWAUKEE

Polaris Restaurant and Cocktail Lounge

Hyatt Regency Milwaukee
333 West Kilbourn Avenue
Milwaukee
Wisconsin 53203
Telephone: 414–276–1234

All major credit cards
Lunch and dinner
Reservations not required
Jacket not required
Liquor served
Dinner: $10.95 to $18.50
      full 3 courses, without wine
Lunch: $4.25 to $6.50
General Manager: Keith Mangum

Here is the spot from which to see all of Milwaukee. The Polaris Restaurant and Cocktail Lounge are in a revolving dome 22 stories atop the Hyatt Regency Milwaukee.

The 360-degree view of the city, including much of the surrounding area and beautiful Lake Michigan, takes about an hour to see completely as the restaurant revolves.

Although it does attract tourists, the Polaris is the local favorite for celebrations ranging from weddings to anniversary parties. There is no other restaurant like it in Milwaukee.

Favorite times to visit Polaris and enjoy the view are at sunset, during a light evening snowfall (when the view appears to be a beautiful impressionist painting), and whenever there are fireworks for festive and holiday events.

Lunch is served from 11:30 A.M. until 2 P.M. Monday through Friday, and its offerings include salads, sandwiches, and entrées ranging from $4.25 to $7.50 (for Prime Rib *au Jus* —English-cut prime rib of beef on a French loaf with fried onions, served with creamy horseradish and natural juices). A favorite is Milwaukee *En Vuelo* (twin enchiladas topped with sauce ranchero, cheddar cheese, and sour cream, served with refried beans, Spanish rice, guacamole, tortilla chips, and sauce caliente).

Dinner is served every night from 5:30 P.M. until 10 P.M., and entrées include Roast Duck, Lobster Tail, BBQ Ribs, Chinese Walnut Chicken, Chicken Normandy, Baked Lasagna, seasonal fresh fish, and Prime Ribs of Beef *au Jus*. Entrées range from $10.95 to $18.50. A modest dessert selection includes a local favorite, Apple Strudel, and our favorites, Carrot Cake and Mud Pie.

WYOMING
GRAND TETON NATIONAL PARK

Mural Dining Room

Jackson Lake Lodge
Grand Teton National Park
P.O. Box 250
Moran
Wyoming 83013
Telephone: 307–543–2811

All major credit cards
Breakfast, lunch, and dinner
Reservations recommended
Jacket not required
Liquor served
Dinner: $14.25 to $23.75
  full 3 courses, without wine
Lunch: $6.55 to $10
Chef: Robert L. Walton

The best of the places to eat in Jackson Lake Lodge is the Mural Dining Room, not only because of its extensive menu, but also because of the scenery it offers.

The Mural Dining Room is so named because its walls are covered with murals based on the work of artist Alfred Jacob Miller, who in 1837 made watercolor sketches as he traveled with Captain William Drummond Stewart on a fur trading expedition. Miller's sketches were converted to today's murals by Carl Roters; they depict scenes from a trapper's life, such as camping under the Tetons and the annual trading fair where trappers exchange their pelts for the supplies they need to survive in the wilderness.

The dining room features popular American cuisine. Among the specialties are Smoked Trout, vegetarian dinners, Prime Rib, fresh pastries, and fresh strawberries. You share the dining room with guests from all parts of the United States as well as from many parts of the world.

U.S. VIRGIN ISLANDS
ST. CROIX

Brass Parrot Restaurant

The Buccaneer
P.O. Box 218
Christiansted
St. Croix
U.S. Virgin Islands 00820–0218
Telephone: 809–773–2100

All major credit cards
Dinner
Reservations suggested
Jacket required
Liquor served
Dinner: $30 to $50
*   full 3 courses, without wine*
Chef: Thene Derima
Maitre d': David Wager

The view from the Brass Parrot Restaurant is as full of history and beauty as the island of St. Croix itself. Overlooking picturesque Christiansted harbor, the first structures on the hotel property were built by Charles Martel in 1653 for the Order of the Knights of Malta, whose flag is one of seven which have flown over St. Croix. Later, Estate Shoys, as it was called then, served as home to young Alexander Hamilton and his mother.

The Buccaneer Hotel was opened in 1947 and is the premier luxury hotel on St. Croix today. From the Brass Parrot Restaurant is a hilltop view of all of Christiansted harbor, the historic Christiansted town, as well as the islands of St. Thomas, St. John, and the British Virgin Isles to the north dotting the horizon like splendid jewels. The Caribbean, surrounding all, washes gently on the shores of Cutlass Cove just below the restaurant.

The food here is enjoyable, with Caribbean specialties such as Island Lobster and Shrimp Bahia (large shrimp sautéed with garlic butter and topped with brandy and pineapple liqueur). And, for a sweet end to it all, there are Banana Flambée and Crepes Suzette.

ST. THOMAS

The Agavé Terrace

Point Pleasant Resort
Smith Bay
St. Thomas
U.S. Virgin Islands
Telephone: 809–775–4142

All major credit cards
Breakfast, lunch, and dinner
Reservations requested
Jacket not required
Liquor served
Dinner: $11.95 to $20 à la carte
Lunch: $3 to $8
Chef: Bruce W. Kraus
General Manager: Robert Walling

The Agavé Terrace Restaurant is situated on the grounds of a luxury resort, beautiful Point Pleasant. Some say that the view from the Agavé Terrace is one of the world's most beautiful. There are good grounds for such a claim. As you look from the restaurant, you see not only scenic grandeur but history as well.

Looking over Pilsbury Sound and down Drake's Passage, one can see the international boundary between American and British territories, as well as the U.S. and the British Virgin Islands themselves. This is an historically important view because this passage is where Sir Francis Drake and his British ships met and defeated the Spanish Armada. Thus began the decline of Spanish power and influence in this part of the world and the ascendency of Britain as a naval and world power.

Along with this magnificent panorama, the Agavé Terrace has an elegant menu. Among the highlights are Shrimp Agavé with gingered pineapple sauce and Fresh Fillet of Red Snapper, poached in court bouillon and served with delicate creamy tarragon sauce.

Bay Wynds

Wyndham Virgin Grand Beach Hotel
St. Thomas
U.S. Virgin Islands
Telephone: 809–775–1510

All major credit cards
Dinner
Reservations necessary
Jacket required in season (November–April)
Liquor served
Dinner: $15 to $30
    full 3 courses, without wine

By the time you read this book, the Bay Wynds restaurant will be in business. As this piece was being written, it was under construction and scheduled to open by February 1986.

Bay Wynds is a stylish 130-seat hilltop restaurant featuring Continental and Caribbean cuisine. It is set 150 feet above sea level on the 32-acre estate of the site of the new Wyndham Virgin Grand Beach Hotel in St. Thomas. As guests dine, they have a spectacular view of Water Bay, St. John's Island, and the Caribbean.

The Wyndham Virgin Grand Beach Hotel is situated on a 1,000-foot white sand beach on Water Bay on the northeast shore of St. Thomas, just seven miles from downtown Charlotte Amalie and nine miles from the Cyril B. King Airport.

Worldwide

Royal Viking Star
Royal Viking Sky
Royal Viking Sea
of the Royal Viking Line
One Embarcadero Center
San Francisco
California 94111
Telephone: 415-398-8000

Breakfast, lunch, and dinner
Meals are included in the
   price of the cruise; wine and spirits are extra
Dress: usually formal
Corporate Chef: Daniel Durand

We have always been bothered by the fact that so many cruise ship dining rooms do not permit many of their guests to enjoy the view to dine by at sea or in port. The Royal Viking Line is different. The immense window-walled dining rooms of each of the line's three luxurious vessels offer scenic views at mealtime. What can be seen obviously depends upon where the ship is: among the possibilities are the endless sea, the setting sun, a distant horizon, passing ships, or an exciting harbor scene.

Dining on a Royal Viking vessel is a delight. In an unprecedented action, the line recently became the first cruise line inducted into the prestigious Swiss and Austrian hotel associations. The chefs and culinary staff are all members of *La Confrerie de la Chaine des Rotisseurs,* the world's oldest food and wine society. For three years in a row, readers of *Travel/Holiday* rated Royal Viking as having the best ship cuisine in the world.

At breakfast, lunch, and dinner, passengers enjoy unharried single seating in a window-walled dining room. All meals are cooked to order and presented with an elegant flair. Fine china, crystal, and flatware add to the luxury of dining. Each ship has two waiters for every twenty passengers and a total of four headwaiters to handle tableside preparations for such dishes as Caesar salad and Cherries Jubilee. There are eight wine stewards and a maitre d' in each dining room.

The executive chefs aboard the three Norwegian-registered vessels spend at least three years training in European hotels and restaurants. Following an apprenticeship, they hold full-time positions in top European establishments. They must also train in hotels and restaurants in the United States. This background produces what Ulrich F. Baur, the line's vice-president of hotel operations, calls "Americanized European Cuisine." He feels that the American palate doesn't want heavy sauces every day of a two-week cruise.

Passengers enjoy a different lunch and dinner menu every day. The chef accommodates dietary needs and prepares special orders if given 24 hours' notice. The menus reflect the itinerary. The chefs try to use the finest local ingredients, which assure freshness and a variety in international accent. Certain items, however, they cannot do without, and they are flown by plane to the ships around the world. Among these are American beef, Norwegian smoked salmon, California wines, Swiss and Austrian chocolate, and live cold-water lobster packed in seaweed and delivered fresh from a New York supplier.

There is a superb wine list, with 95 percent of the items on it available no matter where in the world a ship may be. Imagine, a fine wine cellar on a ship! Passengers enjoy a Norwegian specialty called *Linie Aquavit,* or the "water of life." The line stores the *Aquavit* on each ship, bottling it with a specially designed label. Fine on its own, with tomato juice it creates an extraordinary "Norwegian Mary."

In addition to a well-varied selection of items at the Norwegian Day Buffet (the culinary highpoint of every cruise), available on each cruise are ten varieties of homemade bread, more than 30 pastries and desserts, and a cornucopia of fresh fruit. Truly a feast for the eyes, the buffet tables are decorated with ice and butter sculptures and silver trays resembling Viking ships. The buffet is served at noon, and during dinner there is Norwegian music and folk dancing.

Royal Viking has its own pastry shop. Passengers enjoy homemade breads and muffins, buttery Danish pastry, delicious cookies, pies, tarts—all created from European recipes and products.

Royal Viking vessels sail to six of the seven continents and more than 220 ports, 43 of which are new destinations for them in 1986.

Index of Restaurants